LITERARY CRITICISM AND CULTURAL THEORY

Edited by

William E. Cain
Professor of English
Wellesley College

T0352761

A ROUTLEDGE SERIES

Literary Criticism and Cultural Theory

William E. Cain, *General Editor*

Parsing the City

Jonson, Middleton, Dekker, and City Comedy's London as Language

Heather C. Easterling

Routledge
Taylor & Francis Group

NEW YORK AND LONDON

Routledge
Taylor & Francis Group
711 Third Avenue
New York, NY 10017

Routledge
Taylor & Francis Group
2 Park Square
Milton Park, Abingdon
Oxfordshire OX14 4RN

First issued in paperback 2014

Routledge is an imprint of the Taylor and Francis Group, an informa business

© 2007 by Taylor & Francis Group, LLC

International Standard Book Number–13: 978-0-415-97950-4 (Hardcover)
International Standard Book Number–13: 978-0-415-54187-9 (pbk)

Library of Congress Cataloging-in-Publication Data

Easterling, Heather C.
    Parsing the city : Jonson, Middleton, Dekker, and city comedy's London as language / Heather C. Easterling.
        p. cm. -- (Literary criticism and cultural theory)
        Includes bibliographical references (p.) and index.
    ISBN-13: 978-0-415-97950-4 (alk. paper) 1. London (England)--In literature.
    2. English drama--17th century--History and criticism. 3. English drama
    (Comedy)--History and criticism. 4. Language and languages in literature. 5.
    Sociolinguistics in literature. 6. Urban dialects--England--London. 7. City and town
    life in literature. 8. Literature and society--England--History--17th century. I. Title.

PR678.L58E37 2006
820.9'32421--dc22   2006025978

Visit the Taylor & Francis Web site at
http://www.taylorandfrancis.com

and the Routledge Web site at
http://www.routledge-ny.com

For my parents

Contents

Acknowledgments

I must warmly thank Sara van den Berg, John Webster, and Anne Curzan, for being tireless, generous, and insightful teachers, readers, and mentors over many years, and for helping me to shepherd this project from its earliest impulses to the present. Throughout, they have made this better work than it would have been, otherwise. They are not, of course, responsible for any remaining mistakes or oversights—those are all mine.

I must acknowledge my colleagues, first at the University of Washington and more recently at Gonzaga University, for their friendship, both personally and professionally, as well as their curiosity about this project at crucial times that bolstered my own.

I wish to thank my students at the University of Washington, whose questions and frustrations with Jacobean city comedy prompted valuable thinking about the project of these plays.

I recall first thinking about Ben Jonson while reading *The Alchemist* with the late Arthur Homan in 1984 at Emma Willard School, but I know that I first must have read Jonson with my father, whose love for Jonson's poetry is great. So I thank my Dad for first reading me "On My First Son," and both my parents for the love of reading they instilled in me early, and, more recently, for their unflagging support, including a willingness to postpone visits and cheer for me from a distance.

Deepest thanks, finally, to Gordon, for great patience, grace, and occasional rescues over the initial years of this work; for unfailing belief in me; and for choosing the perfect year to sail around the world, leaving me space and time for this journey of my own.

Spokane, Washington

Preface

A preface offers a frame, sometimes a new frame, for the work it accompanies. In contemplating what prefatory remarks I might offer for this book, I mainly have reflected on the value of time spent, over the past two years, reengaging with different portions of what has become this book, solidifying my readings via fresh interrogation of a range of works, and reading widely: in and out of early modern studies, sometimes with an ear deliberately attuned to conversations on Jonson and early modern drama, just as often finding new and resonant ideas through pure serendipity. It is this combination of the considered and the fortuitous which characterizes most scholarship, of course, and the chapters that follow have benefited enormously, since their first completion as a dissertation, from additional time spent with emboldening new questions and conclusions emerging from such renewed activity with my own and others' work.

This project coalesced around a desire to bring together disparate strands of inquiry, specifically literary criticism, study of the history of English, and the study of gender and language, all for the insights this dialectical combination could bring to reading some already well-known Jacobean drama. A certain critical hybridity already was evident in literary studies as I began, but I felt real trepidation, nonetheless, in proposing the value of an historicized criticism of Jacobean city comedies whose historicizing involved the integration of ideas—about gender and language and about the early modern English vernacular—from the social sciences as much as the humanities. Since my first efforts along these lines it has been enormously inspiring to witness the appearance of more and more studies whose express aim is to forge updated, literary-critical readings via the combining of heretofore distant fields. In late 2003, the appearance of Margaret Ferguson's *Dido's Daughters: Literacy, Gender, and Empire in Early Modern England and France* offered brilliant testimony to the value of drawing on unlikely or new fields of inquiry, with this book's exploration of gender and early modern imperialism via current work in literacy studies. Literacy itself has been redefined, thanks to literacy studies-scholarship, in terms of a shifting set of power relations that has also been starkly gendered throughout western history. In arguing for the relevance of such new work for our approaches to historical matrices of gender, education, and power, Ferguson models the insights made possible by the attentive incorporation of non-literary ideas and practices.

In her prefatory remarks, Ferguson asserts that such new, inherently hybrid fields like literacy studies have "a great deal to teach us in literary studies" (Ferguson 13), and her book and recent others, in turn, have taught me a great deal during an opportune period of rethinking. As my own preface, the present study aspires—humbly and imperfectly—also to teach in this way, and to point the way to what more there is to be taught when the inquiry of literary studies is augmented by diverse and newer critical approaches. In the pages that follow, this study of city comedy and the genre's relationship to London, gender, and the early modern English vernacular offers an updated reading of this drama, a reading made possible by sophisticated and eclectic new directions in early modern studies.

Introduction

We free our Language from the opinion of Rudenesse, and
Barbarism,wherewith it is mistaken to be diseas'd.

Our English tongue is above all other very hardy and happy; joyning
together after a most eloquent manner sundry words of every kind of
speech.[1]

This study investigates Jacobean city comedy as a genre by way of three
significant plays and their shared, profound concern for the vernacular in
early modern London society. It situates city comedy's engagement with
early modern London in terms of the central and thematic role the genre
assigns to language in the world its plays stage. Jacobean city comedy was a
phenomenon of the expanding early modern city, and its consistent subject
is London and the complex problem of the changing, at times incoherent
city.[2] Central to this problem, I contend, is the English vernacular, also in
flux in the period via a combination of great lexical expansion and calls for
lexical and grammatical regulation.[3] The vernacular's adequacy becomes a
question of its ability to encompass or cohere the prodigious city in many
texts of the period, and particularly in the city plays of Ben Jonson and his
contemporaries Thomas Middleton and Thomas Dekker.[4] Terence Hawkes
has described drama as "represent[ing] a formal enactment of a culture's language" (Hawkes 32). I would argue that city comedy not only represents but
interrogates the language of Jacobean London in plays that regularly stage
the city precisely as language or languages. Jacobean city comedy thus offers
important traces of early modern attitudes toward their evolving language
and society.[5] In this study, I first will describe a climate of heightened language consciousness in which London was of special note and concern, and
then closely read three of these plays as documents of attitudes toward the

vernacular, and specifically of a preoccupation with the city as a landscape of semiotic instability troped in distinctly gendered terms.

Such an approach to the power and progress of language as an organiz-ing idea (and an idea that is never static) recently has grown in prevalence within early modern studies, with critics increasingly treating the vernacu-lar as a contested idea and ideal with material dimensions and consequence. This emphasis is not to be confused with Linguistics scholarship, though, as I will describe below, it does build on a historical attention to language traditionally distinct from literary criticism. In *Broken English: Dialects and the Politics of Language in Renaissance Writings* (1996), for example, Paula Blank carefully distinguishes her study's focus and methodologies from the field of Linguistics. She describes her work's emphasis as "the history of ideas about the English language," elsewhere referred to as the study of "attitudes towards language."[6] Blank's editors, Tony Crowley and Talbot J. Taylor, also signal a distinct emphasis on "the role of language in the social, political, and ideological realms,"[7] fueled by advances in cultural criticism's purview. Recent work on Ben Jonson's *The Irish Masque at Court* (1613) detailing the linguistic elements of the playwright's Hiberno-English renderings, offers some additional definition of the parameters of my study of city comedy. Jim Sullivan reconsiders *The Irish Masque* and its representations of spoken "Irish," in the process detailing the range of technical language components that created "Irish" on Jonson's masque-stage (Sullivan 2). A literary-critic, Sullivan nonetheless offers more of a linguist's highly detailed study of Irish and English language features. My point is not to dispute the value of histor-ical-linguistic work like Sullivan's—it augments and complicates a range of critical questions about Jonson, language, and nation, to name but a few— but to highlight the difference between his approach and my own, which is not technically descriptive. I seek to interrogate early modern representations of and attitudes toward vernacular English in London for the literary, social, and imaginative projects they index. I am not concerned with the actual and precise linguistic evolution of English in the period so much as with ideas and concerns about the vernacular and its capabilities, and the literary repre-sentations of and confrontations with it that were the result.

The impetus for this project originated in repeated observation of Ben Jonson's striking preoccupation, throughout his diverse works, with the ques-tion of language's relative ability or adequacy to supply or create community, connection, even a stability for truth. My epigraph from Jonson's *English Grammar* provides a brief glance at this question at work in an explicitly pre-scriptive mode. The English vernacular, for Jonson, problematically retains hallmarks of its recent inferiority; it requires "free[ing]" from its perceived crudeness, implicitly a corrective action, but simultaneously it is celebrated by Jonson as "hardy and happy" for its eclectic expressiveness. There is inevitable tension in a text purporting to further both linguistic revision and expansion, and a distinct anxiety about the vernacular lurks in this duality. For Jonson, there is tension on the discursive as well as the linguistic level. The distinctive "centripetal motion" of Ben Jonson's poetry, masques, and prose-works contrasts starkly with the heedless centrifugal energies of his comedies. Noting this, Thomas M. Greene argues that this reveals an important tension in Jonson himself. In the exactingly calibrated, centered self of *Discoveries* Greene detects a kind of horror of "a self too-often-shifted, a self which risks the loss of an inner poise" (Greene 330). Yet there exists a simultaneous interest in and even envy of the potential brilliance of this shifting multiplicity. Jonson's desire for neoclassical unity and precision—clearly evidenced in his poetry and in works like *Discoveries* and *The English Grammar*—is matched by a fascination with instability, mutation, and improvisation demonstrated in his works for the public stage.[8]

In *Epicoene* Jonson exploits this uncertainty in a satire of language's use as merely a social tool. He takes a more tolerant but also existential approach to the same tensions in *Bartholomew Fair*. Set against Jonson's *Grammar* and his volume of pensées, *Timber, or Discoveries,* both non-dramatic prose works on language in society, the two prose comedies' varied engagement with similar concerns is placed in relief.[9] I seek to model a literary-critical study of Jonson that engages with this varied oeuvre, and with a more complete picture of the author and his complex view of his society and his art. Jonson's vivid stylistic views and neoclassical interest in rhetoric have meant that questions of language, rhetoric and representation in his work have been addressed before by such scholars as L.C. Knights, Jonas Barish, and others.[10] The most interesting recent development along these lines has been scholars' identification of principles and anxieties in Jonson about language's stability that are suggestively deconstructive in character. Douglas Lanier, for example, reads Jonson's notoriously finicky stylistics in terms of anxieties over a perceived instability of the sign. Jonson's uneasiness about semiotic indeterminacy is strongly gendered, Lanier argues: words are slippery, ornamental, and feminine, while ideas—matter—is masculine.[11] Lanier's reframing of Jonson according to both early modern and twentieth-century language questions proposes a provocative critical conversation in which this study aims to participate, bringing together Jonson's dramatic language, his perceived attitudes toward language against a backdrop of larger language concerns at the time, and the urban milieu in which he lived and worked. My study participates in a tradition of parsing Jonson's discernment of language, but will combine this with a consideration of the city, arguing that no reading of Jonson's city comedies, especially his two prose comedies, is complete without an understanding of their particular imbrications with London as a landscape of language.

Jonson was far from alone, however, in his concern for the role of language in London's urban and increasingly diverse landscape, and a broader, generic concern is part of my thesis here. A play like Thomas Middleton and Thomas Dekker's *The Roaring Girl* signals a diversity of perceptions of and proposed solutions to language's adequacy in maintaining community or in creating stability. Reading *The Roaring Girl* alongside *Epicoene* and *Bartholomew Fair* complicates any claim for a generic project, for while *The Roaring Girl* unquestionably is concerned with London as a linguistic landscape whose social coherence is at stake, its characters, its tone, its approach to language and discourse, and its conclusion differ from both of the Jonson plays under consideration. But this is a useful divergence. *The Roaring Girl* possesses a comparative romanticism, even idealism, which challenges too uni-dimensional a hypothesis concerning contemporary responses to early modern London and its vernacular's role and capabilities. *The Roaring Girl* and the two better known, often more highly regarded, Jonson comedies comprise an idiosyncratic subject of study that is part of the point. Such an unlikely grouping signals broad concern for a chaotic city and for the role of the vernacular in this setting; the complexity of response comprised between them makes these plays a compelling subject of study, more so than comparisons of city comedy with Shakespeare regularly suggest.[12] My study's hypothesis of a 'project of the vernacular' initiates new consideration of the variety and the depth of city comedy's exploration of its relentless, urban world. In a careful study of these city plays by Jonson, Middleton, and Dekker, I hope convincingly to signal city comedies' centrality as documents of early modern English attitudes toward social and linguistic change in that emblematically changeable setting, London.

CRITICAL FRAMES

With the current preeminence of cultural studies and its emphasis on the materially eclectic dimensions of culture and identity, it is no longer remarkable for a literary-critical project to bring together diverse strands of disciplinary inquiry. It is nevertheless proper to clarify the critical stakes and methodologies of my study via some discussion of the several fields of inquiry upon which I have drawn for this updated reading of city comedy's engagement with London. My critique has been shaped by literary-critical treatments of Jonson and of city comedy, by historical study of the English language, by socio-linguistic and historical approaches to gender and language, as well as by the new frames for conceptualizing language and identity that have emerged from the late twentieth-century philosophical turns of post-structuralism and deconstruction. One tenet of my argument and approach is that we are better equipped, now, critically and especially theoretically, to fully comprehend city comedy's significance and its interrogation of a fragmented and expanding urban world, than at any time since the early modern period. As Paula Blank and others brilliantly have explored in recent years, language itself lay at the heart of debates both literary and political during this time, and never more vividly than in the increasingly heterogeneous center of England, London. The range of critical strands I strive to synthesize enables an important new reading of city comedy's role in early modern drama and in its historical, cultural moment.

Literary-Critical Context

Critical interest in Jacobean city comedy as a subgenre of early modern drama and thus, also, as a group of interrelated plays, truly began with Brian Gibbons' *Jacobean City Comedy* in 1968, and its distinction of city comedies' "critical and satirical design" and the "sordid realism" of their depiction of their audiences' everyday reality.[13] Though Jonas Barish's monumental study of Jonson's popular drama preceded Gibbons by eight years, Gibbons' interest in Jonson as one among a number of fellow-dramatists accomplished a kind of "retrospective genre-building" (Mehl et al 2) that placed city comedy unequivocally on the late twentieth century's critical map of English drama. Critical interest in Jacobean city comedy has surged in recent years with the publication of several major studies; the attention of both established as well as new scholars is evidenced in the number of recent dissertations addressing aspects of Jacobean drama and city comedy.[14] Such renewed critical interest has been linked by others to cultural studies' materialist lens, which has "only increased . . . attention because city comedy is so clearly a product of a Jacobean London in the throes of . . . emergent [forces] that challenged social order and stability" (Aasand, Rev. 947). There is an inherent competitive ethos to the genre, then, an understanding that has been reinforced by attention to the contemporary phenomenon of the *Poetemachia* and its direct implication of a highly competitive dramatic 'market,' as well. But city comedy's development within a climate of flux and instability also suggests a collective response or project. The present study's focus on several plays' discursive interrogation of the early modern vernacular in society joins a current conversation that explores such collective, ideological possibilities for these plays as a distinct category.

Since Gibbons, interest in city comedy regularly suggests the genre's complex relationship with its society, as critics often find themselves describing both how its plays did and did not neatly fit into their social and ideological setting. Anne Barton scrutinizes city comedy's interrogation of the city, its organization, and ideologies via a focus on civic pageantry. City leaders, she observes, relied on annual, civic spectacles to help animate London's powerful ethos (Barton, "London" 162). In ironic contrast, the same London authorities broadly disapproved of the commercial theaters, not only for their reputations as dens of iniquity, but particularly for the irreverence of the drama they presented. Satiric comedies in particular, and their unpredictable querying of civic life, were no allies of power structures (Barton, "London" 161). Ben Jonson, Thomas Middleton, and Thomas Dekker thus constitute a group of writers whose work city officials alternately commissioned and deplored; their comedies provided their city audiences with a decidedly less honorific parsing of the urban world than their pageantry. Lawrence Manley similarly observes important aspects of city comedy by virtue of its departures from convention, whether dramatic or discursive. Studying renaissance-era chorographies, Manley notes their surge in numbers in the early 1600's, and their strongly formulaic containment or ordering of the city (Manley, "Matron" 347). By contrast, Stow's *Survey of London* (1598, 1603)—a contemporary of such chorographies as well as of the emergence of Jacobean city comedies—radically departs from convention, according to Manley, revealing through its innovation the outdated ideology of chorography as a genre ("Matron" 363). In its second half, Stow's ward-by-ward perambulation of London depicts a complex and chaotic city, and Manley highlights the significance of this new, realistic perspective by suggesting its alignment with city comedy, which was already defying accepted ideologies and addressing the city's "monstrosity" ("Matron" 350).

Others also have recognized that city comedy importantly stages the problems of city life. Susan Wells reads the genre as an attempt to work out representational strategies for reflecting an increasingly indeterminate city, its development perhaps hinging in part on the growing disjunction between the official ideology of city pageants and conventional topographies on one hand, and the realities of city life on the other.[15] Jean Howard takes this view of the genre a step further still, arguing that city comedies succeeded sixteenth-century chronicle plays as sites of negotiating English identity.[16] In the face of an increasingly urban, English identity in the early seventeenth century, such negotiation comes to be a matter of posing and providing imaginary solutions to the problems of urban life. The genre's urban engagement is in the terms of the ideological and the discursive by these arguments, with the vernacular itself incidental or a stand-in for larger social concerns. Such metonymic power is evident in contemporary sources, as well. The vernacular is an evocative place-holder for social concerns and questions of identity in prose-tracts like George Puttenham's *The Arte of English Poesie* (1589), drama like Shakespeare's *Henry V* (1599) or *The Tempest* (1611), and in Edmund Spenser's famous letter to Gabriel Harvey, in which he demands, "may not we . . . have the kingdom of our own language?"[17]

But the vernacular functioned as more than a place-holder for other social anxieties, I would propose. At the heart of plays like *Bartholomew Fair* and *The Roaring Girl* is an interest in theorizing the role of language as the central, material component of city life. Such an assertion participates in recent emphasis on extending materialism's purview to attend to language as a component of people's material lives, and there is a range of critical support for this, including attention to a contemporaneous materialism which encompasses language itself.[18] Douglas Bruster recently has called for renewed attention to early modern England's own materialism as the most valuable focus of the current literary-critical purview. Bruster explains:

> When we think, for instance, of the intensive focus on the material world in such writers as Thomas Nashe, Ben Jonson, John Donne, and Thomas Middleton—to name only a few—we are forced to admit that these authors "theorized" objects, and people's relation to them, in quite complicated and compelling ways. Theirs was a culture that thought almost constantly of the material, even when in the midst of its greatest imaginative leaps: "[M]ay we cram / Within this wooden O the very casques / That did affright the air at Agincourt?" (Bruster 238)

Bruster's points are suggestive for the present study in several ways. Most obviously, in his explicit mentioning of Jonson and Middleton as purported theorists of their seventeenth-century material surroundings, Bruster proposes the value of more fully recognizing and precisely comprehending both playwrights' critical engagement with their society. Bruster points less directly to the specific "material world" or society whose material dimensions were these writers' concern, but the city-world of London becomes the crucial site, not just through the reference to natives such as Jonson and Middleton, but also through mention of Thomas Nashe and his parodic but vividly mercantilist paean to the red herring, as well as of the woefully insufficient London playhouse of Shakespeare's *Henry V*. The present study's focus on the relationship between city comedy, early modern language questions, and the growing city, extends Gibbons' legacy of generic critique and also strives to update our understanding, per Bruster and others, of city comedy through its incorporation of the valuable, newer purview of materialism and cultural studies.

The Idea of Language

In addition to this literary-critical frame, I am approaching city comedy and the role of language in society—both real and imagined—from a critical stance that situates this project within several non-literary frameworks concerning language. One of these is the study of the history of the English language, including ideas about English. The historical language-studies, first, of R.F. Jones, and subsequently of James Earl Joseph, Richard Bailey and James and Lesley Milroy, are the contemporary foundation of this field,[19] and all of these language-historians describe the early modern period's significance as a time of unprecedented lexical expansion as well as concerted and conflicting efforts at standardization. Scholars like James Earl Joseph, after R.F. Jones, pinpoint phases of the English vernacular in this period with observations highly relevant to my study's focus. Joseph notes an elaborative phase in the second half of the sixteenth century that coincided with the production of a national literature that was both aim and sign of such elaboration,[20] followed by a regulatory phase beginning around 1600 whereby the first appearance of numbers of grammars and monolingual dictionaries tracks the movement of the vernacular into a stage of standardization. Richard Bailey, foremost in *Images of English* (1991), surveys the ideas about the vernacular that coincided with the descriptive phases Joseph observes. Acknowledging that linguists typically have little interest in laypeople's notions or images of language, Bailey counter-argues for the great value of common practices, beliefs, and ideas concerning language to understanding not language technicalities, but rather language-in-use and as a shaping social, political, and imaginative force (Bailey ix). Like Joseph, Bailey notes the appearance and then surge of books on words and usage in the late sixteenth-century and sees evidence of a coalescing image of English as a national, authoritative language in its own right (Bailey 36).

Providing both descriptive surveys of linguistic change and histories of cultural change, the kinds of questions history-of-English scholarship has helped raise concerning perceptions of language, including language change, are now central modes of early modern socio-linguistic and literary inquiry. Subsequently, younger scholars interested in vernacular history and culture have troubled the apparent seamlessness of change sometimes implied in these earlier studies. Writing most recently in the new *Cambridge History of Early Modern English Literature* (2002), Paula Blank argues that early modern England grappled with a 'questione della lingua' as much as any other European nation in this period, and that the "linguistic exuberance" so readily attributed to this era of literary output must be reconsidered in terms of a fairly anxious process of vying ideals of expansion and discrimination.[21] The lexical expansion of English between 1580 and 1630 was unprecedented, Blank acknowledges, but what was most significant about such vernacular enrichment was its "relocat[ion] of the contests between the vernacular and Latin within the English language itself" (145). Language, more than anything, is thus a changing and contested field, in this period, a concept boldly and continuously asserted in the city comedies at the center of this study.

The links between gender and language increasingly are central to inquiry concerning uses and perceptions of language as well as discursive effects, both historically and in the present, and in recent decades the study of gender and language has become its own field of inquiry, incorporating the practices and scholarship primarily of Philosophy, Linguistics, Sociology, English Language and Literature, and History, among a range of relevant disciplines. Gender and language scholars, accordingly, are disciplinarily diverse: the field's body of work ranges from the highly theoretical work of French feminists like Helene Cixous and Luce Irigaray and their search for a language outside patriarchal structures and ideology;[22] to descriptive and empirical research on language structure and categorization;[23] to socio-linguistic observation and theorizing of the gendering of matters of language politics, both current and historical, such as standardization.[24]

Sociolinguists like Deborah Cameron, Robin Lakoff, and Lynda Mugglestone, to name a few of the most established scholars in the field, all devote research to varied dimensions of the connections between language and gender, including Mugglestone's work on the historical prescription of "proper" female speech that offers evidence of the embeddedness of gender in the attitudes and expectations that surround language use.[25] Mugglestone's study of eighteenth- and nineteenth-century preoccupations with proper accent and speech as crucial components of true gentlewomanly status begs pertinent questions regarding the nexus of gender and language even earlier, amid the fraught language consciousness of the English Renaissance. Mugglestone observes the subtly prescriptive collapse of what is "ladylike" into what is "standard" (non-localized, grammatically correct) in the eras she studies, finding a strong cultural and socio-symbolic significance attributed to female speech as a wellspring of perfection and purity.[26] What kind of relationship exists between women and language, then, in an earlier period where the ideal and actuality of 'standard' English was as yet significantly unresolved and a central concern? The implications of Mugglestone's findings, as well as fellow scholar Suzanne Romaine's assertion that, "debates about language are really about issues of race, gender, class, or culture" (Romaine 293), suggest the relevance of gender and language questions to situating city comedy's staging of the city as a language contest. Gender and language scholars emphasize the complexity of language and strive to understand and articulate the ways it shapes the social landscape as well as how we use it in negotiating that landscape. It is with this kind of sophisticated, socially contingent understanding that valuable new readings can be made of earlier texts and the language debates that informed them.

The work of scholars such as Mugglestone now form a kind of canon of gender and language study, and the breadth of this inquiry reaches into literary studies, as well, with feminist scholars interested in women and minority writers and in understanding non-privileged subjectivities from earlier periods turning with interest to traditionally sociolinguistic methods of inquiry and scholarship. The fruitful nature of this hybridity for generating new knowledge about the early modern period is evident in recent work by Margaret Ferguson, for example, whose *Dido's Daughters: Literacy, Gender, and Empire in Early Modern England and France* (2003), reframes the imperial projects of early modern England and France and the contributions of early modern women writers like Elizabeth Cary and Aphra Behn, by way of careful and sustained attention to ideologies of literacy. What did the term "literacy" signify in a period when authoritative "masculine" languages like Latin were ceding ground to the vernaculars and a "standard" language was a contested, overtly ideological enterprise? Taking a strong cue from gender and language scholarship and methodologies, Ferguson seeks to insert historical women and cultural theory regarding gender difference into our accounts of literacy as a part of the modernizing process of England and France (Ferguson 13).

Another instructive example of this feminist-critical incorporation of sociolinguistic questions and the reinvigorated inquiry within early modern studies that results, is Juliet Fleming's "Dictionary English and the Female Tongue," a groundbreaking study when it appeared, in 1993, in its surveying of the first English dictionaries and the discursive function of a much-emphasized female readership to these texts' shaping of attitudes toward English and even of the language itself. Fleming's interest in early dictionaries and their purported female audience is by no means a-historical, but her work marks a departure from more descriptive historical studies by its emphasis on theorizing gender's role in the discourse of dictionary-English and language standardization using twentieth-century, philosophy-of-language criticism. Gesturing explicitly to Foucault's theorizing of language and of the mechanisms of discourse in society, Fleming trains a cultural materialist's lens on early seventeenth-century "hard word guides" and identifies their frequent address to women, "not because [women] cared to ascertain the correct use of English, but because they could be used to represent its problems" (181). Women, Fleming argues, were interpellated to represent lexical extravagance that thereby justified regulation: these earliest dictionaries provocatively enact the process whereby a discourse first produces a disruptive other as the ground on which to assert its own adequacy.[27]

At the heart of the new knowledge being generated by approaches like Fleming's and Ferguson's is not, typically, a new set of primary source materials but rather new sets of critical assumptions and questions, including gender and language practices as well as, fundamentally, a theoretical turn whose value as an analytical paradigm is perhaps especially great for the early modern period because of the centrality of language and language-concerns to its cultural expressions. The turn to which I refer is the late twentieth-century 'discovery' of language as a constructed and contestatory field of human identity, expression, and epistemology, first through Structuralism and, even more importantly, through Deconstruction.[28] Contemporary literary-critical and sociolinguistic scholarship relies on implicit acceptance of the politics of language, but the work of Fleming, Ferguson, or indeed of Raymond Williams and Michel Foucault, all derive from a now mostly unexceptional understanding of the need for confronting language itself as indeterminate, more a surface than a substructure of human identity and society, and as the preeminent dilemma of twentieth-century thought about human existence.

The contested state of the vernacular in early modern England and the range of its expression are compelling sites which we may comprehend with greater insight, thanks to these latter day ways of conceptualizing language and its function. Among the valuable observations of critics working along these lines is a clearer picture of an early modern age with an analogous linguistic self-consciousness, grappling with its own, at times deconstruction-like suspicions concerning the role of the sign and the stability of linguistic signification as well as other semiotics.[29] Keir Elam, for example, writing in the early 1980's as part of the first flush of literary-critical work influenced heavily by the turns of Structuralist and Post-Structuralist theory, argues for a thorough re-assessment of Shakespeare's comedies as pure speech-acts, with a meta-linguistic attention to language as a semiotic game as their preeminent theme (Elam 10–12). Elam explicitly confronts the formalism inherent in his meticulous quantifying of speech-acts and linguistic play by gesturing to the historical context of Elizabethan England, in which "language occupied a central place in all areas of cultural endeavor and socio-political conflict"(1). His point is not simply to detail language-games, he asserts, but, in such detailing, to emphasize that Shakespeare's pervasive "exploration of linguistic concerns . . . can be seen as a powerful response to the most important epistemological crisis of the . . . age" (22). Elam's work invaluably suggests further study of early modern drama and culture via newer theoretical parameters, offering, as it does, a fully realized literary re-reading via contemporary language thought and philosophy. As if to spark critical endeavors in this vein, Elam explicitly mentions Jonson as comparably interested in the "self activity of the word" (2). Drama, it seems, is unquestionably ripe territory for observing and theorizing the uses of language and meta-language in the period.

Elam's 1980's-era study also is instructive in its exposure of how critical and theoretical stakes have evolved since his writing. With the emergence of the New Historicism and Cultural Studies as well as, significantly, a range of feminist critical practices, we have learned to consider not just the contingency of what makes up identity and experience, but the politics of such contingency, with language at the center in both cases. Elam provocatively characterizes Shakespeare's language-games as responses to an Elizabethan epistemological crisis but stops short of querying the political as well as the material implications of such responses. As evidenced in the work of Fleming, Ferguson, and Blank, all described above, since the 1980's critical engagement with language and literature increasingly seeks to query the stakes—epistemological, but also social, political—of discursive constructions and debates, including meta-linguistic and meta-discursive habits. The work of these current scholars, as well as the present study, are indebted to forthright, theory-driven projects like Elam's, but no longer is the linguistic or semiotic assumed to operate un-constitutively with gender and a range of other discursive and political dimensions.[30] In configuring an approach to city comedy that combines the range of inquiry surveyed above, my object is to observe but also to critically query the acute language consciousness evident in a group of plays as well as the implications of this staged consciousness for our understanding of early modern literature, gender, and culture. What was at stake, for Jonson, Middleton, Dekker, and their peers, in staging language concerns and in portraying the city as a set of such concerns? What are the stakes, today, of reading in this way? My study proposes the importance of being alert to such questions in reading city comedy.

CHAPTER OVERVIEW AND OUTLINE

Three chapters, each devoted to an individual play, follow an opening chapter that establishes Jacobean London as a society of enormous growth and change that was distinctly animated by a related ethos of linguistic or discursive proliferation and fragmentation. On both counts, the vernacular already was a powerful topos for other urban phenomena or concerns. To establish this, in Chapter One I will draw upon such primary texts as Stow's *Survey of London* (1598); the range of Grammars, orthographies, and other language-manuals that first began to appear in great numbers between 1580 and 1620; some of the pamphlets of the time (a new form of print and circulation) concerning propriety and excess in apparel and diction; and anti- theatrical tracts such as Stephen Gosson's "The School of Abuse" (1579). These print artifacts I combine with recent critical discussions of such cultural components as a heightened linguistic consciousness surrounding the Scots-speaking James I, and an increasingly commercial City whose traditional guild-identity and civic symbolism no longer meshed with its reality, a characterization that is a matter of some dispute but that nonetheless points up critical interest in a period of change.[31] Matthew R. Martin places city comedies within a distinct social and political milieu when he describes them as concerned with "the making and interrogation of self and society," not on the peripheries of royal power, but in the city's social reality, which was undergoing "subtle and not so subtle reconfiguration" in this period (Martin 18). Drawing from such a diversity of texts and ideas, Chapter One frames city comedy's cultural context. The chapter opens consideration of the plays' preoccupation with language at both the discursive and linguistic level by virtue of their embedded-ness in the daily life of a city itself so-preoccupied.

Chapter Two turns to Jonson and argues that *Epicoene* configures contemporary concerns surrounding the vernacular in terms of a city of prodigious talk. City talk is staged in gendered terms, and in *Epicoene* questions of language and the city above all become questions of women and language, as speech is queried via *topoi* concerning literacy/eloquence and language as fashion. Concern for the status and work of language in society is concentrated in the problem of women's use of, and perceived abuse of, English.

The titles of two of the three plays treated here, Jonson's *Epicoene or The Silent Woman,* and Middleton and Dekker's *The Roaring Girl,* explicitly question women's decorum and speech. Both plays map concerns for language and society in terms of women, specifically aspects of female speech, and both signal their particular project or lens through oxymoron: *roaring girl* and *silent woman*. Each title on its own expresses little more than a sardonic commonplace of the patriarchal culture that derived it. The two taken together, however, reveal telling elements of their culture's paradigmatic distrust of women: first, that this uneasiness is centered in female speech and language; and second, based on these two contradictory titles, that women were in an impossible situation. "The Silent Woman" plays on the perceived impossibility of female silence; "The Roaring Girl's" oxymoronic tang stems from its seemingly inappropriate but threatening linkage of "roaring" with "girl," and not "boy." 'Roaring boys'—carousing, master-less young men unruled and unconcerned for propriety—were an accepted, if deplored, feature of London city life. A "roaring girl" derives its significance and humor both from its incongruity and its potential for threatening titillation, as well as its cynical link to the notion of a "silent woman." Women simultaneously are expected to be and considered incapable of being decorous and silent, and their speech is automatically sensationalized and condemned as "roaring."

There is additional irony in the fact that each play's eponymous woman is not at all what she seems. In Middleton and Dekker, "the roaring girl's" roaring is vividly philanthropic and civic-minded, Moll a singular figure unthreatening to the status quo because of the work she performs to shore it up, albeit from the margins. The "silent woman" appears to offer unimaginable perfection but empties this out entirely. In the end there is neither real silence nor even a real woman. The "roaring girl," on the other hand, seems to offer unimaginable disorder but empties this out, too: 'disorder' is in service to order, and 'roaring' is re-imagined as orderly, systematic, and legible. As Chapter Three will argue, Middleton and Dekker's play is an enigmatic fable of a semiotically cohered London, betraying anxieties about linguistic representation and coherence already observed in *Epicoene* and in the contemporary climate more generally.

Placing *The Roaring Girl* between *Epicoene* and *Bartholomew Fair* also places their differences in bold relief. *Epicoene*'s conclusion somewhat nihilistically asserts that language is indeed but a commodity, and perhaps is irrelevant as an all-but-silent plot triumphs over impotent railings and witty rhetorical flights alike. In contrast to such entropy, *The Roaring Girl* ultimately is a fantasy about the city cohered by the unlikely and otherwise unruly sources of Moll Cutpurse and the underworld language of cant. With Chapter Four, *Bartholomew Fair* provides an additional contrast, for while many of its Smithfield characters share the lowlife world of Moll Cutpurse and the canting of *The Roaring Girl*, the latter Jonson play famously is unified only by the ever-changing Fair. In *Bartholomew Fair* there is little to no shared discourse and nothing inclusive about language unless it is understood as a game.

Bartholomew Fair asserts that any trust in language's truth or authority is unwarranted, but the comedy's festive mood celebrates rather than condemns the meaninglessness of language that is just play. *Bartholomew Fair* is closely tied to *Epicoene* and *The Roaring Girl* as a document of the vernacular, or of vernacular concerns, but it is unique in its existential creation and exploration of a world seemingly free from anxieties over language's significance. Written later than *Epicoene,* and as the final work among his major plays, *Bartholomew Fair*, I will argue, marks an evolution in Jonson's attitudes and anxieties in its more genial limning of a society in which order is subdued by the Fair, and in which the constraints of coherence are repeatedly defied and the most preposterous figures are those who take too seriously language's import or decorum. Whether for purveyors like Knockem and Ursula the pig-woman or visitors like Wasp or John Littlewit, language is a game, explicitly and implicitly; it does not truly cohere anything, but this is of no matter.

Epicoene and *Bartholomew Fair* both belong to a group of plays, including *Volpone* and *The Alchemist*, which reflect Jonson at the height of his comedic powers.[32] *Epicoene* (1610) closely follows *The Alchemist* (1609); *Volpone* (1606) and *Bartholomew Fair* (1614) bookend this great period. It is clear that Jonson became more interested in London as a specific locale following *Volpone*. While *Volpone* shares some urbane affinities with successive plays, *The Alchemist* vividly and rather claustrophobically localizes us in London's Blackfriars, and *Epicoene* and *Bartholomew Fair* continue this new precision and exploration of place. Even more tellingly, Jonson's 1616 *Works* includes a reworked *Every Man In His Humor* (1598) with its scene newly relocated from Italy to London. Jonas Barish suggests two plausible dates for this revision: 1605, because of a revival at court, or 1612 (Barish 130). In either case the correspondence in time with Jonson's transition to a London scene in his greatest comedies is suggestive. More than simply using 'the urban' as a generic backdrop for his satirical purposes, Jonson increasingly engages with London's particularities, in comedies which exploit but also query urban idiosyncrasies, personalities, and, especially, anxieties. Despite their clear affinities with *Volpone* and *The Alchemist*—most notably in the energy of their plots and dialogue and the grasping worlds they sketch—*Epicoene* and *Bartholomew Fair* stand out because they are completely in prose, apart from scattered passages in each of deliberately clumsy poetry.[33] Particularly for a stylist like Jonson, this shift to vernacular prose and its everyday locutions demands scrutiny of what is being explored in such deliberate terms.

If the two Jonson plays unambiguously rank among his best and most important work, Dekker and Middleton's well known *The Roaring Girl* occupies a more idiosyncratic place in the work of each of its collabora-tors. Thomas Dekker's most well-known drama is *The Shoemaker's Holiday* (1600), a late-Elizabethan, highly sentimental comedy whose common attri-bution as a 'city comedy' is somewhat perplexing because of its early date and its romantic characterizations and tone.[34] After this play, we come across Dekker mostly as a dramatic collaborator, with Middleton on *The Honest Whore*, Part I (1604) and *The Roaring Girl* (1611), and with John Ford and William Rowley on *The Witch of Edmonton* (1621).[35] That these few plays remain of the more than seventy in which Dekker apparently had a hand suggests both the value of *The Roaring Girl* as well as the difficulty in assess-ing its true place among Dekker's dramatic works and ideas. The play depicts diverse echelons of London society and engages with actual city concerns and enticements through its heroine, Moll Cutpurse. In its more romantic elements the play is recognizably Dekker's, with its clear echoes of Dekker's sensationalist, underworld handbooks like *The Gull's Hornbook* (1609), by far his biggest success as a writer.[36] Where the romantic city gives way to less sanguine visions we perhaps should detect Middleton's hand.

Middleton's best comedies possess the exuberant but slightly acerbic energy and commentary that define Jacobean 'city comedy' as a genre. *The Roaring Girl's* unsentimental examinations of London life fit coherently beside other Middleton plays like *Michaelmas Term* (1604–6), *A Trick to Catch the Old One* (1604–7), and *A Chaste Maid in Cheapside* (1613).[37] But Middleton is more well known and more frequently read for his later tragedies, *Women Beware Women* (c. 1625) and especially *The Changeling* (1622). While the potential for analogous domestic tragedy certainly exists in *The Roaring Girl's* sub-plot of citizen wives and their seducers, this is never realized in the midst of this earlier play's different interests and tone. The abject despair and hor-ror that have long fascinated readers and audiences of Middleton's tragedies nowhere is in evidence in *The Roaring Girl*. Middleton's interest in the social languages of London and in language as an important fabric of his society is clear in the language-policing of *A Chaste Maid in Cheapside* and in *Mich-aelmas Term's* depiction of the micro-community of the Inns of Court and its jargon (Covatta 81, 85). With *The Roaring Girl*, this interest combines with Dekker's more genial vision to depict a linguistic fabric that is comfort-ingly benign. That this fantasy does not quite succeed, thus complicating too simple a reading of "The Roaring Girl's" apparent utopianism, may be Middleton's most interesting dramatic triumph.[38]

Chapter One

"Noise of a Thousand Sounds": Anxious Plenty, Language, and London

This chapter aims to establish London c. 1610 as a setting and society self-consciously experiencing great change with a distinct, accompanying ethos of proliferation and fragmentation. Language historians like R.F. Jones and Richard Bailey have taught us to understand the early modern period as one during which "consciousness of the vernacular was so keen and widespread that it is manifested in all kinds of writing . . . [but] the potentialities of the language were in large measure concealed."[1] I see a crucial relationship between this concern for the vernacular and its authority and the problem of encompassing the increasingly urban world of London in the same period. Jacobean London's preoccupation with the urban and the excessive overwhelmingly focuses on the linguistic itself. In text after text, we may witness the extent to which the vernacular is not only a trope of the particular *copiae* of seventeenth-century London, but is a central concern of the society; words are as much the root as the symbol of the society's sense of proliferation and fragmentation. The instability of such urban copiousness is signaled by the alternate celebration and condemnation observable in any survey of works from the period. The combination of exuberance and anxiety with which London's burgeoning variety and modulating identities are discussed is striking, as is the diversity of discursive sites animated by this ethos of proliferation. Social and political concerns are language concerns; the discourses of fashion, of decorum, of nationalism, of sexual roles and differences, of political hierarchy, are all self-conscious vocabularies—what makes London London, in this period, is its representation via a profuse vernacular. It is a ubiquitous *topos* of the period, holding distinct implications for reading urban literature like city comedy.

It is important to foreground this climate within which seventeenth-century city comedy evolved in England. This connection between the urban, perceptions of the profuse, and the still-stabilizing vernacular is key to understanding both the genre's taking up of the linguistic and discursive as modes of considering its society, and its plays' preoccupation with language by virtue of their embedded-ness in the daily life of the city. Urbane, satiric comedy has a long, classical history—in its focus on city life Jacobean city comedy is not unique; as well, many writers in other modes in this period express a corresponding interest in questions of the vernacular. The city comedy of the early seventeenth-century is nonetheless a unique phenomenon in its explicit imbrication of language and the city in the culturally potent forum of the theater, and in its consistent situation in the contemporary city, not a foreign or ancient locale. A significant element of English city comedy's work, according to Jean Howard, consisted of "posing and providing imaginary solutions" to the problems of the city and of city life.[2] The problem most consistently and diversely confronted in city comedy, I contend, is the vernacular and its ability to cohere an increasingly incoherent world. Jacobean city comedies are self-conscious responses to their society's coincident preoccupation with proliferation and with language.

The work of this chapter first will consist of surveying a range of materials and events from the period, and discussing each one's reflection of the issues sketched above in order to establish the climate within which city comedy's language-project developed. Beginning with such an obvious source as the language and word-guides that began to appear in great numbers for the first time in the period, it will move to consider the antitheatrical tracts of Philip Stubbes and Stephen Gosson, John Stow's *Survey of London*, some educational institutions, and the influence of a Scots king. Following this, the chapter concludes by focusing such a spectrum of vernacular concern more directly in terms of the three playwrights whose selected plays are the focus of this study: Ben Jonson, Thomas Middleton, and Thomas Dekker. All three wrote non-dramatic works for publication; Middleton, for example, was as well-known for his authorship of civic pageants, particularly the annual Lord Mayor's installation, as for his stage-drama. A brief reading of Jonson's *Discoveries* and *Grammar*, selections from Dekker's numerous pamphlets, and the range of Middleton's focus on London all offer insight into these writers' interest in language and the city, and into their use of city comedy as a distinct means of thinking through this interest.

LANGUAGE ANXIETIES IN PRINT, CITY, COURT

City comedy takes up the vernacular as its means of examining urban society at a time when London, and especially its burgeoning variety, was being widely noted. Statistically and historically, early modern London was the site of enormous growth and change in the period from 1580 to 1640, and particularly following the accession of James I in 1603.[3] People flocked to the city's economic opportunities from outlying regions; the city's traditional guild structure and governance, though still in place, increasingly were inadequate to the contemporary realities of new populations, new civic needs and pressures, and the growing predominance of wealthy merchant-trade interests. London was unrivalled as an urban setting, both within England and without. It was "the Epitome and Breviary of all Britain,"[4] according to William Camden, the period's great historian and chorographer, a description whose implication of orderly significance was more wishful than actual, for there was heightened concern among officials regarding the "problem of order," according to historian Keith Wrightson. "The times seemed out of joint," even to contemporaries.[5] London life had no comparable equivalent elsewhere in England, and its singularity rested not simply on its size, but on its accompanying mutability and questionably coherent setting.

We can observe in a range of Jacobean works a marked response to this question of coherence in the form of varying methods and targets of ordering and classification. If, as Richard Helgerson has argued, Elizabethan writers collectively engaged in the "writing of England,"[6] the early Jacobean climate focused on the scrutinizing and organizing of England, specifically London. And just as with Helgerson's Elizabethans, the central component of any English work was English itself. Camden, for example, whose *Brittania* (1587) Helgerson sites as an important component to the Elizabethan generational project of England, published a distinctly different kind of book in 1605, *Remaines Concerning Britain*.[7] The *Remaines* is an encyclopedic study of the language, not the land, of Britain. Tracing the *Remaines'* origins, its editor R.D. Dunn characterizes it as a work "born of the same patriotic impulse which lies behind so much of Elizabethan culture" (xvi), but the same editor later notes that the *Remaines* in fact proceeds differently than *Brittania*:

> In the *Brittania* Camden was interested in languages as the 'surest evidence of the original of a nation' . . . This preoccupation with national identity has given way [in *Remaines*] to a . . . consideration of languages in general, their characteristics and development, beginning with the 'confusion of languages out of Moses.' (xxii)

This, I would argue, is a Jacobean project, exhibiting desire for an ordered vernacular simultaneously with self-consciousness of a variety resistant to order. In the same text, Camden complains, "I may be charged by the minion refiners of English, neither to write State-English, Court-English, nor Secretary-English, and verily I acknowledge it. Sufficient it is for me, if I have waded . . . in the fourth kinde, which is plain English" (*Remaines* 36). Making sense of a city and society in flux depended on making sense of a vernacular widely perceived as itself changing and as profuse an emblem of Englishness as London. A broad range of texts, whether explicit or implicit in their treatment of the language, establish this context for Jacobean city comedy in which societal order and disorder become questions of the linguistic or discursive.

The First Dictionaries—

Sixteenth-century precursors like William Bullokar's *Booke at Large, for the Amendment of Orthographie for English Speeche* (1580) and Richard Mulcaster's *Firste Part of the Elementarie* (1582) already were in circulation, but when the first true dictionary of vernacular Englishwas published in 1604—Robert Cawdrey's "A Table Alphabetical"—it ushered in a flurry of additional efforts which mark the early seventeenth-century as a period of particular concern for vernacular standardization.[8] Language historian John Earl Joseph, argues that the crucial vernacular development phases of expansion and stabilization fairly exactly correspond with the latter sixteenth-century and the seventeenth-century, respectively. Joseph is summarized by Juliet Fleming:

> In the first phase, attention to the perceived "inadequacy" of a native tongue gave rise to a period of rapid elaboration, during which structural or lexical elements were added to make the language adequate to new needs. In the second or restrictive phase of standardization regulations were introduced to stop unsupervised elaboration and make variation less a matter of choice than of fixed rules.[9]

The vernacular elegance of Elizabethan poets 'proved' the eloquent potential of English by 1600, but the language remained unruled. The transition of English into the second and restricting, "standardization" stage "can be plotted by the gradual yielding of sixteenth-century works on rhetoric to the grammars, orthographies, and dictionaries of the seventeenth-century" (Fleming 184). The language and word guides of the seventeenth-century were a direct response to a perceived abundance, even over-abundance, of the lexicon. Their project, whether implicitly or explicitly announced,

was the ordering and containing of such linguistic excess. The very proliferation of these same guides, however, had the ironic effect of amplifying
vernacular concerns and the impression of copiousness. In the brief survey
here, I will suggest that such an epochal project of reform, if ultimately
it produced the sought-for coherence, mainly belied significant doubts
about its subject, English itself, as a language of stability, much less of
privilege.

Cawdrey's *A Table Alphabetical* is presented as: "conteyning and
teaching the true writing and understanding of hard usuall English wordes,
borrowed from the Hebrew, Greeke, Latine, or French, etc., with the interpretation thereof by plaine English words, gathered for the benefit and
helpe of Ladies, Gentlewomen, or any other unskillful persons" (Blank
20). Cawdrey's presentation of English in terms of its legion new words
from foreign tongues is striking. In his *Preface*, Cawdrey renders this problem in more intimate terms: "Some men seek so far for outlandish English,
that they forget altogether their mothers [sic] language, so that if some of
their mothers were alive, they were not able to tell, or understand what
they say" (Fleming 195). There are several problematic layers to this figuring of language-change in familial terms. Most obvious is the anxiety of a
newly unnatural vernacular that distances its speakers from their home and
identity, but there is also the anxiety of an outdated but native language
(that of an older, mother's generation) that has been abandoned for a more
elusive, unstable medium. If Cawdrey's goal in such prefatory words is to
critique the influx of foreign, "hard" words, what his *Table* in fact accomplishes is a codification, or attempt at ordering—at "Englishing"—such
words. His project, echoed by those that followed him, reveals the coincid-
ing enthusiasms for a certain copiousness and for coherence (for language
as a cohering system) in the period. Cawdrey's *Treasury or storehouse of sim-
ilies* (1600), a text that predates the *Table* by four years, makes this vivid
in its figuring of a storehouse for similes "for all estates of men in general."
This is systematized knowledge for all to use, made available by way of
a vast receptacle for quantities of an explicit commodity. Apart from the
striking mercantilist terms, what is emphasized, I would suggest, is sheer
quantity for consumption.

Cawdrey's *Table* was followed, and copied, by John Bullokar's *English
Expositor* (1616), Henry Cockeram's *The English Dictionary: or an Interpreter
of hard English words* (1623), and Thomas Blount's *Glossographia* (1656),
each one typically crediting its predecessors while also announcing its own
innovation.[10] Thus, the complete title of Cockeram's *Dictionary* reads:

> The English Dictionarie: or An Interpreter of hard English Words.
> Enabling as well Ladies and Gentlewoman, young Schollers, Clarkes,
> Merchants, as also Strangers of any Nation, to the understanding of the
> more difficult Authors already printed in our Language, and the more
> speedy attaining to an elegant perfection of the English tongue, both in
> reading, speaking, and writing. Being a Collection of the choicest words
> contained in the Table Alphabetical and English Expositor, *and of some
> thousand words never published by any heretofore.* (title page, italics mine)

The melodramatic flourish of the last phrase curiously contradicts the earnest,
taxonomic quality of the title up till that point; the urge to standardize and
the titillating inclusion of yet more and more words once again coincide to
place in relief the anxieties and pleasures of the transitioning vernacular. If
Cockeram's title suggests a text that alternately orders and expands, his prede-
cessor Bullokar's *English Expositor* accomplishes both at the same time. In his
"Instruction to the Reader," Bullokar clarifies his purpose in focusing only on
"the hardest words used in our language," making explicit that his text is not
a guide to common usage. Instead, "if a word bee of different signification,
the one easie, the other more difficult, I onely speake of interpretation of the
hardest, as in the wordes *Tenne, Girle, Garter,* may appear" (title page "Instruction"). In apparently organizing and codifying these hard words, Bullokar also
succeeds in multiplying the different words' possible significations, a provocative if accurate practice that seems guaranteed to augment popular perception
of vernacular change and slipperiness, not contain it.[11]

These and several other early English dictionaries explicitly invoke
a female readership in their dedications, which Juliet Fleming reads not
simply as good patronage-politics, but in fact as evidence of "gender difference . . . provid[ing] a conceptual grid within which the English vernacular
came of age as an authoritative tongue" (178). By such regular appeals, the
female reader and speaker comes to represent problems of the vernacular, a
key assertion of Fleming's that re-frames early modern discourse itself, and
discursive constructions of women, particularly urban women.[12] Cultural and
feminist critics, for example, have long noted commonplace conflations of the
extravagant or excessive with the feminine. Excess, whether sartorial, cosmetic,
libidinal, or—significantly—rhetorical, has been identified as part of early
modern discursive shaping of gender roles, figuring of femininity and effeminacy, and containment of women.[13] Fleming's work, however, adds a provocative dimension to such cultural and literary studies of women and gender as
well as to the study of the vernacular in the period. Positioned as the primary
audience of the first organizing compendiums of the vernacular, described

above in all their cross-purposes, female excess becomes explicitly linguistic, and vice-versa. The hard-word guides represent an attempt to order and contain language on behalf of women readers, but their offerings also defeat containment in their extension of the female appetite for more and more.

Women already were ascribed a slippery position with regard to the vernacular that predates the seventeenth-century guides discussed above. John Florio, a language scholar with his own influential Italian-English Dictionary (*Worlde of Wordes*, 1598), reflects a sixteenth-century Humanist commonplace when he asserts that women guard the wellspring of vernacular purity.[14] This assignment of vernacular preservation to women derived, sentimentally, from the fact that Latin was the proper linguistic domain of men (among the educated) in medieval and early modern England, and thus the language in which prestige activities of the culture were carried out. Such apparent maintenance of English by women was also highly problematic, however, as Walter Ong notes in his work on Latin-study as a 'puberty rite' of renaissance youth.[15] Ong quotes Sir Thomas Elyot's admonition: "After that a childe is come to seven years of age, I holde it expedient that he be taken from the company of women" (Ong, *Latin* 110). More than simply unhelpful to a boy learning Latin, Ong observes, the vernacular world of women posed a genuine linguistic threat to boys' admittance to the non-English world of men. The vernacular and women's use of and influence over it both were freighted with ambivalent, vividly gendered significance well before the seventeenth-century, when English's rise and Latin's diminution as a prestige language complicated its usage, perceptions, and anxieties the more.

Fleming's sense of the importance of women in the standardization of the vernacular in the period has significant implications for city comedy. One would expect the plays' female characterizations to be complexly bound up with questions of the vernacular, and I will argue that this is in fact the case, particularly in *Epicoene* and *The Roaring Girl.* The early dictionaries' most vivid motif of copia—of the copiousness of the vernacular's new lexicon—is as importantly a signal of femininity as of urbanity, and often both simultaneously. To fully comprehend the potency and ubiquity of this motif and its associations, I turn now from dictionaries to another genre of ordering and containment through words, this time of the city itself: the topography, specifically John Stow's *The Survey of London.*

Stow: London as Language

Stow situated his project of the *Survey of London* (1598, 1603) firmly within the precincts of other "perambulations," of Kent (by William Lambert) and of Middlesex and Hampshire (by Christopher Norden), respectively.[16]

Though he uses the terms "shire" and "county" to distinguish the work of surveying Kent from his own "countrie" of London, Stow does not remark on any difference in the particularly urban work of his "discovery of London, my native soil," musing that all such surveying, collected, might "make up a whole body of the English chorography" (xxiii). Richard Helgerson's work on Tudor chorographies makes no closer distinction, either; as part of his appealing thesis of an Elizabethan generation's project of "writing England," Helgerson provides no sense that Stow's detailing of London was any kind of departure from a larger, national project (Helgerson 126). But the *Survey* is, in fact, a departure in a couple of ways. Notable, first, is Stow's emphasis on London as his "native soil and countrie," thus the city as a region in its own right with its own distinct identity. Despite the proliferation of maps and views of London in the Tudor/Stuart period, a development that can be ascribed to a growing sense of London's singularity, a chorographic focus solely on the city was new. In an extended look at the genre of "topographical description" that emerged in the sixteenth and seventeenth centuries, Lawrence Manley highlights Stow's *Survey* as the only such text focused solely on London.[17] Stow is secondly a departure in the innovation of its street-level "perambulation" of the city. Manley is interested in the early modern evolution of figurations of London away from a unified, personified ideal, and reads Stow as playing an important role in this process when he devotes the second half of the *Survey* to a street-by-street detailing of the city. Manley observes:

> By perambulating the city, [Stow] transformed what was, in the personifying rubrics, essentially a blazon or at best a triumphal procession of the city attributes into an extended *voie* or exploration of the landscape. This not only allowed for more intimate detail but also introduced an historically situated observer into the landscape. ("Matron-Monster" 363)

Such an individual, newly historicized perspective depersonalizes the city as it personalizes the individual's view of it; the ordering and idealizing schema of the chorography gives way to a sensibility more closely allied with city comedy and its interest in street-level profusion and in London's alluring monstrosity. Stow is intent on providing an accurate depiction of the diverse arrays of the city, both over time and in his present day. As he begins his ward-by-ward descriptions, for example, he devotes three full pages to a delineation of the geographical divisions of the city, natural and man-made, and includes a carefully updated list of all twenty-five city wards. London's profusion is for him not a monstrosity, but an urban marvel and engrossing subject for his taxonomic attention. The shift away from traditional chorographic modes of description, however, marks a shift in understanding of the city itself. It is, by this, all detail and no schema, a sense underlined by Stow's continual use of lists and series: whether of church monuments, Lord Mayors, city wards, Roman antiquities found under Bread Street, goods brought in via Billingsgate harbor, and so on. Careful articulation of the variety of the city's trades and their changing locations, below, is compelling for its precision and its amplification, simultaneously, of both urban plenty and changeability:

> For whereas mercers and haberdashers used to keep their shops in West Cheape, of later time they held them on London Bridge, where partly they remain. The goldsmiths . . . are now for the most part removed into the south side of West Cheape, the pepperers and grocers of Soper's Lane are now in Bucklesberrie, and other places dispersed. The drapers of Lombard street and of Cornhill are seated in Candlewick street and Watheling street . . . the stock fishmongers in Thames street; wet fishmongers in Knightriders street and Bridge street . . . The Brewers for the more part remain near to the friendly water of Thames; the butchers in Eastcheape, St. Nicholas shambles, and the Stockes market; the hosiers of old time in Hosier lane, near unto Smithfield, are since removed into Cordwayner street, the upper part thereof by Bow church, and last of all into Birchoveris lane by Cornhill. (74–75)

This description goes on to describe, in succession as above, shoemakers, curriers, founders, cooks, poulterers, bowyers, pater-noster makers, bead makers, text-writers, patten-makers, laborers, horse-coursers, and sellers of oxen, sheep, swine, "and such like." Karen Newman, reading another of the *Survey's* series-laden passages, this one describing luxury goods for sale in London shops, sees Stow as a conservative critic of a burgeoning consumerism devoted to such "knickknacks, though to no purpose necessary."[18] Such lists effectively trivialize their contents, she argues. While new-fangled, fashionable items such as "Owches, Brooches . . . Girdles of the *Spanish* make, Cards, and Puppets"[19] might well be frivolous to Stow, Newman's materialist consideration neglects other points of significance to this series. Specifically, the apparatus of the series clearly becomes, for Stow, the only adept rhetorical mode with which to attempt a survey of London. Such detailing serves mainly to suggest that such profusion—of streets, places, things, words—ultimately is un-encompassable.

This is made explicit when the Survey shifts to include descriptions of wards "without" the city walls as well as "suburbs" even further without the city itself but nevertheless a contemporary aspect of London in its entirety. Stow takes pains to explain the curious existence of wards lying outside the historically organizing and delimiting boundary of the city walls, such as "Faringdon Extra, or Without," its Latin suffix providing an additional implication of excessiveness which Stow wishes to regulate. The Survey's inclusion of a lengthy discussion of "the suburbs without the walls" demonstrates, by its very mention, the problem of encompassing an expanding city. Stow sums up the city via a by-now-characteristic list whose variety and number belie its apparent orderliness:

> Having spoken of this city, the original, and increase, by degrees: the walls, gates, ditch, castles, towers, bridges, the schools, and houses of learning: of the orders and customs, sports, and pastimes: of the honour of citizens, and worthiness of men: and last of all, how the same city is divided into parts and wards: and how the same be bounded: and what monuments of antiquity, or ornaments of building, in every of them, as also in the borough of Southwark: I am next to speak briefly of the suburbs, as well without the gates and walls as without the liberties, and of the monuments in them. (374)

London is listed for us in this paragraph, yet the *Survey* remains incomplete without some discussion of the city's newest districts—outlying areas that are not actually 'London' but unequivocally signal the city's expansion and proliferation.

Social Critique and Other 'Languages'

There are myriad possible sources to marshal in credibly establishing the extent of early seventeenth-century perceptions of the urgent need for ordering, stabilizing, or reforming an incoherent society, and the extent to which the language itself became the focus of much of this anxiety. Early dictionaries make the concern and its language-connection explicit, of course; a work like Stow's, and the irresistible combination of its announced goal and subsequent use of copious language to enact the city, reveal this as vividly if more implicitly. I turn now to consider a pair of texts that will add yet another dimension to this purported climate: the social critiques of Philip Stubbes and Stephen Gosson.[20] Both works were extremely popular, going through several editions following their initial publication, and thus remaining influential into the seventeenth century. Stubbes' *The Anatomie of Abuses* (1583) is a wide-ranging indictment of his Elizabethan society's vices, particularly its obsession with the fashionable apparel that was "a primary site where a struggle over the mutability of the social order was conducted."[21] Stubbes' text provides indisputable evidence of the importance of this semiotic system: for Stubbes, according to Jean Howard, "transgressions of the dress code don't just *signal* social disruption; they *constitute* social disruption" (Howard, "Crossdressing" 422). Gosson's *The Schoole of Abuse* (1579) specifically condemns the theater and its players. My chief interest in these two works lies in their shared anxiety over a perceived lack of order in society, and in their similar expression of this anxiety in ways that reflect a fascination for the illicit or excess, and that fetishize not just items or practices, but words themselves.

Early in the *Anatomie's* depiction of the conversation between the interlocutors "Spudeus" and "Philoponus," the latter (the expert on "Anglia" and the critical voice of the text) compares others nations' with England's obsession with apparel. Philoponus explains:

> The Muscovians, Athenians, Italians, Brasilians, Affricanes, Asians, Cantabrians, Hungarians, Ethiopians, Dutch, French . . . are so farre behind the people of England in exquisitenesse of apparell, as in effect, they esteem it little or nothing at all . . . Other some meanly apparelled, some in beasts skinned, some in haire . . . some in one thing, some in another, nothing regarding either hosen, shooes, bandes, ruffes, shirts, or any thing els. (Stubbes 68–69)

The listing of foreigners emphasizes their numbers as their nationalities underline their otherness. In characterizing these others' limited interest in "exquisite" apparel, Stubbes also cannot help himself, zealously providing us with a list of all the items of clothing these others either do not possess or have no knowledge of. Shortly thereafter, Philoponus recites a short series of fabrics—"Silkes, Velvets, Satens, Damaskes, Sarcenet, Taffeta, Chamlet, and the like"—that will become a motif, repeated over and over again throughout the text, sometimes three or four times within one passage. The effect is artificial, and almost incantation-like, with Spudeus dutifully repeating the list back to Philoponus regularly.

Spudeus's questioning enables ever more elaborate detailing of fashion minutiae; his curiosity provides the forum for Stubbes' extensive descriptions in the person of Philoponus. At the request of Spudeus, Philoponus, for example, embarks on the London fashion equivalent of Stow's ward-by-ward reporting. Philoponus responds to Spudeus with zealous earnestness:

"Your request seemeth both hard and intricate, considering the innumerable **Meryades** of sundry fashions dayly invented amongst them. But yet . . . I will assaie . . . to satisfy your desire. Wherefore to begin first with their Hattes" (Stubbes 90). And with this, the text goes one to describe, one by one, "hatttes," "cuffs," "shirts," "doublets," "hose," "stockings," "shoes," "coats," "jerkins," "cloaks," and "boothose," all before ever reaching the even more elaborate and numerous categories of women's apparel. In his vigor and concern to enumerate every excessive element of English fashion, Stubbes' containing critique actually amplifies his subject, a fact noted by his most recent editor, Margaret Jane Kidnie. She observes:

> Stubbes is himself swept away by an excessive prose style . . . [that] preserves in print the very practices he so strongly opposed . . . The extent to which he savors, even revels in, his writing is obvious. Stubbes is a severe critic of disorder, whose unchecked verbal profusion reveals him to be . . . tainted by the very abuse against which he writes.
>
> (Stubbes 21–22)

Also notable, above, is the text's highlighting of the word "meryades," a feature true to every original edition, in which many words were demarcated in contrasting type. Stubbes was very interested in the visual impact of his words on the page, according to Kidnie, and set apart the myriad foreign words and phrases he used, neologisms and quotations, and expressions he wished to emphasize. Such an effect betrays a desire in Stubbes to control the readers' experience of his text, an interesting dimension to a text whose didacticism is focused on the sartorial. The demarcating effect also calls attention to words as words, I would suggest, setting them apart but also, curiously, creating out of them another kind of fetishized series or list.

One of the most widely quoted judgments from the *Anatomie* reads: "But now there is such a confuse mingle-mangle of apparel in England, and such horrible excess thereof, as every one is permitted to flaunt it out, in what apparel he listeth himselfe, or can get by any meanes" (Stubbes 71). Given Stubbes' apparently primary concern for the sartorial and not the linguistic, his use of the term "mingle-mangle" is striking because of its more well-known use by Ralph Lever in an earlier prose tract on vernacular reform. In *The Art of Reason* (1573), Lever constrasts his proposed method of compounding "ancient English" words with the method of "they that with inkhorn terms do change and corrupt the same, making a *mingle-mangle* of their native speech and not observing the property thereof."[22] Stubbes transposes this colorful term from an explicitly lexical context to his own concerning fashion's problematic excess and ambiguity, creating a suggestive bridge between Lever's text and his own as well as between Lever's subject of the spoken and written vernacular and Stubbes' central concern with the sartorial.

Stubbes' concern for abuses of fashion and apparel has been character- ized by Matthew R. Martin as a concern for a "failure of this ideal social language" of clothing, a language in which "each person's outward appear- ance is an unequivocal expression or sign of his social position determined by birth."[23] Stubbes' indignant, and at times anguished, reports of a soci- ety-wide breakdown in this ideal connection of signifier and signified thus represents a kind of semiotic rupture. Stubbes' solution in his *Anatomie* is to attempt to stop the semiotic confusion, never to question the notion that such an ideal language is possible. Belief in such a possibility for languages— whether visual or verbal—and the inevitable anxieties deriving from such an ideal, constitute a central problem of the language reform movement of the early modern period. Stubbes' *Anatomie* suggests the range of venues where this problem was treated and disputed.

The hypocrisy in the *Anatomie* makes for humorous reading. What is most important, however, is not the hypocrisy, but the source of it: the energy of profusion and change that is both irresistible and worrisome. Stubbes' at times comically righteous indignation is rooted in a profound anxiety con- cerning the excesses and instability he reads in terms of the sartorial. But his urgent and ardent dissection of this excess reveals the excitement of such profusion—of clothing and of the words to describe it.

Stephen Gosson's *The School of Abuse* was the first of several invective tracts by the author, whose chief target was the theater but who devoted his popular *Pleasant Quippes for Upstart Newfangled Gentlewomen* (1596) to a critique of women's apparel, as well.[24] Gosson's anti-theatricalism was a reformed position; having written for the theater himself for a time, he became contrite and outraged at its social and moral dangers—for Gos- son, the theater was a threat to social and civic order similar to the fashions he and Stubbes also condemned. *The Schoole of Abuse* is prefaced with an epistle, "To the Reader," that is structured by an alimentary conceit worth unpacking briefly. The epistle begins by figuring hypocrisy in terms of a profiteering ascetic's diet: "Gentlemen and others, you may wel think that I sell you my corne and eat chaffe, barter my wine and drinke water, sith I take upon me to deterre you from Playes, when mine owne woorkes are dayly to be seene upon stages," (7). Gosson preemptively reassures his readers against such a view of him; his intention is not to offer them a diet he him- self eschews. Rather, he entreats them to be his best readers, to know fully his reformed perspective, to be the few who will not "misconster" him. It is the ignorant who will "swallow" the faults leveled against him and "digest them with ease"; he hopes his gentler readers will not follow this example. Gosson's dietary idiom here is self-consciously clever, of course, but it is also a striking metaphor in a work whose central concern is social order and the theater's dangerous undermining of this. Gosson' epistle purports to preempt charges of hypocrisy and acknowledge the risks of publication to a broad audience, but his imagery betrays an anxiety over control, literally of 'taste,' with its emphasis on careful asceticism and its concluding evocation of ignorant gluttony. That which will be either sparingly or overindulgently tasted will be Gosson's words, bringing us again to an anticipation and anxiety over language as a commodity.

Gosson's aim is to "school" his readers in the perils and poetic heresies of the theater drawn from his own reformed authority as a former denizen, as well as from classical predecessors' distrust of poetry. Gosson is wary of poetry's "siren's song," yet his own ability to resist the pleasure of words and proverbial discourse is minimal. Early on, he describes the dangerous experience of entering a playhouse:

> I shoulde tell tales out of schoole and bee ferruled for my fault, or hyssed at for a blab, yf I layde all the orders open before your eyes. You are no sooner entred but libertie looseth the reynes and geves you head, placing you with poetrie in the lowest forme, when his skill is showne too make his scholer as good as ever twangde: he preferres you to pyping, from pyping to playing, from play to pleasure, from pleasure to slouth, from slouth to sleepe, from sleepe to sinne, from sinne to death, from death to the Divel, if you take your learning apace, and pass through every forme without revolting. (14–15)

Gosson warns of the seductive trajectory brought on by the bad poetry of the theater, but his own language, tinged with Puritan rhetoric, betrays his seduction by the musicality of the very language he suspects elsewhere. The perils of the playhouse are fetishized by Gosson in a manner similar to Stubbes' treatment of fashions. In the act of describing the experience of attending the theater, Gosson's use of series and unnecessary, repetitious descriptions betray as much delight in the excess of words as fascinated disgust in the practices he relates by them:

> In our assemblies at playes in London, you shall see suche heaving and shooving, such ytching and shouldering to sytte by women; such care

for their garments that they be not trode on; such eyes to their lappes
that no chippes lighte in them; such pillows to their backes that they
take no hurte; such masking in their eares, I know not what; such
geving them pippins to passe the time; such playing at foote saunt
without cardes; such ticking, such toying, such smiling, such winking.
(25)

The theater presented a threat of social and moral degradation,
according to its critics, for several reasons, including the way it blurred
social strata with its costumes and its inherent demand for impersonations
that spanned these strata. Gosson's critique in *The Schoole* focuses on the
theater's poetic verse almost exclusively, but a brief foray into the sartorial
dimension of the theater's dangers further reveals his text's reflection of a
broad sense of semiotic instability and a fascination with its various profu-
sions. He remarks:

How often hath her Majestie, with the grave advice of her whole
Councel, set downe the limits of apparel to every degree, and how
soone againe hath the pride of our harts overflown the channel? Howe
many times hath accesse to theaters beene restrained, and howe boldly
againe have we reentred? Overlashing in apparel is so common a
fault, that the verye hyerlings of some of our players . . . jet under
gentlemens noses in suits of silke, exercising themselves to prating on
the stage, and common scoffing when they come abrode, where they
looke askance over the shoulder at every man of whom the Sunday
before they begged at almes. (29)

The problem of sartorial or sumptuary instability combines with the
theater's other licentious threats—including discursive license—to create a mini-drama of class conflict within the playhouse gallery. Even a
"hyerling"—a kind of theatrical day-laborer and not even an acting-com-
pany member—can get a silk suit and some false discourse for the stage
and thereby better himself past the very gentlemen whose recent charity
acknowledged the laborer's true lowliness. Gosson's indignation at these
phenomena of excess and disorder does not curb his own rhetorical over-
abundance. His repeated questions and meticulous detailing of social
affronts promoted by and in the playhouses constitute an ironically analogous profusion.

The Schoole of Abuse concludes with yet another self-consciously rhetorical series whose effect is more self-indulgent than poignant; midway,

the gustatory conceit is reprised, this time suggesting that we must taste what's needful, not just what is delicious:

> These are harde lessons . . . nevertheless, drinke uppe the potion, though it like not your tast . . . resist not the surgeon, though he strike with his knife . . . The fig tree is sower, but it yeeldeth sweete fruite: thymus is bitter, but it giveth honny: my Schoole is tarte, but my counsell is pleasant, if you imbrace it. (51)

The scriptural tone is not coincidental, for Gosson was an installed rector by the 1590s; *The Schoole* as a whole is full of the vitriol and cumulative flourish of Puritan preaching. By this it is no less significant a reflection of the preoccupations of the city and its topoi. The excessive—in substance and amount—language of the Puritan as an element of 'the city' will be immortalized by Ben Jonson's creation of 'Rabbi' Zeal-of-the-Land Busy, as we will see, in his most highly textured evocation of London, *Bartholomew Fair*.

Language and the King

These different textual sites where the London ethos of proliferation was figured were discursively influential, but offer only partial evidence of the social/cultural moment of perceived flux I am attempting to establish. There were other phenomena and other distinct linguistic pressures in existence in Jacobean England, the most obvious of which, perhaps, was the king himself, a Scots-dialect speaker with a sometimes uneasy relationship to English. It is true that the larger populace would never have encountered the king in such a way as to make his Scots-dialect or Scots-inflected English a vivid street-level concern. Nonetheless, James and his courtiers' evident Scottish difference, along with familiarity in centers like London with the Scots accent and dialect suggest the important, additional component of this king to the complex language-ethos of early seventeenth-century London.

James's Scots-English, and its potential role in the way the Jacobean vernacular was perceived, is the central concern of Patricia Fumerton's reading of dialect-speech in Ben Jonson's masque, *For the Honour of Wales* (1618).[25] Beginning with the question, "What does it mean to speak the "King's English" under a Scottish/English king?" Fumerton rehearses Deleuze and Guattari's theory of authorized (or "majoritarian") languages' unceasing influence by the minor languages or dialects they apparently superceded. In Deleuze and Guattari's words, "the more a language has or acquires the characteristics of a major language, the more it is affected by continuous variations that 'transpose' it into a minor language."[26] An authoritative language, thus, is never permanently bounded: dialects, earlier versions, even slang continue to work off of it and make inroads to its lexicon and usage. For Fumerton, this hypothesis precisely captures Jacobean England's precarious sense of its vernacular's vulnerability to variation, especially from a dialect like Scots. A Scots-speaking king only heightened such a sense of mutability, and the masque-form of this king's court notably dramatized it. The courtly masque evolved significantly under James's patronage of Jonson; within his lifetime, Jonson's greatest artistic stature and success derived from his masque-writing career under James and Charles I. That it was in this explicitly courtly form that Jonson created his most fully realized stagings of dialect speech—Welsh, also "Hiberno-English" in *The Irish Masque at Court* (1613)—is no coincidence. The Welsh-speaking anti-masquers in *For The Honour of Wales* distinctly enact the effect, or collaborative influence, of 'minoritarian' languages like Welsh, Scottish, or Gaelic on English, and perhaps reflect, in a comedic mode, the reality of the Jacobean court.

The tension of James' Scots-English is evident elsewhere, as well. James I's most important prose work, the *Basilikon Doron* (1599), was successively "Englished" over the several editions that followed its initial manuscript edition in Scots, but the king's prose and speech remained "everywhere thickly strewn . . . with images and phrases . . . full of a pawky Scottish humor," according to Jacobean historian C.J. Sisson.[27] James's preference for the more homely expression of his native dialect seems perfectly natural, but is made notable by the simultaneous concern for transposing his written work into the 'higher' register of English. And as we have seen, this was true at a time when the English vernacular itself consciously was being shaped to a higher, more authoritative form. James' persistent use of a 'low' medium amid concern for higher expression and authority presents a complex linguistic picture at court. The London underworld 'dialect' of cant created a parallel low-high tension. Canting, and popular response to it as an underworld alternative to English, also pointed up fissures in the vernacular's stability and in its authoritative hold on signification. William N. West, addressing canting's unsettling changeability, ultimately identifies it as "language that produces an effect solely through its form . . . [that] produce[s] affect free from any . . . content—to reveal the work that words do, purified of reference to things."[28] West is interested in the erotics of such a "perlocutionary" force of language,[29] but as significant here is how this abject language both reveals similar properties in all language, especially English in this case, and, per Fumerton, is always potentially present and influential with its "major" counterpart, English. Canting, thus, also was a significant component of the seventeenth-century climate within which city comedy evolved. Cant is a key element in more than one city comedy, and in particular features in Middleton and Dekker's *The Roaring Girl*, to be treated in depth in chapter three, below. As we will see there, canting is staged as one important element of the city's inscrutability, but it also becomes an important vehicle of the play's fantastic resolution or domestication of such urban-linguistic chaos.

The three plays that are my subject fit provocatively into the social and discursive context diversely sketched here. It is also important to place these dramatic works into contexts each playwright created as a commentator on his society, his city, and his society's vernacular through other published works. Specifically, each produced additional work that engaged with London and/or questions of language in prose modes, or, in Middleton's case, in a dramatic mode of civic encomium quite distinct from city comedy. Together they create a convincing ethos of concern for coherence, whether civic, social, artistic, or explicitly discursive and linguistic.

JONSON, DEKKER, MIDDLETON: THE FRAME OF OTHER WORKS.

Jonson and An Unstable Vernacular: Discoveries *and* The English Grammar
Ben Jonson's published works included an *English Grammar* (1640, probably composed much earlier) and a volume of *pensées*: *Timber, or, Discoveries* (1640), addressing matters for poets, notably speech and language-decorum.[30] Both of these texts contribute to the climate sketched above, and together they also comprise a specific frame for Jonson's dramatic work. Though differently, both reflect Jonson's acute consciousness of English as a language in transition, as well as his dynamic, dual interest in precision and tradition. In conversation with one another, his non-dramatic and dramatic works manifest an extreme ambivalence about this vernacular play and about language itself. A new generation of Jonson critics recently has signaled a need for greater accommodation of the poet's prodigious and varied oeuvre and, arguably, multiple careers. The Jonson who emerges from such scrutiny is no longer an either-or figure, "Classical Humanist" or "Romantic Populist," but an artist who is "alert to the . . . contingencies of his age(s)."[31] The present study's investigation of Jonson's potential contributions or, indeed, qualifications to the early modern "language project" aims to participate in this limning of a latter-day Jonson via an attention to his two prose-works on language and a connection of their preoccupations with the city comedies.

One of the most frequently quoted passages in Ben Jonson's *Timber, or, Discoveries*, is usually understood in terms of its corrective attitude towards it subjects: language and "Custom." Though "Custom is the most certain mistresse of language," Jonson declares, by this he refers not to "vulgar custom;" instead, he means "that I call custom of speech, which is the consent of the learned; as custom of life, which is the consent of the good" (622). Here is Jonson the famously neoclassical scholar-poet, who elsewhere in the same text stipulates that using language or words to talk and using them for eloquence are two different things. There is too much nonsense, he complains, and instead approves of "pure and neat language . . . yet plain and customary" (620). Again, Custom is a central fixture of his prescription, though a carefully delimited custom of language and verbiage. Though it is possible to locate a thread of anxiety in the recurrent delineation of what constitutes proper Custom, overall the Jonson of *Discoveries* communicates certainty, both in the opinions he expresses and the stability/authority of the proper vernacular language and language-decorum espoused therein. But custom of language—language itself—was for Jonson a far more ambiguous subject than his firm pronouncements here might suggest. Evidence of this, I will argue, is borne out in the plays, and particularly in the two comedies whose prose-composition signals an interest in quotidian speech. But the *English Grammar* provides evidence as well, as does *Discoveries*, once its efforts at seamlessness are acknowledged and reconsidered. Jonson's relationship to language and to vernacular custom was never as "pure and neat" as *Discoveries* implies.

The tension between the two customs—colloquial, popular "custom" versus custom as the consent of the learned—which I will argue is one component of Jonson's interest in and anxiety about language, quickly is apparent even in the *Grammar*, his most unambiguously prescriptive work. Jonson's *Grammar*, throughout, is an uneasy blend of the directive with the customary, the learned with the colloquial. The title page announces its intention to be "for the benefit of all strangers," such a specific sense of audience indicating a clear, didactic purpose. The phrase that follows somewhat undercuts this emphasis on formalism, however, ascribing authority to "observation of the English language now spoken, and in use." Custom is the ultimate arbiter; it is colloquial and functional, though not necessarily the most correct.

And yet Jonson's explicit concern here is "to the end our Tongue may be made equall to those of the renowned countries, Italy, and Greece" (501). The Preface to the text asserts this specifically in the terms of an anxiety over "our Language," which "is mistaken to be diseas'd . . . [with] Rudenesse; and Barbarism." The vernacular's "matchablenesse, with other tongues" is the stated object, and the grammar's heavy reliance on Latin examples and epigrams, throughout, reinforces this. The *Grammar* also reveals an abiding interest in colloquialisms, however, detailing the words of "rustic people," and lamenting the loss of Anglo-Saxon letters like "k" for the newer "q." The text's complex attitude towards language-use, change, and custom, is conveyed in a series of vivid metaphors. Here is Jonson's description of the consonant "q":

> "Q" . . . is a Letter we might very well spare in our *Alphabet*, if we would but use the serviceable *k.* as he should be, and restore him to the right of reputation he had with our fore-fathers. For, the *English-Saxons* knew not this halting *Q.* with her waiting-woman *u.* after her, but exprest: *quest* by *kuest, quick* by *kuick* . . . Till *custome* under the excuse of expressing enfranchis'd words with us, intreated her into our Language, in *quality, quantity, quarel, quitescence*, &c. And hath now given her the best of *k's.* possessions. (488,491)

Not only is Custom personified here as an over-ambitious meddler, but the two consonants, "k" and "q," also are transformed by this same technique. "K" is figured as male, ancient, dependable, and unfairly dispossessed; while "q" is female, a foreign interloper, untrustworthy, pampered by her ubiquitous attendant, and the undeserving beneficiary of "the best of *k's.* possessions." Contemporary dynamics of gender, social upheaval, and conflicting language reform movements, all in circulation in these images, emphasize a proper and native English tradition sullied by foreign influences, themselves the result of a pretentious, ambitious, and unscrupulous custom. It is significant that here in his own contribution to vernacular regulation, Jonson invokes "Saxon" orthography and phonemes, and the problem of "expressing enfranchised words." With this, he situates himself at the conservative end of a spectrum of linguistic opinion which included Ralph Lever's earlier appeal to 'ancient English,' as well as others more inclined to the importation of foreign terms.[32] A not-nostalgic-enough-Custom, here, is the most problematic enemy of English, despite its importance as well as its basis of Jonson's authority at the outset.

Jonson further complicates custom and his own conservatism by his professed admiration for "the vulgar and practis'd way of making [words, meaning]," which he does not wish "abolish'd and abdicated, (being both sweete and delightful, and much taking the eare)" (501). At the opening of the second book of the *Grammar*, he further asserts the importance of custom in language, and particularly the preeminence of spoken language, over its printed or written form, for the determination of what is proper.

Quoting a passage from Chaucer's *Troilus and Criseiyde* as a syntactic example, Jonson explains:

> The first kind [of contraction of vowels with apostrophes] then is common with the Greekes; but that which followeth, is proper to us, which though it bee not of any, that I know, either in Writing or Printing, usually express'd: Yet considering that in our common speech, nothing is more familiar, (upon the which all Precepts are grounded, and to the which they ought to be referred) who can justly blame me, if, as neere as I can, *I follow Natures call.* (529, italics mine)

This implies a different custom, a benevolent, natural force, honest in its familiarity and inevitability. In *Discoveries*, Jonson asserts that "Speech . . . is the instrument of society" (620–21), and in the passage above this same notion is straightforwardly emphasized. The affable tone, here in particular and throughout much of the *Grammar*, however, belies the subtly fraught nature of the project for Jonson. He confronts the tensions present in the language at this time, from questions of its status alongside Latin and Greek, to conflicting views of the numbers of neologisms and "inkhorn" words entering the vernacular, including borrowings from foreign tongues like French. More specifically, the *Grammar* reveals Jonson's particularly conflicted relationship with the vernacular, in which custom is to be embraced for its colloquial delights and the authority of its familiarity and use, but such use potentially is unsophisticated and unstable. This anxiety over linguistic composition and stability, and by extension, language's cohering powers, combined with his poet's relationship to language and custom, is key to reading the prose comedies of Jonson's mature work.

Compared to the *Grammar*'s self-proclaimed investment in the colloquial and that text's depiction of the different ideals exerting pressure on the language at the time, *Discoveries* offers a far more composed representation of language in use and proper decorum. This latter work is a very different genre of text from the *Grammar,* of course; most accurately characterized as a "commonplace book" or a compendium of selected passages from classical and some contemporary sources, *Discoveries* at times appears to reflect little original thought of Jonson's. This has been a significant critical problem over the years, following an early tradition of reading *Discoveries* as no less than Jonson's "spiritual autobiography."[33] Ian Donaldson offers a corrective to both views of the text, arguing that we must understand its extensive literary borrowings in terms of Jonson's interest in "the ethical problem of literary discoveries" (xiv). The imitation or borrowing of not only ideas but language is inherent in this notion of discovery of another's work and thereby one's own; the ideals and 'opinions' presented thus participate in a process of imitation, even impersonation, that is both all-important and problematic for Jonson, as his concerns in the *Grammar*, above, make clear. Borrowing is "requisite" in a poet or "maker," according to Jonson, but it must be accompanied by discernment to make choices and to "digest" selectively. Such appropriation of the best of others' thoughts and words points to a custom of the learned and a disdain for the injudicious that is quite unambiguous. Critics typically have located the caustic and profoundly satiric voice of Jonson's popular drama in these overt distinctions in *Discoveries*, and there is no question that some of this text's strongest and most jaundiced critiques of linguistic or stylistic offense are re-enacted in the different species of gulls, fops, and impersonators skewered in the plays.

Despite the temptation to read *Discoveries* as a transparent primer to the plays' satiric objectives, however, the seamless ease and precision in matters of decorum and custom of language espoused in *Discoveries* are nowhere evident in the plays. All of them problematize linguistic Custom and its coherence in their bounty of colloquial speech, linguistic 'deformities,' and humorless, proper stylists. In recent work on Jonson, John Creaser observes that "in practice, Jonson's conservative theorizing merely emphasizes the multitudinous inventiveness of his work, as a plumb-line reveals how a wall is out of true."[34] This, to me, more accurately describes the relationship of the poet's self-consciously formal prose works to the plays for us. Though Creaser does not address the problem of language and custom specifically, his observations about "license" nonetheless suggest the kind of ambivalence identified above in terms of language use and the role of custom of speech. Creaser writes, "Jonson's drama moves continually between the two poles of 'licence,' from precedent and authority to licentious outrage. The opposites are continually attracted to one another" (106). This emphasis on Jonson's polarities is helpful, but runs the risk of relegating him as a grotesque. Such contrasting, even contradictory energies map the bounds of a social-linguistic landscape whose popular but decorous, coherent middle ground he seeks, albeit in vain.

The power and problem language holds for Jonson is captured in his famous assertion that "Language most shows a man: speak that I may see thee" (625). This statement is glossed with the Latin, *Oratio imago animi*, or "Speech is the image of the mind"; both phrases enunciate language's referential properties: what one speaks directly figures one's true self and this self's qualities. This idea summons more than one valence to the issue of coherence in language, as the importance of language as a stable system of organizing and articulating experience is joined by the apparent and important role of language in precisely articulating identity and the inner self. Jonson shifts to the *topos* of apparel in this same passage, with it signaling instability and potential incoherence precisely where he has just asserted the importance of their opposites. "No glass renders a man's form, or likeness so true as his speech," Jonson continues, with the sartorial standing in for the linguistic or discursive when he adds, "Would you not laugh to meet a great councilor of state in a flat cap, with his trunk-hose and a hobby-horse cloak, his gloves under his girdle, and yond haberdasher in velvet gown, furred with sables?" (625–26). This is not just a picturesque trope, for the sartorial recurs frequently in *Discoveries'* discussions of speech and language. The regular collapsing of one notoriously ill-regulated and untrustworthy sign-system (apparel) for another belies the text's confident claims. Such problems as the *English Grammar* and *Discoveries* reveal and present are the irresistible raw materials for plays like *Epicoene* and *Bartholomew Fair*, where Jonson's language theorizing will continue.

The context provided to *The Roaring Girl* by the other works of Dekker and Middleton is both more and less clearly relevant compared with the correspondences between Jonson's plays and prose. That is, while Dekker's extensive career as a pamphlet-commentator of London's underside is an obvious link to *The Roaring Girl's* canting and depiction of the layers of city society, neither Dekker nor Middleton published in prose or verse on the subject of language or decorum itself, as Jonson did. For Dekker and Middleton, the explicit subject is always the city, a distinction from Jonson's more oblique and theoretical explorations in *Discoveries* and the *Grammar*. Such a city focus is, of course, valuable and interesting in itself, both as an element of the climate this chapter aims to establish and as a framework of ideas within which the authors collaborated on *The Roaring Girl*. Dekker's lifelong preoccupation with the language and culture of London's lowest classes, as represented in pamphlets like the "Lantern and Candlelight" series (1608); together with Middleton's eclectic output of a gothic verse "moral" and more than a dozen civic pageants combine to sketch two additional interests and investments in the diffuse city, and in the questionably cohering powers of city languages, both underworld and ritualistic.[35]

Dekker's Frail Fables

Dekker began writing prose for the pamphlet trade in 1603, when an outbreak of the plague not only postponed the official Entry procession of the new king indefinitely (Dekker co-created the procession's festivities with Middleton and Jonson), but closed the theaters for so long that writers like Dekker had to find alternative income.[36] Most of Dekker's pamphlet-writing occurred between 1603 and 1609, a period that immediately preceded the writing, performing, and publication, in 1611, of *The Roaring Girl*. Not coincidentally, given the play's characters and subject, much of Dekker's pamphlet-work concerned disclosure of a seamy, secret London: his works often are credited with a journalistic realism in his depiction of the city whose bounds he never left over a lifetime. But such reportage, along the lines of Stow's *Survey*, was not Dekker's aim, according to E.D. Pendry, who sees in Dekker's non-fictional 'realism' a distinct moral vision: "Dekker's feeling for London is moral poetry . . . [He] is a sentimental upholder of aristocracy and gentry. But he admires workpeople . . . All classes and vocations in his view have their dignity, their duties and their rights . . . [a] place in the scheme" (*Wonderful Year, etc.* 12). Dekker is a conservative critic who envisions London as a community and is invested in this community's coherence. His interest in cant and his popular canting pamphlets are enigmatic evidence of this concern for coherence coupled with a fascination with cant's function in his beloved and belabored city community.

The "Lantern and Candlelight" pamphlets were a second series of 'reports' apparently disclosed via the fictional and popular "Bellman of London," a pamphlet-conceit first created by Robert Greene and Thomas Nashe.[37] Dekker's adaptation became a series of underworld exposés grounded in the first chapter's lesson on canting, a familiar device to which Dekker added an opening history of all languages' origins, including cant's, in the destruction of Babel and of monolingualism. The description of English that precedes the story of Babel's fall is striking in its figuration of the English vernacular as a minimally literate, shy woman who is nonetheless an able cultivator of others' linguistic charity:

> Neither were the strings of the English speech in those times untied. When she first learned to speak it was but a broken language. The singlest and the simplest words flowed from her utterance, for she dealt in nothing but in monosyllables, as if to have spoken words of greater length would have cracked her voice; by which means her eloquence was poorest, . . . [and] not regarded amongst strangers. Yet afterwards those noblest languages lent her words and phrases and, turning those borrowings into good husbandry, she is now as rich in elocution and as abundant as her proudest and best-stored neighbors. (*Wonderful Year, etc.* 187)

The explicitly female vernacular's current richness and adequacy is the result of English cunning, thrift, and hard work, not natural abundance. This is a point of pride in Dekker's working-man's sensibility, of course, but it also signals a certain instability: the wealth of the language is ever reliant on a similar diligence and labor, perhaps on additional 'handouts' from abroad. Dekker's primary focus will be cant, so this brief and ambiguous view of English seems an odd inclusion. English is not a safely privileged language, perhaps, in its coexistence with cant, and its vivid gendering only adds to its vulnerability and ever-present insufficiency.

Dekker's addition of the Babel-story is notable to his editor, Pendry, who points out its emphasis on "a decay in the function of language from communication to mystification" (*Wonderful Year, etc.* 20). Such an idea of language seems contradicted by Dekker's intended clarification of canting, however; in its purported effort to reveal and delineate canting and its speakers, the pamphlet distinctly mythologizes the notorious vagrants' dialect, beginning with the initial segue to its existence:

> But I am now to speak of a people and of a language of both which, many thousands of years since that wonder wrought at Babel, the world till now never made mention. Yet Confusion never dwelt more amongst any creatures. The Bellman in his first voyage which he made for discoveries found them to be savages, yet living in an island very temperate, fruitful, full of a noble nation and rarely governed . (*Wonderful Year, etc.* 189)

The existence of cant and of an underworld 'nation' of canters had been the subject of sensationalist tracts at least since Thomas Harman's *A Caveat for Common Cursitors Vulgarly Called Vagabonds* in the 1560's, thus Dekker's re-introduction is purely melodramatic or sensationalist.[38] Also worth noting is the anthropological language and tone—Dekker evokes the discovery idiom and tone of Richard Hakluyt's Elizabethan voyage chronicles, and we can perceive his influence on later writers like Defoe in the simultaneous and almost contradictory mysterious and disclosing approach he takes.

Dekker's description of cant trims between the language's barbarous lack of "any certain rules," and its "kind of form . . . [and] salt tasting of some wit and some learning" (*Wonderful Year, etc.* 191); he supplies detail but not necessarily for clarification. His is a labor against excess, it seems, for language is "nothing else than heaps of words orderly woven and composed together," and there is a risk in making his readers "surfeit on too much." His canting lesson will rather be delightful if we can "gather [words] by handfuls"(192), an apparently ameliorative image that only faintly diminishes a sense of these "heaps." On the other hand, Dekker introduces his "Canter's Dictionary" a page later, with the announcement that "none of those canting words that are Englished [earlier in his report] shall be found, for our intent is to feast you with *variety*" (*Wonderful Year, etc.*193, italics mine). The danger of language-excess must be balanced with the public's appetite for canting words. Dekker concludes his brief canter's dictionary in "Lantern and Candlelight" with remarks that make explicit the view of words as commodities implied in so many works of the period, as we have seen: "And thus have I builded up a little mint where you may coin words for your pleasure" (195).[39] Canting words are more than language or 'things,' they are literally currency, a kind of wealth for the initiated.

The canting pamphlets decode cant; despite the emphasis on stores beyond the dictionary's scope, the strongest announced aim is accessibility. With "O Per Se—O" (1612), the last of the "Lantern" pamphlets, this shifts. The title alone is an inscrutable phrase used as a stand-in for real, potentially prurient, information, as demonstrated by Dekker's pointed use of it, early on:

> So that what intelligence I got from him or any other trained in the rudiments of roguery I will briefly, plainly and truly set down as I had it from my devilish schoolmaster, whom I call by the name of *O per se—O.*

> For if you note them well in their marching, not a tatterdemalion walks his round . . . but he hath his *mort* or his *doxy* at his heels (his 'woman' or his 'whore') for . . . this 'law' they hold when they come to strike a doe: if she will not *wap* for a *win*, let her *trine* for a *make* (if she will not . . . *O per se—O* . . . for a penny, let her hang for a halfpenny). (*Wonderful Year, etc.* 286)

When he finally offers an explanation, several pages later, his clarification defeats signification on linguistic, discursive, and even moral grounds: "I will teach you here what *O per se——O* is, being nothing else but the burden of a song set by the Devil and sung by his choir; of which I will set no more down but the beginning because the middle is detestable, the end abominable, and all of it damnable" (289). The repetition of "nothing" to describe something suggests the problem of words that signify either nothing or such a surfeit that they are untranslatable. "O per se——O"'s nothingness is not empty, but in fact replete with possibilities, all of them titillatingly illicit and none of them nameable, a phenomenon that William N. West observes in discussing the erotic charge of cant's otherness: "The operative principle is that when you cannot understand what people are saying, it must be because they're saying something dirty . . . [but] the "secret" content is not as important as the eroticism of the form of secrecy" (West 246). The language "husbandry" Dekker evokes early on seems powerless in the face of this kind of signification.

This kind of tension too often is obscured in readings that perceive only the romance or sentiment of Dekker's pamphlet-tales. Cant appeals as a parallel language to the English vernacular, and as apparently ancient in origin and capable of ordering its outlaw society. But English itself is not authoritative, according to Dekker's description: the over-determined nothingness of 'words' like "O per se—-O" threatens the ordering fable of cant and its apparent accessibility as a code with exact and unambiguous correspondences; and if cant's existence evidences a society of threatening diversity and disorder, it also points up the potentially fearful multivalence of the vernacular itself.

Middleton's London

Thomas Middleton's relationship to London in terms of its vernacular is less transparent than Dekker's, although his work in city comedy is more substantial and better known. Middleton was not a pamphleteer, perhaps in part because his theatrical fortunes were never as capricious as Dekker's. His dramatic works, though also often described as realistic, lack Dekker's sentimentality. In addition, there is no 'prose context' to his dramatic work. Most useful to consider as a frame to Middleton's part in *The Roaring Girl* and in city comedy's language project, I would contend, are his contradictions. His only non-dramatic publication is enigmatic: *The Blacke Booke* (c. 1600) was a satirical mix of verse and prose and an obvious continuation of earlier work by Thomas Nashe and Robert Greene.[40] The familiar hero, Pierce Pennilesse, and *The Blacke Booke's* moralizing, if satirical, tone distance it from the author's nimble city comedies. By far Middleton's greatest contemporary fame derived from his long career as the author of the annual pageants marking the new Lord Mayor's accession. Middleton gave loyal service and sanctioned representation to the same city that he treated as more of a "predatory trap" than an ideal community on the commercial stages (Martin 21). Various titles from these numerous Lord Mayor's pageants attest to an ideal of stability, virtue, and civic coherence in the City of London and its administration. Beginning with 1613's *The Triumph of Truth*, successive years showcase, seemingly without irony, the values and foundational principles his comedies so vividly call into doubt.[41] *The Triumph of Integrity* (1623), *The Triumph of Honor and Industry* (1617), and *Civitates Amor* (1616) possess none of the oxymoronic tang of the rhetorically similar equation of *A*

Chaste Maid in Cheapside (1613), for example. Middleton was indisputably of London, and the city was not only the source of his livelihood, but also of his identity, authority, imagination, and skepticism throughout his career.

Recent work on Middleton's comedies (excluding *The Roaring Girl*) emphasizes their fundamental skepticism, rooted in their author's self-conscious awareness of the business of representation in his urban society, especially in the theater. Matthew R. Martin distances his view of Middleton's skepticism from the more "moral thesis" of earlier critics. It is too simple to call Middleton a moralist or a didact, Martin argues; Middleton's best plays, like Jonson's, are "fictions of unsettlement" (Martin 21) that derive interrogative energy from the epistemological difficulties or ruptures created by a changing city. For Anthony Covatta, this important characteristic in Middleton is not "skepticism" but irony. The accomplishment of plays like *A Chaste Maid*, Covatta insists, is their ironic vision, their suggestion of the inherent dualism of contemporary life.[42] *A Chaste Maid in Cheapside* is completely organized around several paradoxes, the most central and most obvious being that suggested by its title: the possibility of a chaste young woman in the notoriously prostitute-laden locale of Cheapside. The fact that the "maid," Moll Yellowhammer, is still chaste by the time of her wedding at the end of the play is countered by the irony that she has maintained this chastity in spite of her family's plotting.

The artisan's family, that bulwark of respectable middle-class London, is dissected and critiqued in the play via a series of paradoxical family-arrangements, licit and illicit, but all initially accepted. The rearrangement of these relations over the course of the play and their affirmation, even in the face of a society unchanged in its appetites and potential for corruption, concludes *A Chaste Maid* on an ironic but genial note. With his daughter Moll happily and modestly married, despite his own efforts, and his son Tim also married to a Welsh "heiress" who turns out to be a common prostitute, Yellowhammer Senior closes the play with a humorous pragmatism that injects realism into the ideal bliss of Moll's just victory in love:

> So fortune seldom deals two marriages
> With one hand, and both lucky. The best is,
> One feast will serve them both. Marry, for room
> I'll have the dinner kept in Goldsmiths' Hall,
> To which, kind gallants, I invite you all.[43]

A Chaste Maid's denouement emphasizes marriage, companionship and continuity, but does not proffer "happily ever after." The irony of the play's working out of relations both paradoxical and problematic is encompassed by these last lines' reminder that we're still in Cheapside, still needing to work the system whenever possible. Such dual impulses to the noble and the grasping are part of the city world as Middleton presents it.

According to Covatta, in both comedic and ironic modes, you are "at two" (as opposed to "at one with") with another, whether a person, an idea, or a society (Covatta 51). The ironist more or less patiently confronts the 'at-two-ness' of social life while the satirist or moralist condemns and seeks solutions to duality. Acceptance of irony is not the same thing as anarchy, but the ironic perspective can encompass anarchic energy as an aspect of human impulses. This ironic lens in Middleton, as briefly exemplified in *A Chaste Maid's* thematics, importantly frames his work in *The Roaring Girl* and the latter play's engagement with language and society. Indeed, though Covatta never mentions the larger irony of his subject's dual career—his personal "at-two-ness"—as city poet and city 'parser,' this even more fully frames Middleton's vivid exploration of language's dualism in *The Roaring Girl* with Thomas Dekker.

The overall effect of this brief survey of early modern language and city concerns is not intended to be seamless or without contradiction. What makes this society and its London-focused drama compelling are the tensions evident in the concurrence of pamphlets giving the minutiae of cant with the progressive "Englishing" of King James' *Basilikon Doron*, with Cawdrey's word-guide, directed to aid "Ladies . . . and other unskillful persons," with Florio's inverse opinion that women were stewards of "vernacular purity." What clearly emerges from such an otherwise eclectic mix is a profound and widespread interest in the English vernacular that betrays anxieties over linguistic authority, stability, and this language's role within its rapidly changing society. As this chapter attempts to demonstrate, there are numerous contemporary venues within which to study this early modern phenomenon. City comedy's particular combination of quotidian realism, language-conscious literary art, and the culturally potent early modern stage suggests the unique value of the lenses this dramatic genre trained on its society. Given these three artists' thorough and diverse engagement with their city and their vernacular, the city comedies of Jonson, Middleton, and Dekker emerge as compelling sites of contemporary thought about the vernacular and its role in the city.

Chapter Two
Epicoene, Women, and the Language of the City

Epicoene is a play about talking. Witty talk, foolish talk, talk suffused with affectation, eloquence, gossip, or innuendo—*Epicoene* encompasses them all in its vivid equation of the city and talking. Such a structuring of London by speech is an exuberant as well as uneasy proposition, and this tension is central to *Epicoene's* significance as a staging of the relationship between the vernacular and the city. On one hand, everyday speech, and by extension its setting, is vital and human; any society that can exist without the intercourse of speech is, at best, arid and, at worst, sociopathic. On the other hand, the same speech easily becomes excessive, noisy, and threatening of order in its unruliness. As described in chapter one, this concern was not unique to Jonson, but *Epicoene's* configuration of this urban tension in particularly gendered terms makes a significant connection of gender to language as an additional variable of social coherence. This chapter confronts *Epicoene's* city talk in terms of the growing role of women as 'city-talkers,' arguing that the play's concerns for language and the city reflect anxieties about women's place in a changing society that are encompassed by women as speakers. The "silent woman" is not simply an ironic joke; it evokes and sets in motion a whole set of issues about women and language that includes questions of speech, silence, and levels of literacy, as well as the gender-inflected problem of language treated and commodified as mere fashion. The words, below, of one of the play's memorable female speakers provide a useful encapsulation of these topoi with which to begin:

> Yes, sir, anything I do but dream o' the city. It stained me a
> damask table-cloth, cost me eighteen pound at one time, and
> burnt me a black satin gown as I stood by the fire at my Lady
> Centaure's chamber in the college another time. A third time,
> at the lord's masque, it dropped all my wire and my ruff with

wax candle, that I could not go up to the banquet. A fourth time,
as I was taking coach to go to Ware to meet a friend, it dashed me
a new suit all over—a crimson satin doublet and black velvet skirts—
with a brewer's horse, that I was fain to go in and shift me, and kept
my chamber a leash of days for the anguish of it.[1] (III.ii.57–66)

With these words *Epicoene*'s Mistress Otter offers us a London characterized
by both fashion and social mishap. A preoccupation with fashion dominates
this picture, and Mistress Otter vividly uses the sartorial in her approximation of sophisticated discourse. The Mistress's confused attempt to make
sophisticated conversation with the gentlemen Truewit, Clerimont, and
Dauphine reflects her striving through language that is literally fashion as she
describes fine "damask," "black satin," and the hazards of elaborate ruffs and
their structuring wires. There is a *non sequitur* quality to her speech as she
launches unbidden into this description of her sartorial misfortunes at the
hands of the city. But the inanity of this woman's effort to style herself via her
language also offers an implicit critique of a language that is itself styled by
fashion. Mistress Otter is in some respects an ancillary figure to the central
plot of *Epicoene*. These brief lines signal her centrality to the play's thematics,
however, as they frame concerns with language as fashion and with levels of
eloquence and literacy.

The London Mistress Otter describes is a city of significant contrasts. Its
masques and "college(s)" of literate ladies are set against details that bespeak
a city still reliant on older and oral modes of communication, organization,
and order that is nonetheless also the home of sophisticated, hyper-literate
young men like Truewit. Levels of literacy—vernacular and learned—are
set in tension with distinctly oral elements of city life. Mistress Otter, for
example, describes a "brewer's horse" spoiling her urban finery, a detail that
gestures to a communal, public-house element of city life not traditionally
structured by print or dominated by sophisticated society. Finery of "crimson
satin"—which the play's editor R.V. Holdsworth notes as usually associated
with the nobility[2]—gestures faintly to sumptuary laws which once strictly
regulated sartorial vocabulary and display, but were scarcely enforceable in
Jacobean England, given the increasing wealth and power of urban middle
class Londoners like Mrs. Otter and her husband. Of Jacobean sumptuary regulation, historian Jane Schneider notes that England "had no formal
clothing ordinances on the law books after 1604."[3] Such a juxtaposition of
modes of oral and more than one literate culture expresses some contradictions within Mistress Otter's world and character and also points up another
aspect to this *topos* of literacy in the play: the tension of a social climate (and

historical moment) where different levels and valuations of literacy exist as social and gender markers.

Mrs. Otter's speech is in response to the gentlemen's bemused queries; her tumbling narrative is an attempt to be a suitably urbane equal to these visitors, her social betters. But her speech comes across as mere chatter, the confused pronoun references in the first, fifth, and seventh lines all underlining her lack of syntactic as well as discursive control and the vast distance between her rambling and the eloquence she seeks. This contrast will be a theme in the play's examination of eloquence and literacy, as well, with its subtitle, "The Silent Woman," adding silence to the signifying spectrum of eloquence and chatter.[4] This places women's silence and its understood opposite, chatter, at the center of *Epicoene*, but it is not just Epicoene and rather women more generally, who are central to the play.

Epicoene was Ben Jonson's first exclusively prose comedy as well as his first play explicitly set in contemporary London.[5] As such, it represents a new engagement with the vernacular for Jonson, not simply with its rhetorical uses, but with the particular linguistic and discursive practices of the everyday. If, as we have seen, Jonson's expository prose confronts linguistic and stylistic concerns and attempts to elide or neutralize the conflicts, in prose comedies like *Epicoene* these concerns become the overt subject. Mistress Otter's "dream o' the city" speech offers a useful précis of the language-based and, I argue, highly gendered tensions animating *Epicoene*. One is the contemporary transition to an increasingly literate, print-based culture from a significantly oral one, combined with the question of eloquence, its relationship to silence, and the relationship of 'chatter' to both of these. Another concerns the adequacy of language or discourse to create or sustain legitimate social coherence when it becomes fashion or commodity only. Emerging from the mouth of one of the more vivid women characters in the play, these concerns of fashion and of the triangular dynamic of literate eloquence, silence, and chatter, are here presented, literally, in terms of women and their speech in the urban, language marketplace of London.

Querying *Epicoene*'s reflection of language and society has a significant critical history. Jonas Barish explicitly focused his landmark study of Jonson's public drama on the syntactic and stylistic effects of its language (Barish 3). In *Ben Jonson and the Language of Prose Comedy*, Barish uses Shakespeare's more rounded, Ciceronian style and affect to clarify Jonson's rejection of balance or parallelism in favor of a "winding and knotty" prose style Barish terms "baroque" (59, 48). Prose and linguistic satire go hand-in-hand in Jonson, Barish argues, signaling the significance of *Epicoene*'s prose for mapping and mocking the locutions of polite London society. Arnold Preussner challenges

Barish in his own consideration of language and society in *Epicoene*. Preussner traces "Jonson's movement of mind in *Epicoene* . . . by analyzing the play's verbal development" (Preussner 9) and concludes that the play "depicts a verbal wasteland" (15) rather than the more benign, if ambivalent world of compromise between societal acceptance and rejection that Barish ultimately hypothesizes. Preussner and other, later critics are notable for their desire to push analytically and theoretically on Barish's mostly empirical categorizing of Jonson's linguistic patterns, and to consider the implications of these patterns for our understanding both of Jonson as an artist and of the projects of his plays.[6] Douglas Lanier, for example, reads *Epicoene* as an exposition of Jonson's fantasy of a masculine stylistics, a style that "needs no ornamentation, that can subdue differences between writer and reader, language and thing" (Lanier, "Masculine" 8); more recently, J.A. Jackson invokes Barthes' work on the post-structuralist reader to characterize the audience's role of filling in the gaps in meaning inherent in language which *Epicoene* sharply exposes by its conclusion (J.A. Jackson 11).[7]

In *Epicoene,* language and the question of legitimate linguistic behavior become "the subject of the play itself" (Hawkes 157), according to Terence Hawkes; and Gale Carrithers' singles out *Epicoene* as the play in which Jonson "moved oppositions and variations of orality and literacy from frame . . . to predominant central action" (Carrithers 340). Carrithers is interested in the ways that city comedies, notably those of Jonson and Thomas Middleton, depend on different levels of literacy for their comic and contemporary *topoi*, including such typical polarities as wit vs. dullness. The real action in *Epicoene*, according to Carrithers, is the enactment of vying levels of literacy, magnified in the urban setting of London, and the re-framing of "wit" along explicitly (and relatively new) linear, syntactic, textual lines. *Epicoene* depicts a London where one's mastery of and control over a proliferating vernacular in an ever-burgeoning society—that is, one's literacy—dictates all.

This scholarship now must be brought together with more recent work on early modern language and gender in order to assess questions of language and literacy in a play subtitled "the silent *woman*." Juliet Fleming, for example, studies the earliest English dictionaries and what they reveal about "configurations of the relationship between the feminine and the vernacular at the inception of the English dictionary" (175), and suggests the centrality of women's use of English—and concerns about women's usage—to the earliest reformist thinking about the vernacular.[8] Fleming notes the almost invariable directions to women in the titles and prefatory dedications of sixteenth- and seventeenth-century "hard word guides" (precursors to "dictionaries"), and asserts the importance of this association between women and the vernacular in the creation of a standardized language. In a claim that suggests the value of studying other linguistic and discursive sites in terms of their concern for "female language," Fleming argues that the "female user of English" was used to represent vernacular problems or concerns. Gender difference, she suggests, "played a . . . fundamental role in the production of that set of linguistic assumptions and practices that we now call standard English" (178). Uncovering this linkage of gender difference with linguistic practices and ideologies in the period is Margaret Ferguson's aim, as well, in recent work on literacy as a component of early modern imperialism, and gender's role in shaping ideas of vernacular literacy at a time when a standard language was a contested, ambiguous ideal (Ferguson 11–12). Ferguson seeks "to disrupt the still-dominant scholarly consensus that neither historical women nor cultural theories of gender difference had much to do with changes in literacy that have been seen as causes—or effects—of the modernizing process (13), thus offering a précis of her book that implicitly avers the importance, not just in gender and language study but in all study, of recognizing the power but also the contingency of language ideology. For language, sociolinguists like Rosina Lippi-Green have taught us in recent years, is "a flexible and constantly flexing social tool for the emblematic marking of social allegiances" (Lippi-Green 63), and thus never distinct from the wielding of power in discursive terms. "In the simplest terms," she explains in a gesture to Foucault, "the disciplining of discourse has to do with who is allowed to speak, and thus, who is heard . . . Language . . . becomes the means by which discourse is seized" (Lippi-Green 64). It is such re-conceptualizations of language from non-literary fields, in recent years, that have aided the fruitful interdisciplinary work of scholars like Fleming and Ferguson.[9] The model they provide for nuanced re-readings of a range of texts suggests the value of revisiting other language-forums with an updated set of critical questions, weighing Fleming's word-guides' concerns and elisions, for example, against other, less overt, documents of language such as *Epicoene*.

In *Epicoene*, questions of language are in fact questions of women and language. Concern for the status and capabilities of vernacular speech in society is concentrated in the problem of women's use of, and perceived abuse of, English. Each of these tensions of literacy/eloquence and fashion will be a frame through which to read the play. I begin with the 1616 folio edition's dedication and first Prologue, then move on to the play itself to examine, first, the significance of literacy in Act One's exposition of the play as well as in the play's portrayal of the Lady collegiates; next, the dynamic of eloquence-silence-chatter in the characterizations of major characters; and, finally, the problem of discourse as fashion via pretenders like Daw and the

Otters, dandies like La Foole, and strivers like the Lady collegiates. Within these frames and some additional comparisons, I propose, this first prose comedy of Jonson's emerges as a significant document of the vernacular and of the role of gender anxiety in questions and concerns about the linguistic as well as the social coherence of the city.

LITERACY, ORALITY, ELOQUENCE, CHATTER : CONTEXTS

Epicoene's staging of the contemporary dynamic between oral traditions and an evolving, print-based literacy contrasts with recent historical work on orality and literacy in early modern English society. Adam Fox's extensive study, *Oral and Literate Culture in Early Modern England, 1500–1700* (2000), argues there was an easier exchange between the two modes than is suggested by artifacts as well as other studies of their existence and relationship. Carrithers, for example, argues that both Jonson and Thomas Middleton reflect a London that was "uneasily shifting from predominantly oral-aural-memorial culture to an increasingly textual-substantial culture" (Carrithers 339), and were acutely conscious of this shift. *Epicoene* reflects this self-consciousness, I would contend, in its suggestion of an important difference between a vernacular literacy, varyingly rich with oral residue, and an educated, masculine literacy grounded in the Latin available primarily to boys and men. In his study, Fox is careful to describe not a simple polarity but points on a continuum of literacy, but this nevertheless evokes uncomplicated transitioning across a social spectrum of widely varying needs and competencies, an idea *Epicoene* vividly challenges in its rendering of a society where the vernacular is a battleground and social interactions are loaded skirmishes between different levels of linguistic facility and sophistication. Fox, for example, claims "no necessary antithesis between oral and literate forms of communication" (Fox 5) in the period; one did not have to destroy or undermine the other. Print's potential augmentation of spoken word forms appears an unproblematic development to Fox, and not the source of concern or competition that others such as Carrithers have noted. In the play, re-inventions of speech-modes by a text-based sensibility supply much of the humor and sometimes operate quite subtly, as in Act II, scene iii, where Dauphine and Clerimont mockingly attempt to categorize Sir John Daw's crude verses:

> *Dauphine*: Then this is a *ballad* of procreation?
> *Clerimont*: A *madrigal* of procreation; you mistake.
> (II.iii.137–138, italics mine).

Clerimont's mock-serious re-naming is mainly directed towards further sati-
rizing Daw's bombast, but the gallants' distinction between a ballad and a
madrigal also depicts two sophisticates' distinction between oral and literate traditions and these traditions' respective class associations and perceived
levels of sophistication. The ballad, with its roots in an older and less urbane
tradition, is dismissed in favor of the new and far more intricate madrigal,
a written text by necessity, with its complex vocal harmonics and syncopa-
tion.[10] Also important is who is doing the ordering and identifying here, for
it is the two gallants, as men of this new, literate society, who relegate the
ballad to an outmoded genre and world.

Fox details diverse oral and literate practices and is intent on establishing a reciprocity between the two more equivocal than Walter Ong's notion
of "oral residue" within literate cultures (Ong, *Orality* 120). Ong distinguishes between a vernacular literacy and a more elite, school-derived, and
thus male literacy that wished to standardize the organic vernacular of common use. He argues, significantly I think, that this is a moment when *literacy*
meant different things depending on your relationship to language. For more
and more people, language was a text-based commodity, but for myriad others, including most women, language was not yet so concrete and 'thing'-
like (Ong, *Orality* 125). Ong's nuanced depiction of the complexity of this
transition—its unevenness and its at times competing sensibilities—suggests
real tensions between different 'literacies,' and the gendered nature of the
differences.

Epicoene's three gallants typify this new literacy in their wit, which Carrithers has described as being "unawed at any document as a symbolic object"
(337). The play abounds as well with a contrasting type best understood in
terms of Huston Hallahan's reading of the play's opposition of eloquent,
witty speech and chatter, or "chat" (Hallahan 117–118). Hallahan's focus,
while not directly addressing the growth of print in the period, nevertheless
points up oral and vernacular practices and conceptions of speech that were
affected, even challenged, by the augmentation and "reinvent[ion]" (Fox 5)
of language and expression in a burgeoning print culture. Fox's contention
of seamless cultural transition is not borne out in other scholarship or in the
play itself; tensions surrounding the uneven growth of print-based literacy
circulate throughout *Epicoene*.

LITERACY, ORALITY, ELOQUENCE, CHATTER: THE PLAY

Epicoene's opening immediately calls attention to such different levels of literate vs. oral practices, and also depends upon these differences for its import.

The printed edition's listing of "The Persons of the Play" (Herford and Simpson, 5, 162) presents the characters in a standard format that nevertheless highlights elements not as evident in the purely oral transmission of a performance. "Dauphine Eugenie," for example, reveals the print detail of a silent, added "e" on the end of that character's first name, creating not only an incorrect form of the word but an impossible, feminine form of it according to the French from which it derives. This nuancing is not crucial to understanding Dauphine, but the added dimension is only available via the printed text and thus offers a kind of privileged information to that literate readership over the original, theater audience. A similar principle is at work with the listing of characters like "Madame Centaure," with her superfluous "e"; and "Mistress Mavis," with her name's more literate sense from the Italian *maviso*, for *mal-viso*, or "an ill face," less accessible to all. Anne Barton has noted an aspect of the Italian origin of Mavis's name that provides an additional dimension to the oral-literate gap Jonson appears to play with here, as he evokes a text which signals an appetite for new words. Barton points out Jonson's debt to John Florio's *A World of Wordes*, the 1598 translation of an Italian dictionary, adding that "[r]eaders and audiences who had explored this new book for themselves possessed a key to Jonson's play which others lacked."[11] These minor details foreground the possibilities of augmentation provided by print, to which Jonson was meticulously attuned; less directly, they also suggest the gaps in comprehension and knowledge determined by oral and literate abilities at the time.

A more complex framing of the oral and the literate derives from contrasting two other texts from the opening of the play. The text of *Epicoene* in the 1616 *Works*, from which derive all modern editions, includes a dedicatory letter to Sir Francis Stuart and a *Prologue* from the play's 1609 debut that pointedly juxtapose more oral with more literate sensibilities, as well as the different oral and written modes of the play's circulation. The effect foregrounds the social and discursive dynamics of the orality-literacy divide that will animate the play itself. Both the letter and the Prologue develop around central, organizing metaphors of quite different significance. In the letter, Jonson's dedication and reverence are structured by the conceit of judicial censure:

> This makes that I now number you not only in the names of favour
> but the names of justice to what I write, and do presently call you to
> the exercise of that noblest and manliest virtue, as coveting rather to
> be freed in my fame by the authority of a judge than the credit of an
> undertaker. (H&S, 5, 161, ll. 5–11)

Stuart is Jonson's "noblest and manliest" arbiter, rendering his judgment via the act of reading: "Read therefore, I pray you, and censure" (l.11).
In the first Prologue, by contrast, the appeal is both popular and populist, as
the narrow censure of the letter literally gives way to "taste," broadly defined,
in the Prologue's gustatory metaphor:

> Truth says, of old the art of making plays
>   Was to content the people, and their praise
>   Was to the Poet money, wine, and bays.
> But in this age a sect of writers are,
>   That only for particular likings care
>   And will taste nothing that is popular.
> With such we mingle neither brains nor breasts;
>   Our wishes, like to those make public feasts,
>   Are not to please the cook's tastes, but the guests.'
>   (H&S, 5, 163, ll.1–9)

Here we find not the letter's appeal for one sophisticate's "sentence," but
the contrasting of an age when art served and gratified only popular taste
and the present time, when art has become distanced from the people by
a wrongheaded, censorious sophistication. It is a striking reversal of the
literary values that infuse the Stuart letter; the *Prologue* champions the
judgment of "the guests" over "the cook," and compares play-going to the
public feasting that was a feature of an older, communal society. The most
important verbs in the *Prologue* echo this more public, oral ethos, with
"say" appearing twice, including as the action of Truth itself. In the letter,
by contrast, the most repeated verb is "read," with "censure" and "consider" also contributing to a distinctly different sense of value, or the play
itself is distanced from any public, oral 'say'ing, referred to as "this dumb
piece" (5, 161, l.12). Also notable here is the collapsing of oral with oral
in the *Prologue*. This text evokes one orality via another, of eating, tasting,
and relishing food. The simple but significant human pleasure in food is
equated with the oral/aural consumption of the audience, whether simple
or sophisticated. Sensual pleasure is not an apparent value of the literate
domain evoked in the letter to Sir Francis Stuart.[12] In the letter, to read is
to judge properly, an act of discernment far distant from the doubly oral
feasting and satisfaction of the *Prologue*. It is worth noting, as well, that
a *reader* of *Epicoene*—with the printed text's *dramatis personae* and its layers of dissemination—will be alerted from the start to the status and disguise of Epicoene herself. There is an increased informational dimension

to reading the play that fosters informed judgment but also diminished dramatic tension and surprise at the play's denouement. This legibility is privileged in the letter to Stuart, yet the foreknowledge it yields undercuts not only the dramatic/comedic value of the play, but also the significance of the silent, stage-managed deception at the center of the play. The contrast between literate and oral modes of consumption of the play that is created by these two conceits favors neither one, but it precisely captures two conflicting values for Jonson: restraint and judgment vs. expansive *joie de vivre*.[13] In these separate prefaces, Jonson balances and compartmentalizes these two urges and aesthetics in a way otherwise impossible, particularly in the play itself, where the tension between linguistic and discursive restraint versus feminine or feminized dilation becomes the very subject of the drama.[14]

In *Epicoene*, those who are masters of the textual, and of syntactic complexity, triumph. This is placed in sharp relief early on in the play's climate and context of adroit, literate wit among the three "gallants"— new men of the fashionable "town" of the West End. The gallants pit their sophisticated, articulate wit against varied others whose lesser levels of sophistication—whose lesser literacy—they find humorous and worthy of disdain; Act I catalogs the various butts of their ridicule, all of whom can be described as those less able to gain or exhibit degrees of literate facility, and consequently less able to rely upon them. Dauphine's uncle Morose, the first example, is unique in being stubbornly unwilling to tolerate any spoken language at all, sophisticated or not, save his own. The different women described are all dependent on physical attributes, not wit, as is pointed up by the men's regular and sardonic descriptions of the relative virtues of the female toilette. The female "Collegiates" are mocked for their attempts at a literate society; women cannot seem to prevail via either beauty or wit. Finally, Sir John Daw and Sir Amorous La Foole pretend to the gallants' literate sophistication, but achieve only the superficial trappings of wit. Act I introduces the central protagonists of the play and immediately places the triangulation of eloquence, silence, and chatter or noise at the center of the play's action.

Truewit's elocution, specifically his elaborate, literate language, immediately is noticeable. Truewit speaks in texts, his syntax and explication that of printed, not spoken, language, and he derives power from this adroit command of vernacular style, including his ability to wrest meaning from others' speech to serve his own purposes, serious or slight. Truewit's and Clerimont's first conversation is a "conversation" only in the sense that Clerimont's brief lines provide Truewit with fodder for his own rhetorical flights:

> *Cler*: Why, what should a man do?
>
> *True*: Why, nothing, or that which, when 'tis done, is as idle. Hearken after the next horse-race, or hunting-match; lay wagers, praise Puppy, or Peppercorn, Whitefoot, Franklin; swear upon Whitemane's party; spend aloud that my lords may hear you; visit my ladies at night and be able to give 'em the character of every bowler or bettor o' the green. These be things wherein your fashionable men exercise themselves, and I for company.
>
> *Cler*: Nay, if I have thy authority, I'll not leave yet. Come, the other are considerations when we come to have grey heads and weak hams, moist eyes and shrunk members. We'll think on 'em then; then we'll pray and fast.
>
> ---
>
> *True*: Yes, as if a man should sleep all the term and think to effect his business the last day. Oh, Clerimont, this time, because it is an incorporeal thing and not subject to sense, we mock ourselves the fineliest out of it, with vanity and misery indeed, not seeking an end of wretchedness, but only changing the matter still.
>
> *Cler*: Nay, thou'lt not leave now— (I.i.32–46, 50–56)

Edward Partridge points to Truewit's use of the word "fineliest" in these lines as a signal of the character's self-consciously elaborate language (Partridge 174). The moral gravity of Truewit's theme is undermined by the accompanying sense of his greater appreciation for a good turn-of-phrase, a characteristic further suggested fifty lines further on, when he devotes the same wry eloquence to the question of whether or not it is acceptable for women to "paint" and mend themselves with cosmetics. With this latter, Truewit directly invokes a paradoxical tradition traceable to Ovid and continued by Donne, Erasmus and others of mock-praising the cosmetic arts of women. Like these poets, Truewit here defends female artifice, though seemingly more out of the rhetorical tradition and challenge this defense represents than any firmly held beliefs. When Truewit pronounces: "Many things that seem foul in the doing, do please, done" (I.i.114–115), it is the proverbial phrasing and precise syntax that animate him, not the notions themselves, a sense confirmed by Clerimont's response: "Well said, my Truewit" (I.i.127).[15]

Clerimont's response to Truewit, above, also points to the literate affect of the wit's expression, though mockingly: "Foh, thou hast read Plutarch's *Morals* now, or some such tedious fellow, and it shows so vilely with thee, 'fore God, 'twill spoil thy wit utterly. Talk me of pins and feathers, and ladies, and rushes, and such things, and leave this stoicity alone till thou mak'st sermons" (I.i.62–66). Clerimont defies Truewit's apparent stoicism and champions the trivial and non-literate pleasures of fashionable society. This society is vividly feminine in Clerimont's description; his reply implies a difference between educated male and female society and pastimes that is fundamentally discursive, and dependent on literacy. The two gallants spend their time talking no less indulgently than ladies spend theirs with hats and feathers, but the gentlemen's talk is nimble, full of sophisticated wit. Their literate talk also is unrestrained, but is not the disorder that disorders the most in this world.

The polarity between literate/verbal and oral/material is sustained as Truewit continues his description of female beauty:

> The doing of it, not the manner: that must be private. Many things that
> Seem foul i'the doing, do please, done. A lady should indeed study her
> face when we think she sleeps; nor when the doors are shut should men
> be inquiring; all is sacred within, then. Is it for us to see their perukes
> put on, their false teeth, their complexion, their eyebrows, their nails?
> You see gilders will not work but enclosed. They must not discover how
> little serves with the help of art to adorn a great deal. How long did the
> canvas hang afore Aldgate? Were the people suffered to see the city's
> Love and Charity while they were rude stone, before they were painted
> and burnished? No. No more should servants approach their mistresses
> but when they are complete and finished. (I.i.113–126).

Here, literate constructions play off descriptions of gilders and the newly rebuilt Aldgate, with its statues of Peace and Charity. Visual impact and popular authority among the masses are suggested by these references, as well as the potency of their apparent splendor to the uninitiated. They constitute ironic gestures to a London of civic symbolism, public pageantry, and guild identities in the speech of a character whose speech-patterns and idiom suggest his very distance from this same London. More of this irony arrives a few lines later, when Truewit describes Morose's intolerance for noise in terms of the drawing-up of "divers treaties"—written texts implying functional literacy and a society organized around literate-practices—with "fishwives and orangewomen, and articles propounded between them. Marry, the chimney-sweepers will not be drawn in" (I.i.149–152). In his combining of "treaties" with these stereotypically least-sophisticated (and presumably least-literate) of trades-people, Truewit expertly portrays Morose's absurdity precisely in terms of oral versus literate practices and the problem or at least the inanity of their mixture.

The remaining scenes of Act I extend this staging of oral-literate dynamics with the arrival of several additional characters, including the third of the three gallants, Dauphine. Dauphine is capable of the literate wit of his fellows, but remains generally taciturn. This is not to be confused with the "dumbness" which Dauphine references at his entrance in I, ii: "How now! What ail you, sirs? Dumb?" (I.ii.1). Dauphine is importantly not dumb, but the humor of his question derives in part from his friends' relative prolixity. His consistent and deliberate reserve is an eloquent silence, an example of rhetorical control as adept as Truewit's, and a feature of the eloquence-silence-chatter spectrum the play dissects.[16] Scene two also introduces Sir John Daw, a knight of the gallants' acquaintance, who is an additional suitor to Epicoene. The gallants describe Daw explicitly in terms of his success or failure as a manipulator of textual knowledge:

> *Clerimont:* They say he is a very good scholar.
>
> *Truewit:* Ay, and he says it first. A pox on him, a fellow that pretends
> only to learning, buys titles, and nothing else of books in him.
>
> *Clerimont:* The world reports him to be very learned.
>
> *Truewit:* I am sorry the world should so conspire to belie him.
>
> *Clerimont:* Good faith, I have heard very good things come from him.
>
> *Truewit:* You may. There's none so desperately ignorant to deny that:
> Would they were his own. God b'w'you gentlemen. (I.ii.74–84)

Truewit's disdain derives not simply from the superficiality of Daw's "learning," or even from its evident commodification, but from the knight's blurring of the distinction between "buy(ing) titles" and genuine knowledge. Daw is more than just foolish or self-deceived; he is emblematic of a "literacy" that is shallowly pragmatic, a symptom of an increasingly market-driven, urban setting where learning is a discursive commodity and little more. Truewit's disdain derives from Daw's mere performance of literate sophistication.

At the end of Act I the arrival of Sir Amorous La Foole even further maps these issues of language, literacy, and the esoteric nature of eloquence.

If Truewit is verbose but eloquent and Dauphine depicts the possibilities of sophisticated restraint, Sir Amorous La Foole embodies the folly of excess without control, the problem of words as display without content. In La Foole, language is foolish, mere affectation, currency in quest of status. Act I, scene iv brims with comic affectation between La Foole's attempts at sophisticated phrasing and Clerimont's mockery of the courtier's locutions:

> *La Foole*: 'Save, dear sir Dauphine, honoured Master Clerimont.
>
> *Cler*: Sir Amorous! You have very much honested my lodging with your presence. . . .
>
> *La Foole*: Excuse me, sir, if it were I' the Strand, I assure you. I am come, Master Clerimont, to entreat you to wait upon two or three ladies to dinner today.
>
> *Cler*: How, sir! Wait upon 'em? Did you ever see me carry dishes?
>
> (I.iv.1–4, 8–12)

This exchange gives way to chatter a few lines later, as Dauphine's mock-sincere interest spurs Sir Amorous to a breathless autobiography filled with inept boasts and affected locutions. La Foole's speech and the scene conclude with a reference to money and status that points up a primary anxiety behind the "problem" of language in *Epicoene*'s society:

> *La Foole*: . . . and now I can take up [with his inherited wealth] at my pleasure.
>
> *Dauphine*: Can you take up ladies, sir?
>
> *Clerimont*: Oh, let him breathe, he has not recovered.
>
> *La Foole*: No, sir, excuse me: *I meant money, which can take up anything*. . . . I'll take my leave abruptly, in hope you will not fail— Your servant."
>
> (I.iv.67–75, italics mine)

In a world where "money . . . can take up anything," traditional hierarchies and class boundaries become fluid; what is better, higher, wiser, matters little in the face of the financial. In this climate, language becomes magnified simultaneously as an additional kind of "currency" but also as a last, crucial gatekeeper. La Foole's mannered and absurd malapropisms represent both his attempts to affect an eloquent status via language and his defeat at the hands of an eloquence he cannot even approximate. Amid these specific offenses, La Foole's overt effeminacy must not be overlooked. With his first name's evocation of the type of the lover, and his surname's combination of both a 'Frenchified' construction and the grammatically feminine inflections of "La" and an ending-"e," La Foole is presented from the start not simply as affected and foolish but explicitly as effeminate. Well before our first encounter with any of the women characters in the play, La Foole offers some of the problems of female speech.

Any consideration of language in *Epicoene* must decide what to do with Morose and his aversion to all noise apart from his own voice. Speech, for Morose, is a "discord of sounds" (II.i.3); he commands his servant, appropriately named "Mute," to communicate only with physical motions, not words or speech. Besides the obvious comic value of a character lifting arms and legs as communication, there is a sociopathic bite in this turning away from language that isolates Morose not just from the gallants and their banter, but from the city itself. Such mute communication also proves absurd and impossible, as Morose's attempts to keep his servant silent involve more and more of his own words:

> *Morose*: Answer me not by speech
> but by silence, unless it be otherwise.—Very good.
> And you have fastened on a thick quilt or flock-bed on the
> outside of the door? . . . But with your leg,
> your answer, unless it be otherwise.—Very good. This is
> not only fit modesty in a servant, but good state and
> discretion in a master. And you have been with Cutbeard,
> the barber, to have him come to me?—Good. And he will
> Come presently? Answer me not but with your leg, unless
> It be otherwise; if it be otherwise, shake your head or shrug.
> (II.i.9–20)

Morose's speaks in two modes, according to Barish: his "normal style of self-congratulation . . . and mass of affectation and . . . old-maidish pickedness"(Barish158), and the cruder, repetitive idiom of agitation to which various "torments" bring him. Barish characterizes the first of these modes: "Morose's studied singularity of diction and gratuitous floridity emanate fittingly from one who has shut himself off from the sound of the human voice and must rely upon memory and reading . . . [his style] tend[s] toward pedantry more than foppery" (Barish 159); Act II, scene i, provides an initial showcasing of this affectation: "I see by such doctrine and impulsion, it may be effected . . . an exquisite art!" Immediately after these utterances, however, Morose's smug tranquility is broken by

Truewit's horn (sounded offstage) and his speech shifts shifts to an altogether different register characterized by strings of series, lamentations in duplicate, and a startling abandonment of temperamental balance for crudity: "Oh! Cut his throat, cut his throat! What, murderer, hell-hound, devil can this be? . . . Out, rogue! . . . Pain of thy life, be silent!" (II.i.39–46). This disintegration of "inkhorn" eloquence into graceless complaint heralds the first confrontation between Truewit and Morose, pitting Truewit's eloquence against Morose's verbal impotence.[17] Truewit encircles and overwhelms Morose, whose mannered locutions appear ever more clearly a precarious verbal disguise. The scene plays out a struggle for control of discourse and linguistic practices, a context in which Morose proves barely a player.

ORALITY, LITERACY, ELOQUENCE, AND CHATTER: *EPICOENE'S* WOMEN

Epicoene's staging of the contemporary dynamic of a growing authority of literacy in tension with oral traditions structures the play throughout subsequent Acts. Jonson continually offers us moments and characterizations which hinge on problems of literacy or literacies, as in the example of Mistress Otter with which I began. The choice of Mistress Otter's words to begin this study was not arbitrary, however, for the play's staging of female characters and their speech comprises the heart of its concerns over literacy and eloquence. With the addition of the lady collegiates to the company, questions of literacy even more vividly become questions of female speech.

As surveyed above, Arnold Preussner reads *Epicoene* as a play about language and society in which rational discourse dissolves, Act by Act (Preussner 9–10). Language vividly is forsaken in the play, "the characters . . . are either incapable or unwilling to use speech as the instrument of society" (Preussner 13). There is a case to be made for Jonson's interest in an unwillingness to apply speech constructively, but the play's focus on women and literacy concerns also hints at a problem of inability. This in turn suggests some need for rethinking Preussner's progressive cacophony. For example, in his reading of Act IV—apparently the point where linguistic debasement to noise also becomes physical debasement to violence—Preussner notes how little of the action of the Act is pertinent to the larger marriage-plot that purports to be the center of the play; much of the Act's chaotic energy stems from excess on every level. This sense is unmistakable, but it is possible to read the chaos, apparent irrelevance, and linguistic debasement as an escalation of characters' clumsy and at times shrill gestures toward literate sophistication, to read characters' speech as revealing their differing degrees of understanding of and comfort with textuality. In one vivid example, certain texts are sought as medicinal cures, and several characters strive to exercise a 'literate' familiarity with them:

> *Epicoene*: Gentlemen, for heavn's sake counsel me. Ladies! Servant, you have read Pliny and Paracelsus: ne'er a word now to comfort a poor gentlewoman? . . .
>
> *Daw*: I'll tell you mistress . . . The disease in Greek is called *pavia*, in Latin *insania, furor, vel ecstasis melancholia*, that is, *egressio*, when a man .
>
> *Morose*: Shall I have a lecture read upon me alive?
>
> *Daw*: But he may be but *phreneticus* yet, mistress, and *phrenetis* is only *delirium* or so—
>
> *Epicoene*: Ay, that is for the disease, servant; but what is this to the cure? We are sure enough of the disease. (IV.iv.60–75)

Epicoene appeals for counsel to anyone who has read natural science. Daw is all too happy to demonstrate his learned abilities; Epicoene demonstrates her own sophistication in rebuffing, unfazed, his pedantry. Morose's doleful question highlights the sheer noise of all this "learnedness"; as Preussner argues, the play becomes progressively noisier throughout Act IV. It also becomes progressively more crowded with characters vying for sophistication—La Foole, Daw, and the Lady Collegiates dominate much of Acts IV and V. The Lady Collegiates weigh in with a cure, and the discussion of books and their curative properties progresses to the ludicrous querying of a servant as to which of her parents was "cured" with *The Sick Man's Salve*(1560), a still-popular religious tract in the Elizabethan period:[18]

> *Haughty*: I'll tell you (Mistress) Morose, you must talk divinity to him altogether, or moral philosophy.
>
> *La* Foole: Ay, and there's an excellent book of moral philosophy, madam of Reynard the Fox and all the beasts, called Doni's *Philosophy* . . . I have read it, my Lady Centaure, all over to my cousin here.
>
> *Mistress Otter*: Ay, and 'tis a very good book as any is of the moderns.
> Daw: Tut, he must have Seneca read to him, and Plutarch and the ancients; the moderns are not for this disease.
>
> *Clerimont*: Why, you discommended them too today, Sir John.
>
> *Daw*: Ay, in some cases; but in these they are best, and Aristotles's *Ethics*.

Mavis: Say you so, Sir John? I think you are deceived: you took it upon trust.

Haughty: Where's Trusty, my woman? I'll end this difference . . . Her father and mother were both mad when they put her to me . . . And one of 'em—I know not which—was cured with *The Sick Man's Salve*, and the other with Greene's *Groat's-worth of Wit*.

Truewit: A cheap cure, Madam.

Haughty: Ay, it's very feasible.

[enter Mistress Otter with Trusty]

Haughty: Oh, Trusty, which was it you said, your father or your mother, that was cured with *The Sick Man's Salve*?[19] (IV.iv.81–115)

Truewit's sarcastic response, here, derives its comic punch from the difference between his understanding and use of the *Groat's Worth of Wit* (1592), and Lady Haughty's. Truewit, the easily literate wit, quips on the work's title and in doing so trivializes both the already trivial text and any sincere valuation of it. Lady Haughty's response, however, indicates that she has not noticed his joke or his sarcasm. Her earnest reply implies a different understanding of texts, and certainly of this popular, cheap-print pamphlet, whereby she neither scrutinizes titles nor is adroit enough to treat them playfully. To reprise Carrithers' claim, the exchange here between Truewit and Lady Haughty demonstrates the difference between being "unawed at any document as a symbolic object," and being awed, unable to think about a text or title like Greene's-*Groat's Worth of Wit* with irony, much less treat it in such a way oneself. A similar gap in perceptions is indicated by the servant Trusty's response:

Trusty: My mother, madam, with the *Salve*. . . . And my father with the *Groat's worth of Wit*. But there was other means used: we had a preacher that would preach folk asleep still; and so they were prescribed to go to church by an old woman that was their physician, thrice a week–

Epicoene: To sleep?

Trusty: Yes, forsooth; and every night they read themselves asleep on those books. (IV.iv.116–125)

The value of these works lies in their words, but as semi-mystified curative powers, not for their content. They are also interchangeable with other prescribed 'cures' like church—they bring sleep, not knowledge. In attempting

to display familiarity with texts, these characters in Act IV, scene iv, and notably the female characters like Lady Haughty and Trusty, reveal the degree to
which such literacy is still mysterious to them, and to which books' value is
as objects or titles. Many things are roundly mocked in this scene, but this
discrepant treatment of textual knowledge is crucial to its hilarity; IV, iv is a
highly parodic scene in which women's increasing, real-life literacy—especially in fashionable and urbane London—is depicted in terms of misplaced
debates on natural philosophy and medicine, Ancients vs. Moderns, divin-
ity, and moral philosophy, that improbably and sardonically conclude over
cheap-print 'wisdom' like *The Sick Man's Salve* versus Robert Greene's *Groat's
Worth of Wit*.

Daw and LaFoole also participate in this inanity in the play, of course.
It is the women characters, however, who constitute the scene's center of
gravity. What distinguishes the women-pretenders from the two gentlemen-
fools is their significance to others. That is, Daw and La Foole are mocked
and easily dismissed throughout the play, but their ridiculousness has little impact on the larger plot. They are simply gulls whose literate pretensions create further opportunities for humor at their expense. The women
in the play, however, and the lady collegiates in particular, are never treated
this casually, their ridiculousness is never so easily dismissed. The gallants
mock the ladies—in Act V, scene ii, they bemusedly observe the collegiates'
competitive, affected wooing of Dauphine, the ladies' newest favorite—but
the women and their pretensions also are a source of anxiety for the men in
their fascination. The gallants' rehearsals of different attitudes toward female
beauty appear at intervals throughout the play and serve as a subtle backdrop to their otherwise practiced air of bemusement. Act IV, scene I kicks off
the Act's cacophony by offering a reprise on women that suggests both the
actual influence of the women the gallants would mock, and the anxieties
surrounding the matter of women's shifting place in society. Truewit catalogs
women and their aesthetic challenges:

> If she be short, let her sit much, lest when she stands she be thought to
> sit. If she have an ill foot, let her wear her gown the longer and her shoe
> the thinner. If a fat hand and scald nails, let her carve the less, and act in
> gloves. If a sour breath, let her never discourse fasting, and always talk at
> her distance. If she have black and rugged teeth, let her offer the less at
> laughter, especially if she laugh wide and open. (IV.i.39–46)

In this passage the generic lady become progressively more monstrous, and
Truewit's solutions to her beauty-dilemmas increasingly limit her expression.

Women must take care, most of all, to police their offending mouths, whether in speech, breath, or laughter. What seems at first a standard rehearsal of misogynistic rhetoric, however, shortly modulates to reveal the fascination and trepidation behind the equally misogynistic regulation of women's minds and social place. Questioned as to his knowledge of women, Truewit admonishes his fellows' reliance on fictional romances like *Amadis de Gaule* in favor of real women, declaring that a man "must go where she is" (IV. i.65–66). He describes the proper approach to women:

> If she love wit, give verses, though you borrow 'em of a friend, or buy 'em, to have good. If valour, talk of your sword, and be frequent in the mention of quarrels, though you be staunch in fighting . . . If she love good clothes or dressing, have your learned council about you every morning, your French tailor, barber, linener, et cetera.
>
> (IV.i.97–104)

There is a Machiavellian air in Truewit's wooing advice; woman is a highly dangerous creature who must be managed and controlled: "Then if she be covetous and craving, do you promise anything . . . so you shall keep her in appetite still . . . Let your gifts be slight and dainty, rather than precious. Let cunning be above cost" (IV.i.109–114). The emphasis on controlling female expression and the flow of goods around women in these speeches has been noted by Karen Newman in her account of early modern discourses of femininity, particularly as enacted on the stage.[20] The female was almost categorically associated with excesses both sartorial and linguistic, according to Newman, with each of these coming to signify the other in a symbolic economy whereby the 'talking woman' with her open mouth was equated with an appetite that was traditionally sexual and now also highly acquisitive (Newman, *Fashioning* 134). "Jonson's *Epicoene*," she writes, "is peopled with talkative women whom he portrays as monstrous precisely because they gallivant about the city streets spending breath as well as money" (*Fashioning* 135). This problem of the threat of women moving, spending, and, especially, speaking freely (again, with such speaking synechdochic for other, unrestrained transgressions) is the context for the gallants' exchanges about women throughout the play, including IV, i. In such a context women's speech and changing levels of literacy become as monstrous as the female bodies Truewit describes.

In considering literacy and especially an eloquence-chatter dynamic in terms of women in the play, it is impossible to avoid *Epicoene's* title and subtitle, "The Silent Woman." The entire play revolves around what might variously be perceived as the question or problem or ironically impossible joke of a woman who does not speak.[21] As a joke, it is as anxious as it is humorous: the subtitle describes a silent femininity that never exists in the play and the city world it evokes. The apparently silent woman herself is neither silent nor a woman; the most vivid characteristic of actual woman-hood, throughout the play, is chatter unaffected by class distinction. Mistress Otter, Lady Haughty, and their collegiate companions all contribute a par-ticularly unruly linguistic excess. Truewit's excesses derive from virtuosic self-indulgence, but with the play's women, the noise of their chatter results from overzealous aspiration to a literacy and related eloquence they either parrot or inaccurately invent. Women's speech is cynically idealized as silence in the subtitle, but its actuality in the play is never less than shrill noise. Women are linguistic offenders in a manner which aligns them with Sir Amorous, Daw, and Captain Otter, but are recognized and perceived by others—specifically the three gallants—in a way that sets them distinctly apart as women. As we have seen already, the excesses of Daw and La Foole are ridiculous, those of Morose pathological, but nonetheless comical. By contrast, the noisy chat-ter of Mistress Otter and the collegiates is humorous but also more threat-ening, their speech and its cacophony signaling not just stylistic but social chaos. Many have noted the similarity of Jonson's oxymoronic subtitle to then titles and subject-matter of other popular drama of the day such as Thomas Dekker's *The Honest Whore* (1604/5) and Thomas Middleton's *A Chaste Maid in Cheapside* (1613). Clearly there existed a kind of vogue for these paradoxical expressions of London life. That all these titles make their expression via an explicit female unruliness as well as the rhetorical figure of the oxymoron is important for parsing *Epicoene*'s concern for women and language. "The Silent Woman" is not as obviously sexualizing an expression as these other examples, but its evocation of the silent female mouth—this orifice so commonly eroticized for its metonymic possibilities—points up the central and complex problem of women talking.[22]

EPICOENE'S *WOMEN AND SHAKESPEARE'S WOMEN*

We might further consider the question of women and language in *Epicoene* by contrasting the way Jonson treats women and language, particularly in *Epicoene*, with the way women and language are represented by Jonson's con-temporary and rival, Shakespeare. Shakespeare never wrote any play we truly could consider a London "city comedy," and Shakespeare's particular que-rying of and experimentation with the English vernacular does not belong to city comedy's unique nexus of conversation about language and society in the context of London.[23] Language in Shakespeare typically embodies an ideal of efficacious oral communication; language in Jonson is more material, more quotidian, and more morally indicative, never as graceful an "instrument of society" as in Shakespeare, and expressing notions of humanity that are equally divergent. It is possible to see these two playwrights as involved in distinctly different literary, dramatic, and discursive projects; the role and function of women in their works perhaps reveals this most vividly.

To begin with Shakespeare's women-characters and what their language signals or accomplishes, Lawrence Manley confronts the fact that Shakespeare never wrote true city- comedy by examining the numerous instances in his plays where there is generic disjunction. That is, though Shakespeare never wrote a city-comedy, he signals interest in that genre in plays like *Measure for Measure* (1604), where his interest lies in juxtaposing comedy and romance, and thus exploring generic boundaries (Manley, *Literature and Culture*). Manley comments on this strategy of exposing generic types:

> In such plays, the opposition between different kinds of comic potential is not simply a dynamic that gives definition to form; it is also a medium for self-reflection, a means for giving visibility to the ways in which generic kinds and social relations are structured. (Manley, *Literature and Culture* 455)

Implicit in Manley's discussion of this strategy is Shakespeare's commitment to coherence, to the "meaningful clarity of oppositions" that may be produced in the apparent dissonance of contradiction. The vehicle by which such contradictions are overwhelmingly distinguished, in diverse plays like *Measure for Measure* and *Henry V* (1599), is one or more woman characters. Manley points out the habitual phrase "I understand you not," a "conveniently compact and metrical way of annotating a positional relationship" (Manley, *Literature and Culture* 453), and notes its recurrent utterance in Shakespearean drama: by Isabella in *Measure for Measure*, Hermione in *The Winter's Tale* (1610/11), Marina in *Pericles* (c.1608), the Princess of France in *Love's Labours Lost* (c.1595), Katherine at the end of *Henry V*. Most of these characters speak an idealized language of romance in Shakespeare, but it is compelling to consider, with Manley, that the real power of such female speech lies in its disruption, its revelation of contrasting genres and their possibilities. Women's speech emphasizes coherence in its work of highlighting moments of incoherence. Discussing Marina's response to the vice-ridden cityscape of Mytilene, Manley comments:

> Marina's gesture, like that of Morose in Jonson's *Epicoene* . . . stuffing
> his ears with shoewax, is but her first resistance to the endlessly divid-
> ing and divisive language of the city . . . [Her] resistance stiffens in
> response to the bawd's further anti-romantic advice on the exploita-
> tion of illusion . . . Marina's response to this dissonance is simple and
> straightforward: "I understand you not." The phrase marks a moment
> of transition, in which the possibility of romance is recuperated from its
> demon other, city comedy. (Manley, *Literature and Culture* 462)

In Jonson's dramatic world, by contrast, if he evokes the genre or language
of romance at all, it is never in service to a greater coherence, but only to
further reject such a possibility. Coherence is an anxiety but an absence in
Jonson's world, 'What can cohere society?' a recurring question whose lack of
an answer is the source for his early, acid satires and later, dark comedies. In
Shakespeare, women effect such coherence, and their speech, in particular,
often holds power because of its disjunctive, Romantic mode. In Jonson, and
in *Epicoene*, language explicitly is the opposite of coherent, and the women
of the play act as a kind of anti-center, their speech significant for what it
doesn't achieve—either silence or literate eloquence—in a play whose title
foregrounds both female silence and a femininity that is incomplete.

LANGUAGE AS FASHION

In April 1609, an entertainment devised by Ben Jonson was performed for
the opening of the New Exchange, a new retail complex in the Strand. *The
Entertainment for Britain's Burse* celebrated London's burgeoning marketplace and the new availability of exotic goods in the capital. As Ian W. Archer
argues, however, such an encomium to the city as "the choicest storehouse in
the world" could not completely conceal accompanying concerns about the
sheer consumption, and growing culture of consumption, the pageant and
its namesake also celebrated.[24] It is this tension surrounding consumption,
as well as the most frequent target of Londoners' anxieties over acquisitiveness—women—that I foreground as an additional thematic of *Epicoene*, the
city comedy Jonson would present by the end of the same year. Archer uses
the performance and themes of *Britain's Burse* to parse the material lives of
Londoners in 1609, as well as their attitudes toward the proliferating materialism of their city. I will use Archer's scrutiny of Jonson's pageant, its appearance so close to *Epicoene* in time, to emphasize the pervasive and threatening
imbrications of city, commodities, and women that are fundamental to
Epicoene's querying of language as fashion. Archer cites Karen Newman's

observation that consumption was seen as an activity to which women were conspicuously (and dangerously) prone (Archer 185), and points as well to a 1616 speech by James I, in which the king blames women and their shopping habits for overcrowding in the city:

> One of the greatest causes of all gentlemen's desire, that have no calling or errand, to dwell in London, is apparently the pride of women. For if they bee wives, then their husbands, and if they be maydes, then their fathers, must bring them up to London because the new fashion is to be had nowhere but in London. (Archer 186)

Fashion and women's destructive pursuit of it corrupt men and the larger city, alike. While it might be celebrated in *Britain's Burse*, James's speech underscores fashion's destructive potential as well as women's, by implication. Such a sentiment was not exclusive to James or the court. *Epicoene*, set in the milieu of the modish West End, confronts fashion as both a sartorial and linguistic problem; the play poses the satiric but no less nervous question of what ensues in a society when language has become only fashion. An additional, crucial component of the play's work as the language document I am claiming it to be is this conflation of language and apparel, this connection of language to fashion. We have observed the centrality of concerns about women and language in *Epicoene's* treatment of literacy, eloquence, and its opposites. This tension between literacies, or between literacy and residual orality, and the related social/rhetorical axis of eloquence/silence and chatter, is infused with the problem of language as fashion. Concerns over pretended literacy and aped eloquence stem from an acknowledgment that language can be viewed as a commodity with no other purpose or value beyond a certain sartorial effect. With this urban-charged problem of language as fashion, once again women are the center of the play.

Jonson is preoccupied with style, linguistic and otherwise, everywhere in his works; the very appearance of his *Works*, in 1616, is the self-conscious gesture of a poet intent on styling himself for consumption (Loxley 39–41). Yet such consumption or commoditization is at all times problematic for him. In one of the most familiar of his pronouncements in *Discoveries* he asserts, "Language most shows a man: speak, that I may see thee" (H&S, 8, 625). Language is profoundly revealing, providing exposure that is as anxious as it is enthralling. The passage continues by delineating the myriad physical and intellectual variations of men and the language that reveals them, ascribing a taxonomic orderliness to men and their speech that nevertheless dissolves into a more chaotic show:

> And . . . these styles vary, and lose their names: for that which is high
> and lofty, declaring excellent matter, becomes vast and tumorous, speak-
> ing of petty and inferior things . . . Would you not laugh to meet a
> great councillor of state in a flat cap, with his trunk-hose and a hobby-
> horse cloak his gloves under his girdle, and yond haberdasher in a velvet
> gown, furred with sables? (H&S, 8, 626)

Language can coherently show a man to advantage, but can just as easily
reveal the kind of motley, disjointed self (and disjointed society) depicted
via the apparel analogy, above. In this passage, the main problem appears
to be one of mismatched styles—the issue is more rhetorical than related
to commoditization. But such an explicit reference to the sartorial evokes a
larger Jonsonian concern for representation, fashion, and commodity toward
which the playwright is ambivalent, at best. Language and fashion do go
together in Jonson, but rarely in the ordered, comprehensive terms of most
instances in *Discoveries*.

Douglas Lanier highlights sections of *Discoveries* in terms of what he
sees as Jonson's preoccupation with forging a purely masculine expression
that is distanced from the distinctly feminine and ornamental materiality of
words:

> Right and naturall language seem[s] to have least of the wit in it; that
> which is writh'd and tortur'd, is counted the more exquisite. Cloath of
> Bodkin, or Tissue, must be imbrodered; as if no face were faire, that were
> not pouldered or painted? No beauty to be had, but in wresting and
> writhing our owne tongue? Nothing is fashionable, till it bee deform'd;
> and this is to write like a Gentleman. All must be as affected, and pre-
> posterous as our Gallants cloathes, sweet bags, and night dressings: in
> which you would think our men lay in, like Ladies: it is so curious.[25]
>
> (H&S, 8, 581)

For Lanier, this passage reveals the "feminizing dangers of rhetorical
ornament" for Jonson, and these dangers succinctly are expressed in the
language of fashion—fabrics and the embellishment of such fabric and of
faces. There is continual slippage between fashion and language as *Discoveries*
surveys language, style, and the problem of rhetorical fashions with precise
care. Jonson's pronouncements, many adapted from favorite classical sources,
create an impression of lucid stability: his words can re-organize such
mayhem just by naming it. This may be true in the pages of *Discoveries* itself
(though its length and bricolage-quality call to mind other catalogings—

Stow, in particular—that, as we have seen, ultimately effect the opposite of order). Outside of *Discoveries*, its taxonomic work on both language and fashion is little in evidence: in *Epicoene* the social and rhetorical instability of language as fashion is the central problem, and exercising its worst extremes provides no remedy. Language is fashion, and fashion can be mistaken for sophisticated discourse. The worst offenders—the male gulls and especially the Lady Collegiates—are silenced at the end of the play, but the victory of Dauphine and his two companions is a triumph for fashionable new gentlemen of the town like them, whose sophistication is real but for whom everything is ornamental. This effeminates characters like Truewit, and it is notable, as discussed above, that the most stylistically pretentious character among the men is the thoroughly effeminate, preposterous Sir Amorous La Foole. Language as fashion is not solely a problem of women, but is invariably linked to the feminine.

This linkage and the anxiety inherent to it is established well before any women characters enter the play. In Act II, scene ii, Truewit tortures Morose with an unending catalog of the perils of matrimony that emphasizes the demands placed upon the hapless husband by the wife's unquenchable appetite for material goods and accoutrements:

> You shall lie with her but when she lists; she will not hurt/ her beauty, her complexion; or it must be for that jewel or/ that pearl when she does; every half hour's pleasure must/ be bought anew . . . Then you must keep what servants she please . . . and [to provoke your jealousy, she will] go live with her she-friend or cousin at the college, that can instruct her in/ all the mysteries of writing letters, corrupting servants, / taming spies; where she must have that rich gown for such/ a great day, a new one for the next, a richer for the third.[26] (II.ii.93–106)

A large part of the speech's effect is Truewit's verbal barrage, but it is worth noticing its profusion's similarity to diverse tracts like Stubbes' *Anatomie* and phenomena like the New Exchange and its bounties—Truewit describes women and marriage with a recognizable discursive trope of the woman-consumer that is almost automatically conflated with the city and its excesses.

Truewit emphasizes sheer quantities of wifely demands, but the nature of them also makes connections between fashion and language-use in both explicit and implicit ways:

> If [she is]/ learned, there was never such a parrot; all your patrimony/ will be too little for the guests that must be invited to hear her speak

Latin and Greek, and you must lie with her in/ those languages too, if you will please her. (II.ii.76–80)

[She must] be a states-/ woman, know all the news; what was done at Salisbury, / what at the Bath . . . or so she may censure poets and authors and styles, and compare 'em, Daniel to Spenser, Jonson with the tother youth, and so forth; or be thought cunning . . . and have often in her mouth the state of the question.

(II.ii.114–121)

Knowledge of classical languages, discoursing publicly on current events, making judgment of the literary value of vernacular works—all are collapsed as the frivolous, pernicious, and above all purely fashionable pursuits of the city wife. And while the gallant's objective of tormenting Morose by cataloging the latter's sociopathic fears somewhat qualifies his words, Truewit's rapid listing lends them a quality of 'common knowledge.' This is not just Morose's wretched anxiety, but a more universal concern to which he easily subscribes. Women's appetite for the fashionable is gestured to again, this time as ostensibly sincere advice to Dauphine about women:

Yes, but you must leave to live I' your chamber, then . . .
as/ you are wont, and come abroad . . . to court, to tiltings, public
shows and feasts, to plays, and church sometimes: thither they come to
show their new tires too, to see and be seen. In these places a
man shall find whom to love, whom to play with . . .
The variety arrests his/ judgment. (IV.i.55–63)

Here, Truewit is speaking companionably to his friend, but the implications are the same: women are vividly public creatures in these remarks, primarily desiring to display themselves. They hold outspoken sartorial conversations across the city; their availability is both exciting and intimidating.

Language as fashion is brought to an extreme in the character and speech of Mistress Otter, whose attempts at sophisticated social discourse invariably invoke apparel. In the speech quoted at the opening of this chapter, she relates her experience of the city precisely in terms of her sartorial choices and challenges, and this continues throughout the play. Mistress Otter's most distinctive speech-acts revolve around her comical approximations of a courtly idiom, including near malapropisms and the constant mention of fashions: "I cannot assure you, Master Truewit. Here was a very melancholy knight in a ruff, that demanded my subject for somebody, a gentleman, I think" (III.ii.21–23). Mistress Otter rants to her husband about his improper respect for her and furiously points out the discrepancies between them in status. Her most pointed weapon, revealing, to her mind, her sophistication and sufferings, is her 'learned discourse' of fashion and commodities:

> Who gives you your maintenance, I
> pray you? Who allows you . . . Your three suits of apparel a year?
> Your four pair of stockings, one silk, three worsted? Your clean linen,
> your
> bands and cuffs, when I can get you to wear 'em? 'Tis mar'l
> you ha' 'em on now. Who graces you with courtiers or great
> personages, to speak to you out of their coaches . . . ?
> Were you ever so much as looked
> upon by a lord, or a lady, before I married you? . . . And did not I
> take you up from thence in an old greasy buff-doublet, with points,
> and green vellet sleeves out at the elbows? You forget this. (III.i.38–55)

Mistress Otter is a striver and she is the most egregious linguistic offender among the women of the play. Her studied efforts to adopt the trappings of stature, linguistic and sartorial, signal her character's value for considering the language-fashion-women nexus of the play.

The collegiate ladies' social position is more assured than Mistress Otter's, but their striving is just as energetic. Their pretensions seem more learned: their "college," to begin with, suggests a society for education, and the ladies wield it self-consciously as a component of their sophistication. It appears to have little to do with actual learning and literate discernment, however, and more to do with a vogue for such societies. Truewit describes their club as "A new foundation, sir, here I' the town, of ladies that call themselves the Collegiates, an order between courtiers and country madams, that . . . give entertainment to all the Wits and Braveries o' the time, as they call 'em, cry down or up what they like or dislike in a brain or a fashion with most masculine or rather hermaphroditical authority" (I.i.73–80). Truewit, admittedly, is not a dependably unbiased source; the ladies' own characterization of their college echoes Truewit, however:

> *Haughty*: No, we'll have her to the college: and she have wit, she
> shall be one of us! Shall she not, Centaure? We'll make her
> a collegiate.

> *Centaure*: Yes, faith, madam, and Mavis and she will set up a side.
>
> (III.vi.51–55)

Lady Centaure's suggestion of Epicoene's value as a new member who can complete "a side" for card-playing succinctly trivializes the ladies' College without anyone else's help.

The ladies pursue learning, current events, social engagements, even lovers, because they are fashionable; their speech, though more nimble than Mistress Otter's, is strewn with commodities with which they hope to ennoble themselves. They all determine to woo Dauphine as their next conquest, and their successive encounters with him make their self-importance and its fashionable basis evident:

> *Haughty*: I assure you, Sir Dauphine, it is the price and estimation of your virtue only that hath embarked me to this adventure . . .
>
> *Dauphine*: Your ladyship sets too high a price on my weakness.
>
> *Haughty*: Sir, I can distinguish gems from pebbles—
>
> *Dauphine*: Are you so skillful in stones? . . . I perceive [Centaure and Mavis] are your mere foils.
>
> *Haughty*: Then you are a friend to truth, sir. It makes me love you the more. (V.ii.1–17)

Lady Haughty affects sophistication in her redundant coupling of "price" and "estimation," as well as in her commodity-based idiom: fine-ness of virtue—or of anything else—is a luxury item for transaction. She is attracted to how 'expensive' she perceives Dauphine to be, which she makes explicit in her mention of "gems" in the next lines. Dauphine's responses contribute to Haughty's ridiculousness, as they mock her discourse of fashionable goods with puns like "foils," to which she is haplessly oblivious.

The ladies' preoccupation with fashions and this preoccupation's superficiality extends to Lady Centaure's disparaging of Haughty to gain Dauphine for herself. Unable to come up with any appropriate words of seduction, Centaure turns to a subject she presumably knows well: "Good Sir Dauphine, do not trust Haughty, nor make any credit to her, whatever you do besides . . . Besides, her physicians give her out to be none o' the clearest—whether she pay 'em or no, heav'n knows; and she's above fifty too, and pargets! See her in a forenoon" (V.ii.30–36). "Pargets" means to plaster, with face make-up in this case, an uncomplimentary description of the fashionable but also condemned practice of face-painting in women.[27] Centaure's

lure to Dauphine is the promise of details about face-makeup and her fellows' habits: "If you'll come to my chamber one o' these mornings early, or
late in an evening, I'll tell you more" (V.ii.38–40).

Dauphine, in somewhat disingenuous agony, describes this situation
in which all three ladies "would possess me" (V.ii.54), his judgmental verb
comically accurate given all we have observed. There are plenty of judgmental or inane characters in *Epicoene* whose views represent no true gauge of
social realities—Morose, Daw, even the gallants themselves. Acquisitiveness,
however, unequivocally drives women in *Epicoene*; this is judged or mocked
by others, but is offered to us from all sides, especially by the women themselves. Their appetite for fashionable things is demonstrated to include language, treated by them as yet another thing to acquire for fashion's sake.

As we have seen already, addressing women and language in *Epicoene* must account for Epicoene herself, "the silent woman." The *topos*
of language as fashion seems pertinent but complicated in this case of a
'woman' who is only a woman by the disguise of women's fashions, but
whose speech, or lack of it, successfully passes her with interested parties
like Morose and her collegiate "sisters." The play poses language perceived
as merely commodity as a problem, but all but Dauphine and his boy-
woman are fooled by "Epicoene" as a commodity—a commodity who is
crucially discursive and sartorial—throughout. Perhaps the real joke is on
anyone who considers himself outside of this urban economy of language
and fashion. Jonson's play foregrounds the vernacular by sketching a city
constituted by talk; the city-problems of instability and incoherence thus
are discursive, and the greatest discursive incoherence is threatened by
women. But with 'woman' herself revealed as a commodity at the play's
conclusion, anxieties over female literacy or lack thereof, chatter, or materialism are trumped by the collective appetite for commodities of language
and appearance laid bare in Dauphine's triumph. In the end, the silent
'woman' is the symbol of everyone's unstable treatment of language as a
fashionable 'thing.' Women are the central mode by which *Epicoene* queries
the vernacular in its London society, but in service, ultimately, to a broader
perspective on the role of language in this society.

EPICOENE'S LANGUAGE AND WOMEN, AND THE CONTEXT OF *THE ALCHEMIST*: A CONCLUSION

Epicoene's interest in the quotidian, and specifically in the life of the city
in terms of speech and speakers, is buttressed by some brief comparison
to *The Alchemist* (1610), a play somewhat better known and more readily

recognized as a London-steeped city-comedy.[28] Several elements of *The Alchemist's* rendering of language distance it from *Epicoene* as a project and product of Jonson's social and linguistic concerns. I conclude with a discussion of these differences and how they help to complete a picture of our play.

The Alchemist is written in verse, in contrast to *Epicoene's* unyielding prose. This fact alone suggests different aims in each play, for language and style never are neutral media for their author. For Jonson, to use language was to criticize, to rebuke, to condemn, to ridicule or admire, and the choice of verse also distances *The Alchemist* from everyday speech and thus from explicit vernacular satire. Verse also releases the capacity of language as fantasy, achieving this despite *The Alchemist's* setting in contemporary Blackfriars during a plague episode. Barish comments, "With [*The Alchemist*], the [linguistic] fantasies are . . . screwed up to an unnatural pitch, and this time they vibrate with all the strange resonances of an occult jargon." The play is rendered in a "fabulous surrealistic language. The radically illusory nature of the hopes nursed by rogues and fools alike . . . all require Jonson's most radically hyperbolic blank verse incantations" (Barish 188). Such an incantatory quality—surely one of the pleasures of *The Alchemist*—also distances it from *Epicoene's* interest in more quotidian city talk. *Epicoene's* language evokes a society structured by its relationship to the vernacular and its uses. Characters' language is posed as a commodity in both plays, but in *The Alchemist* the commodity is unreal, spell-like bombast devoted purely to predation; in *Epicoene* language serves vanity, whose traditional association with women makes the play's ending all the more ironic. Jonson undertook a distinct project with each play.

This is clear in considering the differing ways women feature in the two plays. The incantatory quality of *The Alchemist* is extended to its two women, Dame Pliant and, particularly, Dol Common, who personify a host of fantastic women to the various gulls who visit Subtle and Face. Though Dol, part of the corrupt triumvirate with Subtle and Face, holds a proportion of power in the plot and its plottings, she and Dame Pliant function most vividly as ciphers for others' fantasies while the action is loudly dominated by the men's machinations. Dol is a consummate performer, the most noteworthy example being when she enters raving passages of Hebraic prophecy: "And last Gog-dust, and Egypt-dust, which fall/ In the last link of the fourth chain. And these/ Be stars in story, which none see, or look at . . . For, as he says, except/ We call the rabbins and the heathen Greeks" (IV.v.9–13). These mysterious words are not her own on two levels: they are quoted from Hugh Broughton's 1590 *Old Testament* history,[29] and also were given to her by Face for the confuting of Sir Epicure. By contrast, the women of *Epicoene* function as part of a wholly different enterprise, their language vividly, and problematically, their own, much to the chagrin, amusement, and distress of the men around them. When Mrs. Otter does her own rendition of a tirade, her affected but hapless approximation of fashionable diction makes her speech quite *sui generis* in its disarray. Epicoene herself, of course, is an exception—all her speech is a performance coached by Dauphine, we find in the end. But even in this instance, and in the degree to which Epicoene functions symbolically for others' assumptions, the lens of the play is trained on a more quotidian world, and more quotidian, discursive issues, than *The Alchemist* whips up.

Fakery animates both plays. Face deceives his absent master and runs an alchemist's operation devoted to deceit and gain; every character is self-deceived to some degree except Face, who deceives everyone else. Morose is tricked into marrying a woman who has posed as perfectly silent, but who is revealed as a boy at the end by virtue of the meta-deceit of Dauphine, whose trick fools even his close associates. Lesser characters are revealed as fakes throughout; deceit is explicitly linguistic in both. In Act IV of *The Alchemist*, Surly, convinced of the treachery of Subtle and Face and determined to expose them, enters disguised as a Spaniard and succeeds in at least partially duping them by speaking Spanish. In *Epicoene*, Cutbeard and Otter pose as a Canon Lawyer and a Priest. Already notorious as "Latin-ers," the two put their linguistic tics to work in the personifying of professionals and of the Latin jargon of the Inns of Court and the Church:

> *Cutbeard*: Your question is, for how many causes a man may have *divortium legitimum*, a lawful divorce. . . . I answer then, the canon law affords divorce but in few cases, and the principal is in the common case, the adulterous case. But there are *duodecim impedimenta* . . . all which do not *dirimere contractum*, but *irritum reddere matrimonium,* as we say in the canon law.
>
> *Morose*: I understood you before; good sir, avoid your impertinency of translation.
>
> *Otter*: He cannot open this too much, sir, by your favour.
>
> (V.iii.70–84)

What is different in *Epicoene* is that Daw's and Cutbeard's linguistic disguise is more accurately a discursive disguise, their diction a mask of pretended literacy and thus of education, class, and authority in a London milieu in which Latin persisted alongside the vernacular amongst educated men. Surly's Spanish pose, while comical and undoubtedly fraught with implications concerning current relations between England and Spain, is the much more simple disguise of a recognizably foreign vernacular and never evokes the complex, English-Latin, literacy dynamic inherent in Cutbeard's mixing of vernacular speech, English canon law discourse, and law-Latin. The two pretenders' performance is not meant to be sophisticated or seamless, of course:

> *Otter:* That 'a boy or child under years is not fit for marriage because he cannot *reddere debitum.*' So your *omnipotentes*—
>
> *Truewit* [aside to Otter]: Your *impotentes*, you whoreson lobster.
>
> *Otter:* Your *impotentes*, I should say, are *minime apti ad contrahenda matrimonium.*
>
> *Truewit* [aside to Otter]: *Matrimonium?* We shall have most unmatrimonial Latin with you: *matrimonia*, and be hanged.
>
> (V.iii.184–191)

The effect is not one of showcasing language as deceit, but rather of emphasizing the fissures in language's potential as disguise in terms of levels of literacy. Cutbeard and Otter habitually pepper their colloquial speech with Latin adages, but their apparent facility fails them in this literate context, demanding fluency and comprehension, not parroting. Truewit's objections to their errors of prefix and declension make clear that their Latin literacy, and vividly not his, is scripted and incomplete.[30]

It is inaccurate to posit *Epicoene* as a truly realistic portrayal of London c. 1609, of course. There is a hermetic, jewel-box quality to its London houses and drawing rooms that certainly cannot be seen as accurate or attempting accuracy. But its interest, especially by comparison to *The Alchemist*, lies in parsing the city not as a predatory trap set by hack-alchemists, but as a close-set landscape of speakers. The city is its speakers and their language, a problematic idea when city, speakers' literacy, and language itself are in flux. Jonson offers no solution to this problem, and the women-speakers who are the focal point of the play's topoi of literacy/eloquence and fashion are not improved or changed at play's end. But the end of the play does perform some reframing. The revelation of Epicoene's true gender, and Dauphine's/Jonson's successful trick on everyone, including the play's audience, mean that language is fashion and fashion is language for everyone.

Chapter Three

Double-Talk and the Canting Cure: *The Roaring Girl's* Moll Cutpurse as the City

Thomas Middleton and Thomas Dekker's *The Roaring Girl* also confronts London via language and as language, but in a different manner and mood compared with Jonson's *Epicoene*.[1] Middleton and Dekker's play offers a compelling counterpoint to the latter's darker anxieties about language in society, but signals its deep engagement, nonetheless, with questions of the vernacular. The distinction is crucial to emphasize, for my argument in this chapter is not that *The Roaring Girl* provides a similar rehearsal of Jonson's concerns and commentary. *The Roaring Girl's* particular staging suggests the diversity, rather, of city comedy's generic project of interrogating the vernacular in society. Whereas *Epicoene* offers little resolution to the particular problems of the vernacular—and vernacular users—it raises, *The Roaring Girl* constructs a fantasy of legibility within the threateningly profuse city, rendering several otherwise ambiguous semiotics of the city knowable, if not ultimately containable.[2] Such a fantasy betrays anxieties about representation and coherence observed in *Epicoene* and in the contemporary climate more generally. *The Roaring Girl* works hard—with its realistic settings and portrait of an actual and notorious figure—to offer an alternative London, an ideal vision that reveals its points of stress.

Neither Middleton nor Dekker were self-consciously self-making, prose stylists like Jonson; Dekker's populist, often romantically nativist style in particular differs markedly from Jonson's sometimes painstaking classicism.[3] Neither cultivated alternative professional identities as sharply distinct from the playhouses as Jonson did. Much of Dekker's published prose work engages with London and particularly its underworld in a spirit of fascination and disclosure similar to *The Roaring Girl's*, without the skepticism and judgement characteristic of Jonson. And if some of Middleton's best known plays exhibit more of a Jonsonian edge, he was most famous in his own day as the frequent author of the annual civic pageantry surrounding the Lord

Mayor's installation, as well as other similarly festive, city events.[4] Absent the prescriptive contexts, such as *Discoveries* and *The English Grammar,* that frame Jonson's interrogations of language and society on the stage; and given alternative contexts like Middleton's "entertainments" and Dekker's sentimental pamphlets about city life and its underside; *The Roaring Girl* is perhaps less clearly querying language and the city. Such interrogation is as central to *The Roaring Girl*, however, as it is in Jonson. *The Roaring Girl* appears more optimistic in its posing of not just city-problems, but solutions, however insufficient. Its vivid staging of cant, in particular, calls attention to the workings of language in Act V of the play. Moreover, *The Roaring Girl's* fable-like quality (and this fable's insufficiency) clearly points to certain dramatic, discursive conventions and expectations, employing them and then enacting their instability. Middleton and Dekker's play offers a deceptively provocative staging of the city as a series of linguistic and discursive conflicts.

The Roaring Girl confronts urban instabilities by staging three 'languages'—the sartorial, the social (including the double-speak of innuendo and female outspoken-ness), and the vernacular-alternative 'dialect' of canting. All three center on Moll Cutpurse, the play's eponymous "roaring girl" and unlikely heroine; all three represent problems of representation, signification, or legibility. All three will be rendered benign or transparent through Moll. The play can only offer a temporary solution, however. In the end neither the play nor Moll can eliminate the anxious distances in languages, whether between language and truth, or between signifier and signified. This provocative 'failure' must complicate too easy an understanding of Middleton and Dekker's play as a more optimistic occasion of contemporary thought about the vernacular and its capabilities in early modern London. For all its sentimentalism and proffering of Moll as a romantic heroine who mends social ruptures, the play repeatedly stages its own failure to sustain such a fantastic solution to the complexities of urban life and its legion semiotic inconsistencies.

The Roaring Girl inserts Moll Cutpurse into a fairly conventional citizen-plot.[5] Young Sebastian Wengrave outwits his snobbish, greedy father, Sir Alexander Wengrave, who has threatened to disinherit Sebastian if he marries his true love, Mary Fitz-Allard, because of her meager dowry. Sebastian seeks to compel his father's acceptance by pretending affection for Moll, whose unseemly notoriety makes her far less desirable than Mary. The play's subplot involves an equally conventional Jacobean theme: the attempted seduction of middle-class wives by lazy, upper class "gallants." In both plots it is Moll, the roaring girl, whose combination of apparently instinctual moral uprightness and street smarts challenges the treachery of jealous fathers and lascivious gallants, alike. Middleton and Dekker's fictional portrayal of the real-life Moll, Mary Frith, is unconventional as a stereotypical transgressor who in fact upholds conservative social values as part of her cohering function in the play. This important difference is made clearer by comparison with the other contemporary dramatic rendering of Moll, in Nathan Field's *Amends for Ladies*.[6] Field's play presents Moll as a minor and one-dimensional character. She appears only once, as a messenger between a gallant and a citizen-wife. Her arrival with a letter for Mistress Seldom provides the occasion for a thoroughly conventional rehearsal of the fierce, contemporaneous debate over female propriety, dress, and decorum. The Mistress's "hic" and "haec," in the speech quoted below, specifically evoke the *Haec Vir/Hic Mulier* pamphlet war of the time, famous both for its misogyny and its defensive responses in women's behalf:[7]

> *Moll:* By your leave, Master Seldom, have you done the hangers I bespake for the knight?
> *Mis. Sel.:* Yes, marry have I, Mistress *hic* and *haec*, I'll fetch 'em to you . . .
> > Hence, lewd impudent!
> > I know not what to term thee, man or woman,
> > For, Nature, shaming to acknowledge thee
> > For either, hath produced thee to the world
> > Without a sex: some say thou art a woman,
> > Others a man: and many, thou art both
> > Woman and man, but I think rather neither,
> > Or man and horse, as the old centaurs were feigned.
> > > (Field, II.i.17–27)

Moll's reply is similarly conventional:

> Why, how now, Mistress What-lack-ye? Are you so fine, with a pox? I
> Have seen a woman look as modestly as you, and speak as sincerely, and
> follow the friars as zealously, and she has been as sound a jumbler as e'er
> paid for't: tis true, Mistress Fi'penny, I have sworn to leave this letter.
> (Field, II.i.29–45 passim)

This Moll is crude when provoked, defiant of Mistress Seldom's middle-class judgement of her, and no true ally of the citizenry. Field's brief insertion of Moll Cutpurse into *Amends for Ladies* is little more than an occasion to stage the simplest and most anxious points in the *Hic Mulier* debate. Moll's response to Seldom's vitriol reinforces the mistress's parroted stereotypes;

this Moll is every bit as transgressive as her critics, and critics of "mascu-line women" more generally, suggest. She skewers hypocrisy more than social codes, but her momentary appearance mainly unsettles others in the most stereotypical ways.

In *The Roaring Girl,* by contrast, Moll is the central character and pro-tagonist of the play, not a cipher or polemical occasion. She is the site of social anxieties but also of their resolution, at least temporarily. Moll's *sui generis* identity is crucial to the play, and her singularity accords with her function of representing and resolving a set of anxieties that are distinctly urban and semiotic in nature. One of the play's most provocative moves, in fact, is to stage Moll's marginality as at the center of the London society she moves through. Moll reconfigures the center, for a time, as the transgres-sions that would normally place her outside society instead place her at the heart of things as these same transgressions—cross-dressing and canting, for example—become benevolent aspects of her assistance to upstanding others. As the vivid embodiment of several aspects of semiotic uncertainty made legible, Moll becomes a kind of center, herself, a mode of cohering the city despite her marginal status both in the plot and in the reordering that occurs at play's end. Critical readings, most notably of the play's combination of sentimental and citizen-oriented New Comedy elements with the satiric edge of city comedy, have begun to pay attention to *The Roaring Girl's* staging of "cant," the notorious alternative language of the Elizabethan and Jacobean underworld.[8] Canting, however, is only one of the 'languages' of the city this play interrogates. Moll's transgressions signal the languages she, and through her the play, encompasses: 1) the sartorial, as Moll cross-dresses as a man or androgynously in modish combinations of men's and women's clothing; 2) the social, with Moll portrayed as an outspoken, 'public' woman; and 3) the dialect of cant, as Moll plays a spokesperson's role on behalf of underworld "canting" in Act V's extended exhibition. Moll thus embodies the inscrutable city. She is a kind of synecdochic London, and through her domestication and coherence, *The Roaring Girl* attempts to render the city, particularly its semiotic threats, comfortably knowable and unproblematic. Through Moll *The Roaring Girl* constructs a fantasy of coherence in early modern Lon-don that ultimately is a semiotic fantasy encompassing social languages like apparel and innuendo, and renegade 'dialects' like canting.

Beginning with Moll's infamous dress, and its provocations and impli-cations over the course of the play, my consideration in this chapter next will move to a focus on Act V, scene i, the canting scene. I conclude with some discussion of social language in the play, specifically such challenges to order as double-talk and Moll's proto-feminist speech in Act III. Each of these selected aspects represented a significant *topos* of the inscrutable and un-regimented city at the time, as discussed at length in chapter one; each is rendered benign, docile in its legibility by virtue of the play's portrayal of the transgressive Moll as a socially conservative upholder of middle-class values. Moll Cutpurse, the roaring girl, is a curious mix of social defiance and preservation. For Middleton and Dekker, she is a means of posing and resolving the problems of the city's chaotic challenge to semiotic order, if only temporarily. It is their genius to turn Moll, commonly understood to be part of the problem, into the discursive solution to the city.

"HEYDEY, BREECHES!": MOLL AND THE SARTORIAL

In Thomas Middleton's *Epistle*: "To the Play-Readers: Venery and Laughter," which prefaced the print edition of *The Roaring Girl*, the centrality of the sartorial in the play is made concrete: plays are fashionable apparel, playmaking the art of following changing fashions:

> The fashion of playmaking I can properly compare to nothing so naturally as the alteration in apparel: for in the time of the great-crop doublet, your huge bombasted plays, quilted with mighty words to lean purpose, was only then in fashion; and as the doublet fell, neater inventions began to set up. Now in the time of spruceness, our plays follow the niceness of our garments: single plots, quaint conceits, lecherous jests, dressed up in hanging sleeves.[9] (*Epistle* 1–9)

Middleton's conceit nimbly uses the language of apparel to characterize recent and current theatrical trends, in so doing pointing up the double-duty of this language, as well. It is also a pointed conceit in its connection of two common targets of social outrage and reform. Middleton's discursive connection of fashion and the theater makes explicit each one's individual and related significance as an unruly phenomenon and semiotic of Jacobean London. The *Epistle* continues in a conventionally self-deprecating tone, mildly extending the sartorial conceit with, "and for venery, you shall find enough for sixpence, but well couched an you mark it," with the word "couched" also containing two meanings at the time: 'hidden,' and 'embroidered with gold thread,' a playfulness that highlights play in language as well as the affinity of slipperiness between the sartorial and the theatrical.

The latter half of this opening letter to the reader becomes increasingly ambiguous in its references. Its description of "Venus . . . pass[ing] through the play in doublet and breeches" (*Epistle* 15–16) seems to indicate

Moll Cutpurse, though it also suggests a degree of venery in Moll that she herself repeatedly will defy. Additional slippage ensues as Middleton moves between Venus, Moll, and "this published comedy," the book: "The book I make no question but is fit for many of your companies, as well as the person itself, and may be allowed both gallery room at the playhouse and chamber room at your lodging" (18–21). His arrival at the pronouncement: "Worse things, I needs must confess, the world has taxed her for than has been written of her" (19–22) is thus quite enigmatical—the object of this censure would appear to be Moll, but could also be Venus or the published text itself. Most vivid are the ambiguity, the seemingly easy indistinction between play and person, and the magnified problem of slander. This play, according to Middleton, will aspire to treat notoriety with "a slackness of truth [rather] than fulness of slander" (ll. 29–30), foregrounding drama's work of disguise or transformation through language and, importantly, costume. In its opening *Epistle*, *The Roaring Girl* begins its exploration of clothing as an organizing—and disorganizing—system of the city by situating the sartorial's work alongside the equally dynamic theater.

The pre-eminence of apparel as a semiotics in early modern England is a crucial context for *The Roaring Girl's* comedic impact as well as its interrogation of the city's language. In work on the range of "silent languages" at play in Elizabethan England, historian Mary Hazard discusses this society's strident and repeated attempts to police sartorial display and delimit sumptuary imitation.[10] Such efforts, she concludes, "affirmed the silent potency of costume, a power so strong it defeated the word of law" (108), a suggestive phrasing that points up the complex instability at issue: when costume is as powerful as words, just how powerful are words? The explicit implications of this for the period have attracted attention beyond history or literature. From the field of law we have a recent, comprehensive history of sumptuary law, *Governance of the Consuming Passions: A History of Sumptuary Law*, whose title alone suggests the unruly subject of such legislation. Reviewer Peter Goodrich comments: "Legislation regulating dress and the other forms of 'presentation of the self' [p. 7] were crucial aspects of the formation of the social order and most specifically played a vital role in the identity . . . of "imagined communities" and moods of nation, class, and gender" (2).[11] Philip Stubbes' *Anatomie of Abuses* reflects contemporaneous interest in this 'consuming passion,' and Stephen Gosson's pious attacks on the theater for its semiotic corruption were also directed towards women's fashion, as we have seen. The *Anatomie's* obsessive condemnation of English fashions unequivocally reflects the potency and unruliness of the "ideal social language" (Martin 43) of clothing. Taking up Stubbes, among a range of sources, Karen Newman has notably addressed this 'problem' of fashion in early modern London, examining the preoccupation with English prodigality in dress among the period's poets, dramatists, and print-moralists. She locates a collective and sustained anxiety over apparel's ever-decreasing stability as a category of differentiation in the period, ultimately delineating clothing as a discrete semiotic system experiencing, and perceived as experiencing, instability in the period. Mary Beth Rose, similarly interested in the 'problem' of fashion as an unstable signifier, focuses specifically on *The Roaring Girl* and considers fashion in the gendered terms of Moll's androgyny. Rose reads the play alongside the *Hic Mulier* controversy, and highlights affinities between play and pamphlet-debate in order to further reveal "this phenomenon of fashion as the focus of considerable moral and social anxiety" (Rose 368) in this period, in London.[12]

It is this sartorial dimension of Moll that is central to her social definition and lack of definition in the play, and most challenging to those around her, by virtue of how uncertainly defined she is by an androgynous costume. Though notorious for dressing like a man, both popularly and in *The Roaring Girl*, the stage-Moll first appears, and first arouses male interest and female suspicion, in an outfit that blends traditionally male and female garments to distinctive effect. The stage direction for her first entrance in II, i stipulates, "Enter Moll in a frieze jerkin and a black safeguard." This discordant combination, a kind of sartorial gibberish, determines all around it. Indeed, the unvarying manner by which Moll's entrances are accompanied by stage directions regarding her costume makes clear the importance as well as the consistent impact of her dress-configurations. Mary Beth Rose's observation, that "society's effort to assess the identity of this female figure in male attire becomes the central dramatic and symbolic issue of the play"(367), incompletely emphasizes the extent to which Moll's attire is the preoccupation of the play-*text* as well as of her fellow characters. Moll's creators take pains to emphasize that she is *sui generis*, but cannot obscure her larger significance: in Moll's gender-blending dress Middleton and Dekker inscribe the broader anxieties, concerning fashion and sartorial legibility, of a Jacobean London society where sumptuary laws were expired or unenforceable, and where a proto-capitalist merchant-trade was bringing in more luxury goods and styles every day. In her cross-dressing, Moll dramatically embodies one kind of semiotic rupture in a society whose traditional systems of social coherence anxiously were in flux.

Moll's costume and its changes throughout the action of *The Roaring Girl* are vivid—a scene's dialogue need not call attention to her apparel for it to feature as a parallel language to any spoken exchanges. There are also several instances when her clothing, especially her androgynous clothing, is explicitly treated: scenes that feature Moll's own apparel choices and, especially, others' responses to her choices. I read some of these moments, below, to reveal dress as a titillating, unstable language, and a system connected strongly to identity. As the figure at the center of the play's insistent look at representation and coherence, Moll is constantly part of a process, first, of staging the problems of sartorial ambiguity, but then of removing or solving some of that threatening inscrutability by virtue of her frank and unambiguous bearing.

The extraordinary power of costume is evident in I, ii, when the comments of Sir Alexander Wengrave imply its ability to effect not just outward, but physiological metamorphosis. He describes Moll as, "a creature nature hath brought forth/ To mock the sex of woman. It is a thing/ One knows not how to name . . . / . . . 'Tis woman more than man,/ Man more than woman, and—which to none can hap—/ The sun gives her two shadows to one shape;" (I.ii.127–132). In Sir Alexander's description, Moll is monstrous because her clothing signals a biological ambiguity; her sartorial disorder automatically signals a more serious, and permanent, error. Sir Alexander's discomfort stems from a challenge that is linguistic and even ontological: "It is a thing one knows not how to name" (I.ii.129). Moll challenges the seemingly stable words "man" and "woman," as well as the concepts and social structure their apparent stability reifies. The sartorial link to such instability is made clear in III, iii, in a striking articulation of clothing as a semiotics of gender significance. Speaking to Sir Alexander, the henchman Trapdoor offers details of Moll and her supposed relations with Sebastian Wengrave:"Her black safeguard is turned into a deep slop, the holes of her upper body to button-holes, her waistcoat to a doublet, her placket to the ancient seat of a codpiece; and you shall take 'em both with standing collars" (III.iii.25–29). Trapdoor figures Moll's apparent gender shifting using the language of the sartorial as fashion and biology become the same thing. "Codpiece" and "placket" stand in for "man" and "woman," a substitution suggesting both the instability of gender through such ephemeral fashion terms, and the instability of lexical denotation, itself, because of its metonymic tendencies.[13]

In addition to the slippage enacted via sartorial details in this speech, Trapdoor concludes with a detail that encompasses both Moll and Sebastian, the prodigal: "you shall take 'em both with standing collars." How does this fit with the preceding focus on Moll's sartorial-biological metamorphosis? According to New Mermaids editor Paul Mulholland, the standing collar was a high straight collar then in vogue. More important than this literal definition, however, is the collar's associations with upstart, "new-fangled" styles from France—nearly synonymous with effeminacy at the time—and with women's appetite for aping upstart fashions, including men's fashions.[14] The description infers a problematic sexual indeterminacy in both Moll and Sebastian, the effeminate male often provoking an equal level of anxious venom, popularly, as the cross-dressed female. Sebastian's linkage with the un-categorical Moll threatens to render him similarly aberrant.

The threat of women's sartorial androgyny thus lodged centrally in the gender and class ambiguity it created and marked. Related to this was the additional threat, and thrill, of sexual perversity and, especially, availability that this styling seemed to signal to others, particularly men. Noting the Elizabethan William Harrison's diatribes in *The Description of England,* and his railing against improperly (i.e. masculinely) dressed women, Jean Howard highlights his description of the latter as "trulls." "The word 'trull' is important," she comments, "The OED defines 'trull' as 'a low prostitute . . . a drab.' Harrison's diction links the mannish woman with prostitution."[15] We see this discursive dynamic clearly in II, ii, when Sir Alexander is a hidden witness to a series of bawdy exchanges between Moll and a Tailor. The scene is interesting on several levels. There is Sir Alexander's reprisal of the collapsing of sartorial and biological upon learning that Moll is being measured for new breeches: "Heydey, breeches! What, will he marry a monster with two trinkets?"(II.ii.76–77). There is also the Tailor's insistent innuendo, which depends on the titillating fact of Moll's female biology but apparently male appetites:

> *Tailor:* . . . you say you'll have the great Dutch slop, Mistress Mary.
>
> *Moll:* Why sir, I say so still.
>
> *Tailor:* Your breeches then will take up a yard more.
>
> *Moll:* Well, pray look it be put in then.
>
> *Tailor:* It shall stand round and full, I warrant you. (II.ii.81–86)

The juxtaposition of the Tailor's easy and bawdy banter about breeches with his use of "Mistress" when addressing Moll plays up her gender-troubling habits and of course uses this fitting of clothing as an occasion to highlight unruliness, both sartorial and potentially sexual. In Sir Alexander's final words in this short vignette, fashion converges with gender-distinction, sexual propriety, and nationality: "Here's good gear towards! I have brought up my son to marry a Dutch slop and a French doublet" (II.ii.91–3). Moll's 'unnatural' sartorial choices not only imply sexual perversity, but apparently exclude her even from Englishness. The otherness of her dress announces her as sexualized, and the same otherness easily collapses into foreign-ness, a threatening but also thrilling combination.[16] Also important here is the personification of the "Dutch slop" and "French doublet," with the striking implication that clothing itself holds a kind of subjectivity or agency. Moll is reduced to what she wears, in both cases creating a kind of fetish of precisely what is being condemned.

Moll holds her own in this scene, but her lines, considered separately from the Tailor's rejoinders, are interestingly neutral. While each of her lines could be played to heighten innuendo, in and of themselves they are quite innocent or straightforward. Concerning the breeches, above, Moll requests, "Pray, make 'em easy enough" (II.ii.87), a remark that sparks a leering, bawdy reply from the Tailor: "So, I have gone as far as I can go." Moll simply replies, "Why then, farewell" (94–95). Her most provocative act in this scene is not her words, but her desire for male breeches. Her supposed promiscuity, assumed by both Sir Alexander and the Tailor, derives from her fashion, almost in despite of her words. Moll's language features a different kind of double-talk than the Tailor's, and adds a new dimension to the innuendo that is a marked characteristic of much of the play's dialogue. Moll is often as bawdy in her speech as others are in the play, but she indignantly protests the matter of sartorial double-talk wherein others read her clothing as projecting an illicit meaning besides its mere incongruity. Turning the tables on the lecherous gallant Laxton at their 'appointment' in Act III, scene i, Moll berates him for the sexual capitulation they both know he was expecting from her. In denying him, she angrily asks, "What durst move you, sir/ To think me whorish?" (III.i.88–89)—a rhetorical question neither answers, but which points to assumptions based on her provocative dress and deportment. Moll's protests against such prurient 'double-talk,' and her insistent sporting of partially or entirely male clothing by taste and not as disguise, offer a more legible version of the stereotypically transgressive, androgynous woman. Moll's outrage at sexual license, especially presumptions about her own, is a key recuperation of the unregulated and therefore threatening woman she appears to be. Moll's sexual integrity re-frames her unruliness, including her androgyny. Her sartorial choices become the opposite of inscrutable; the lewd, androgynous woman (of *Hic Mulier*, for example, or of Field's play) is rendered legible and benign through Moll's representation of a cross-dressed woman whose clothing-choices are in fact part of her sexual integrity and upright subjectivity.

The importance and simultaneous instability of sartorial appearance are highlighted throughout the play, whenever Moll is onstage. In Act IV, scene I, for example, Moll and Sebastian Wengrave have plotted a secret rendezvous between him and Mary FitzAllard within his father's house, prompting the appearance of both Moll and Mary in male attire. Significantly, only one of them is in disguise. Moll has had her tailor outfit Mary in a page-boy's uniform, thus Mary poses in livery, while Moll herself, dressed as a man, is posing as no one but herself. The two women's appearance together in these clothes creates a striking visual exposition of female cross-dressing that underscores Moll's difference. Mary FitzAllard's androgynous attire provides safe cover for her visit to her male beloved. Mary, a nearly silent and conventionally demure female figure in the play, is suddenly eroticized by her costume. "Me thinks a woman's lip tastes well in a doublet," comments Sebastian upon kissing her as a page, "Every kiss she gives me now in this strange form is worth a pair of two," (IV.i.55–56). Mary's newly ambiguous gender proves irresistible to Sebastian. Her kisses are more potent the less familiar, or the less female, they are, a claim of significant irony given the fact of her disguise and its confirmation of her otherwise limited agency.[17] The potency of her appearance does not lend her any other presence, however; Mary speaks less than twenty words in the whole scene. Her silence and objectification by Sebastian make it clear that she is hiding as a male, not appropriating the subjectivity of a male.

Moll, by contrast, appears as herself, her distinct but normal attire ironically made more transparent and even less problematic by Mary's presence and appearance. Moll's speech in Act IV, scene I, is rife with bawdy innuendo, but such double-talk—with which she and Sebastian banter as equals—emphasizes not her own attire or sexuality, but Mary's as the silent, and seemingly only, woman. That Moll does not consider her own clothing as cross-dressing or as disguise is clear in her response to Sebastian, early in the scene. In response to his remark that Mary's lip "tastes well in a doublet," Moll responds, "Many an old madam has the better fortune then,/ Whose breaths grew stale before the fashion came:/ If that will help 'em, as you think 'twill do,/ They'll learn in time to pluck on the hose too!" (IV. i.47–51). Such a remark signals Moll's exclusion of herself from these others who 'pluck on the hose.' She additionally distances herself by her use of the term "old madams" who will put on this new fashion, in so doing rehearsing the tacit association between whores or sexual license and cross-dressing that she elsewhere vehemently denies and defies concerning herself, as we have seen.

Moll at first embodies the inscrutability of androgyny, but she finally renders such androgyny legible and thereby unthreatening. As we have seen above, set next to another woman's less familiar appearance in male clothing, Moll's sartorial effect is oddly familiar and benign. If her status as a conventional woman remains uncertain and un-codified by the end of the play, she has nevertheless made her own androgyny harmless. The end of the play, and Moll's place within it, are distinctly marked, sartorially. Though her androgyny is now coherent, and indeed a cohering instrument in the play thus far, Moll appears in the final scene in women's garb for the first time. The semiotic complexity of this moment bears some unpacking. First, Moll is not only in women's clothing for the first time in the play, she is also in disguise for the first time. On one level, this 'disguise' very visibly appears to 'solve' Moll for us—she is now completely legible as the woman she is. But disguise typically functions to create misrepresentation, a break or gap between signifier and signified. So Moll, in disguise as a woman, queries the very legibility such a disguise had seemed to lend her. It certainly complicates all clothing as an unstable signifier, since Moll simultaneously is now most clearly female and least clearly 'herself.'

Yet, and this is a third aspect of this resonant moment, her women's garb makes her conventionally acceptable for the first time, despite the fact that this appearance both is and is not truthful. Sir Alexander Wengrave, the play's figure of narrow-minded propriety, confirms this fact with his affable response to the sight of Moll, masked, and in female dress: "Now has he [Sebastian] pleased me right. I always counselled him/ To choose a goodly personable creature:/ Just of her pitch was my first wife, his mother" (V.ii.129–132). Sir Alexander's favorable response is based on this representation of a conventional (and identity-less) woman.

This layered problematizing of the sartorial so near the play's conclusion constitutes a provocative fissure in the play's fable of coherence. This is a faltering that recalls Mary Beth Rose's notion that Middleton and Dekker's unwieldy heroine ultimately supplies or evokes more content than her creators' form can contain (Rose 390), a nod to Moll's complex work in this otherwise fairly standard citizen-plot. But such an argument suggests a lack of control on the playwrights' part over their heroine and their play. Rose is correct that content overmatches form, but I would suggest that this is intentional: the play's fable of coherence ultimately is impossible to sustain. It is clear by the end of this final scene that Moll will not stay in women's dress from now on. The changes she has wrought in others and in the society of the play may be effectual, but she herself is not changed, and her disguise is precisely that. She is not assimilated at play's end, in part because she explicitly chooses not to be. Moll's dramatic change in dress for *The Roaring Girl's* conclusion exposes the stubborn instability of the sartorial, despite much of the play's fable-esque work to render this less problematic. The insufficiency of its fantasy of semiotic coherence—in this case in terms of the sartorial—is staged clearly by the play's conclusion.

It is notable that Moll's cross-dressing, in its style and intentions, is distinct from the more well known cross-dressing of many of Shakespeare's heroines. To put it succinctly, in Shakespeare the cross-dressing of a Rosalind is socially acceptable because it is understood that she will *not* stay that way for long; in *The Roaring Girl*, Moll's cross-dressing is acceptable precisely because she *will* stay that way. *Twelfth Night's* Viola cross-dresses as Rosalind had, her male dress as Cesario a disguise that provides a practical means of survival in a foreign environment. In work that contrasts the cross-dressing in Shakespeare versus plays like *The Roaring Girl* and Heywood's *The Fair Maid of the West*, Jean Howard writes of Viola:

> The audience always knows that underneath the page's clothes is a "real" woman . . . who freely admits that she has neither the desire nor the aptitude to play the man's part in phallic swordplay. The whole thrust of the dramatic narrative is to release this woman from the prison of her masculine attire and return her to her proper and natural position as a wife. (Howard, "Crossdressing" 431)

Howard regards the cross-dressed Viola as a lesser threat than Olivia's lack of a properly disciplined feminine subjectivity. Discussing Rosalind, Howard makes a comment that applies equally well to Viola, observing that "[Rosalind] could be a threatening figure if she did not constantly, contrapuntally, reveal herself to the audience as the not-man, as in actuality a lovesick maid" (434). Despite appearances, cross-dressing heroines in Shakespeare are not necessarily disrupters of social norms and mores. Even Portia, a much more able and willing player of the 'man's part' in *The Merchant of Venice*, is not interested in dismantling the sex-gender system of her society: "Portia's actions [including her cross-dressing] are not aimed at letting her occupy a man's place indefinitely . . . but at making her own place in a patriarchy more bearable" (433). The phenomenon of their cross-dressing, and its distinct difference from Moll's, is neatly summed up by Rosalind herself: " . . . dost thou think, though I am caparison'd like a man, I have a doublet and hose in my disposition?" (III.ii.191–193). Moll, of course, does have a doublet and hose in her disposition; unlike her apparent Shakespearean counterparts, male dress is not her *disguise*, but her preference.

Moll's purpose is precisely *not* to be absorbed in the comic plot; she is crucial, but crucially marginal, in the end, to the society with which she interacts. Howard puzzles over Moll's status and function in the play, accurately observing that "Middleton and Dekker have attempted to decriminalize Moll, to present her as neither thief nor whore, to make her an exception to society's rules concerning women's behaviour but not a fundamental threat to the sex-gender system" (*Crossdressing* 438). While Howard focuses upon the ways that Moll's domestication is not so seamless, it seems to me that the more pertinent issue is *why* domesticate Moll as Middleton and Dekker have done? One answer, I propose, is that Moll functions as a fantasy of coherence, if an imperfectly complete one. Middleton and Dekker intend to make her a cross-dresser with a difference; unlike Shakespeare's cross-dressing women, Moll resists patriarchal structures like marriage permanently. But she is a different kind of project, her function not a standard character's. Moll literally embodies the problems the play poses, including different urban freedoms, and she embodies their solutions by becoming legible in an emblematic way. She becomes a placeholder for (and a solution to) different problems of incoherence, like apparel, though imperfectly.

"ZOUNDS . . . TEACH ME THIS PEDLAR'S FRENCH": MOLL DECODES THE CITY

Act V, scene I of *The Roaring Girl* calls explicit attention to the workings of language well before the famous canting lesson which will be the primary focus of this section. The scene begins with Moll (dressed as a man) and the rake Jack Dapper discussing his recent escape from an overly severe magistrate with her assistance. Moll and Jack are accompanied by two gentlemen, Sir Beauteous Ganymede and Sir Thomas Long, and the action of the scene concerns a progress through London at Sir Ganymede's entreaty to "Come, come, walk and talk, walk and talk" (V.i.32). The arrival of an additional gentleman, Lord Noland, prompts an attempt at polite conversation:

> *Dapper*: Here's most amorous weather, my lord.
>
> *All*: Amorous weather?
>
> *Dapper*: Is not amorous a good word? (62–64)

Finding the right word challenges Dapper, whose curious use of "amorous" could signal a malapropism (certainly a convention of stage-humour at this time) or an "inkhorn" term. This latter would make Dapper more pedantic than feckless, as "inkhornisms," or neologism introduced from languages like French and Latin, were widely condemned as unnecessary and pretentious.[18] In either case, this slight exchange sets the stage for a scene which will problematize and attempt to resolve the signifying stability and potential of words, most vividly by its introduction of cant and its insistence on cant's transparency and accessibility. In a series of exchanges within this lengthy scene, language is foregrounded again and again, culminating in the canting exposition.

Following Dapper's gaffe and its highlighting of the uneasily contextual nature of appropriate discourse, the small company encounters Trapdoor and his vagabond sidekick, Tearcat, who go to elaborate rhetorical lengths to pass themselves off as returned soldiers in need of alms. Questioned as to the nature of their military service, Trapdoor unconvincingly describes service in Hungary and several subsequent misfortunes that he notably supports via two eclectic lists:

> *Lord Noland*: Who served there with you, sirrah?
>
> *Trapdoor*: Many Hungarians, Moldavians, Valachians, and
>   Transylvanians, with some Sclavonians; and retiring home,
>   sir, the Venetian galleys took us prisoners, yet freed us, and suf-
>   fered us to beg up and down the country.
>
> *Dapper*: You have ambled all over Italy, then?
>
> *Trapdoor*: O sir, from Venice to Roma, Vecchio, Bononia,
> Romania, Bolonia, Modena, Piacenza, and Tuscana . . . as
> Pistoia, Valteria, Mountepulchena, Arrezzo, with the Siennois and
> diverse others. (V.i.87–96)

Trapdoor employs these lists of foreign names as both verification and incantatory smokescreen. His lists are not even credibly accurate—he is trying to evoke something he knows little about. He clearly intends his words to perform and persuade merely in their quantity, as commodities of sound. They are offered meaningfully as groups of similar words, but ultimately are invalidated by this same accumulation. Linking "Roma" and "Pontevecchio," "Bononia" and "Bolonia," Trapdoor parrots words without any notion or interest in what they signify. It is this last performance, significantly, that reveals Trapdoor and Tearcat as vagabonds, not soldiers, to Moll, who determines them "mere rogues, put spurs to 'em once more" (V.i.97). The inaccuracy of their lists might well be the tip-off, but an additional clue, I would suggest, is Trapdoor's use of his list as a potent but not signifying noise. One of the more provocative aspects of cant was its abject quality, according to William West: "The work of cant on the Jacobean stage . . . is to produce affect free from any discernible content—to reveal the work that words do, purified of reference to things . . . Cant shows only the perlocutionary force of its words, apart from any descriptive meaning."[19]

Such a 'perlocutionary force' is precisely what Trapdoor's list, above, ineffectually attempts to harness. Moll's recognition of the two 'soldiers' as underworld denizens derives at least in part, I would argue, from such a distinct treatment of language. And when Moll subsequently challenges Trapdoor, saying "I hope then you can cant, for by your cudgels, you, sirrah, are an upright man" (ll.150–151), she is mainly acknowledging what he has already implied by his canting-esque use of English. The scene's segue into a full-fledged canting lesson shortly thereafter is thus prepared for in this instance; the canting exposition continues with an ever more vivid debate over the properties of language.

Cant was an index to all language's potential strangeness and unruliness at a time when English could still be described as "the still-developing standard vernacular that the Tudor dynasty from Henry VIII onwards had consciously labored to produce."[20] Unlike Latin and, very recently, English, with their written grammars, "cant was something changeable, hybrid, and confusing: an unproductive and inexpressive 'gibberish'" (West 230). Such linguistic changeability and hybridity was, of course, one of the fears about the English vernacular itself harboured by those intent on asserting and assessing its authority. The creation of an English grammar (a project undertaken independently by many 16th and 17th century scholars) was but one of the anxious labours of the period devoted to the vernacular, as we have seen. Cant's lack of order was perceived as a persistent threat to this recent stability, and as a persistent reminder of the vernacular's much less authoritative linguistic past (and, arguably, everlingering present). Such a self-conscious project as the creation of an English grammar, its very laboriousness implying not simply patriotic enthusiasm but also anxiety regarding the status of English, meant that cant indeed represented as much a linguistic as a social threat.[21] This "peddler's French" signalled the potential of still greater linguistic instability, as well, in its status as a language consciously intended to conceal rather than express meaning. To return to William West's sense of cant as an abject language, a language of pure affect is a kind of "mirror reflection that reveals [all] language as something strange and alien" (231). Cant had a contentious and threateningly crucial relationship to the vernacular in what it revealed about the latter by its parallel existence.

Cant is thus a potent vehicle of linguistic commentary or critique in *The Roaring Girl* that relates to the play's work with the sartorial. In Act V, scene I, the canting lesson's initial rendering of cant as transparent, unproblematic, and readily translated, asserts an unlikely linguistic coherence in a play full of semiotic ambiguity and vernacular double-talk. While on one level it seems intentionally both parodic and ironic that cant, the transgressive "gibberish" of outlaws, should represent this legibility and containment, on another this circumstance implicitly critiques the standard English that is cant's counterpart, implicating its slippages by the apparent laying wide of cant's "secret" signification. Cant in *The Roaring Girl* is far from the service of misprision; the ultimate double-talk, canting instead becomes an antidote to the layers of innuendo and plays-of-reference in the standard vernacular speech of others in the play. In this reading, cant's subversiveness is re-framed to create a language-fantasy whereby its meaning and significance are vividly knowable, and the complex urban world it evokes—even its most threatening elements—vividly legible.

The "discovery" of cant to a more upstanding and thus un-versed audience is a vivid feature of Act V, scene i's exposition; such cant-lessons were a popular prose genre of the time, with dozens of 'guides' appearing between the mid 1500's and the first decades of the 1600's.[22] Early on in *The Roaring Girl's* canting scene, however, yet another type of discovery is connected to canting's milieu that emphasizes its signifying potential, especially as a rival of English. Moll describes Tearcat as a "whipjack," a canting term, who can "discover more countries to you than either the Dutch, Spanish, French, or English ever found out; yet indeed all his service is by land, and that is to rob a fair or some such venturous exploit" (V.i.131–136). Moll's sarcasm is clear, but the association made between Tearcat's roguery and the period's exploration via the word "discover" adds a dimension to cant. To "discover," in such a context, meant to both find a new land and implied the telling or reporting about such a place to others. It collapses actual with rhetorical or linguistic conquest, and Moll's use of it implies a kind of imperial power in roguery and its canting language. Tearcat's response to Moll furthers this notion as he describes his tutelage of Trapdoor in terms of mapping, sailing, and naming:

> No indeed, Captain Moll . . . I am no such nipping Christian, but a maunderer upon the pad I confess; and meeting with honest Trapdoor here, whom you had cashiered from bearing arms, out at elbows under your colours, I instructed him in the rudiments of roguery, and by my map made him sail over any country you can name, so that now he can maunder better than myself. (V.i.139–146)

Given Moll's evocation of voyaging, Tearcat's description of his "map" and Trapdoor's sailing in this figuration of a rogue's education links such tuition to early modern exploration.[23] Both render a world that is perhaps wider but also straightforwardly knowable, and such worldly canting knowledge is readily accessible: Trapdoor now "can maunder better than myself."

Tearcat's speech is a combination of English and cant, with cant descriptions and phrases like "nipping Christian" and "maunderer upon the pad" colorfully gilding his disclaimers. The irony of cant's illumination of his English speech, as well as of Trapdoor's apparently shining success at mastering the language and practices of the master-less—of 'discovering' using a language of 'covering,' of rogue imperialism within local bounds—all point to anxieties about cant as criminal and inscrutable that the play works to render comical, benign, and knowable.

The most important factor in *The Roaring Girl's* benign presentation of cant and its rendering of it as a language-solution is Moll herself. She is the decoder of these two rogues' underworld allegiances, initially, summoning their cant-identities herself. With this she also becomes a translator of cant, both their usage and her own, for her gentle-bred companions:

> *Moll*: And Tearcat, what are you? A wild rogue, an angler, or ruffler?
>
> *Tearcat:* Brother to this upright man, flesh and blood: ruffling Tearcat is my name, and a ruffler is my style, my title, my profession.
>
> *Moll*: Sirrah, where's your doxy? . . .
>
> *All:* Doxy, Moll? What's that?
>
> *Moll:* His wench.
>
> *Trapdoor*: My doxy stays for me in a boozing ken, brave captain.
>
> *Moll*: He says his wench stays for him in an ale-house . . .
> (V.i.153–160) (168–170)

On a literal level, Moll's translations clarify the meaning of terms like "doxy"; more thematically, Moll's facility and translation of this underworld code render it unthreatening by virtue of its connection with her benevolence. Her companions, all mystified and no doubt initially threatened by these rogues' slipperiness and speech, are reassured by Moll's explication; cant then becomes exhilarating and desirable. Jack Dapper is the most ardent in his response, enthusiastically crowing "Here's old cheating!" (167), and "Zounds, I'll give a schoolmaster half a crown a week and teach me this pedlar's French" (178–179). Sir Thomas Long also reflects this excitement in his treatment of canting as a commodity and performance for his upper-class pleasure, saying "Well said, Moll—[to Trapdoor] Cant with her, sirrah, and you shall have money—else not a penny" (183–185).[24]

Cant is more than this benign amusement, however, and this also is signalled by Moll's interaction with canting in Act V. As an alternative language, cant is a threat to the vernacular's authority in its parallel existence, and in the slippery properties of language it lays bare. If *The Roaring Girl's* and Moll's work initially offer the possibility of cant as easily legible to any as well as mainly benign in its intentions, this geniality is momentarily complicated in a way that pinpoints cant's potential threat to the vernacular. The canting scene will conclude in its more genial temper, but this moment of semiotic confusion interjects a provocative tension into its exposition. At Sir Thomas's invitation, quoted above, Trapdoor launches into the scene's lengthiest canting sequence, yet:

> *Moll*: Come on, sirrah.
>
> *Trapdoor*: Ben mort, shall you and I heave a booth, mill a ken, or nip a
> Bung? And then we'll couch a hogshead under the ruffmans, and
> there you shall wap with me, and I'll niggle with you.
>
> *Moll*: Out, you damned impudent rascal! (V.i.191–196)

To the others, Trapdoor's words provide yet further amusement and interest as this mysterious canting language. Moll, the translator, is greatly offended, however, responding in English to Trapdoor's cant-impudence. Entreated by Lord Noland to explain her anger at Trapdoor's innocuous-seeming gibberish, Moll proceeds with a translation that stops short of conveying the meaning of the canting terms "wap" and "niggle":

> *Moll*: Marry, this, my lord, says he: 'Ben mort'—good wench—'shall
> you and I heave a booth, mill a ken or nip a bung?'—shall you
> and I rob a house, or cut a purse? (V.i.196–198)
> 'And there you shall wap with me, and I'll niggle with you,
> —and that's all.
>
> *Sir Beauteous*: Nay, nay, Moll, what's that wap?
>
> *Jack Dapper*: Nay, teach me what niggling is; I'd fain be niggling.
> (V.i.204–208)

This is not gibberish; like all cant, "wap" and "niggle" have English correspondents that Moll resists decoding, seemingly out of modesty. Moreover, it is clear from her companions' responses that these words possess a provocative and suggestive power as sounds without any English translation. "Niggling," in particular, possesses a titillating 'perlocutionary force,' to use this

term again, whereby it seems to require no definition. Yet leaving it unde-
coded opens the possibility for the space between signifier and signified to
expand indefinitely, as signalled by Trapdoor's ultimate response to the question of what "wapping" and "niggling" mean: "'Tis fadoodling, if it please
you," (211); the words are parallel sexual terms, this seems to clarify. But
"fadoodling," according to editor Paul Mulholland, is a "nonce" or nonsense
word (221, note 211). William West adds, "So obvious seems the sexual
meaning of the terms "wapping," "niggling," and "fadoodling" that it is startling to learn that it is illusory" (245). Wapping is not in fact fadoodling,
since fadoodling means "nothing," and in fact is not even cant.

This is a striking moment in which concepts of words, their meanings, and their participation in systems of words and meaning are implicitly
queried.[25] Sir Beauteous responds to all this with ebullience, saying "This is
excellent; one fit more, good Moll" (V.i.212). Moll complies, and the scene's
more genial treatment of cant resumes, presumably reinforcing the benevolence implicit in the gentleman's request—that canting is fundamentally a
performance, a pleasant song to be reprised. And yet questions of cant's relationship to English have been raised; questions of, 'What counts as a coherent word?' 'As coherent cant?' 'As nonsense?' Moll's ability to domesticate
cant is not complete, and words like "fadoodling" reveal the instability not
just of the vernacular, but of cant, too. And cant as simply song or entertainment has its own implications, pointing as it does to language as sound, not
sense.

Act V, scene i concludes with one more evocation of a gap between
signifiers and signifieds worth reading. The gentlemen inquire about Moll's
considerable knowledge of the underworld and its canting language. The
ensuing discussion focuses less on Moll's potentially troubling expertise than
on her name and the whole issue of names and their inaccurate reflection of
those that bear them.[26] Moll comments on this matter:

> Must you have
> A black ill name because ill things you know?
> Good troth, my lord, I am made Moll Cutpurse so.
> How many are whores in small ruffs and still looks?
> How many chaste whose names fill slander's books?
> Were all men cuckolds, whom gallants in their scorns
> Call so, we should not walk for goring horns. (V.i.341–347)

She continues a few lines later, notably in prose this time, and not verse,
as above, "Good my lord, let not my name condemn me to you or to the

world . . . If all that have ill names in London were to be whipped and to pay but twelvepence apiece to the beadle, I would rather have his office than a constable's" (ll. 353–357). Explicitly evoking the crowded and diverse London world, Moll calls out for recognition of the potential inconsistency between words, specifically names, and the truth. Such a statement encompasses cant's possibilities as a code demanding exact correspondence between words and meaning, as well as the vulnerability enacted with true rogue words like "fadoodling"; it also calls attention to the innuendo or double-talk that is notably absent from the canting-speech, but is otherwise a feature of most other speech in the play.

"SPOKE LIKE A NOBLE GIRL, I'FAITH": MOLL AND SOCIAL LANGUAGE

In the canting scene, Moll decodes cant for her gentleman friends, rendering it docile and sporting, as we have seen. Moll's consternation is considerable, however, over Trapdoor's use of "wapping" and "niggling," and the final definition, "fadoodling," which is neither English nor cant, and signifies nothing but implies prurience. This last phenomenon signals an aspect of language that West observes: "The operative principle is that when you can not understand what people are saying, it must be because they're saying something dirty" (246). Languages like cant possess a particular erotic power based on their claiming a hidden meaning, argues West, but this dynamic is not limited only to 'secret' words or systems. Cant on stage, and its charge, reveals a "discourse in which language itself is recognized as an object of desire" (248). West wants to distance this desire in language from gender, which he sees as an historical/social construct, and despite the fact that language is typically eroticized in explicitly gendered terms. His illumination of the circulation of desire in language is invaluable for reading *The Roaring Girl's* other vivid discursive and linguistic feature, its double-talk. Such a social language, however, makes gender a central consideration, not incidental.

The most vivid characteristic of language in *The Roaring Girl*, by far, is its capacity for innuendo; subtle or not so subtle implication or bawdy double-talk dominates the speech of nearly every character, including Moll herself. So constant is it within the play's vivid evocation of the city and its suggestion of Moll as its emblem, that innuendo becomes a standard mode of 'city talk.' In a play not otherwise preoccupied with aspects of language or the semiotic city, this still would be notable; as it is, this feature of *The Roaring Girl's* dialogue must be read as a significant part of the play's distinctive project. Double-talk—language that is deceptive or contains a secondary, usually bawdy, significance—is posed as the typical mode of communication between men and women, and is a distinct 'social language.' Also part of what I will consider as the social language of this play are instances of speech by Moll that overtly signal their social implications; I will look at two speeches and their curious combination of social transgression and preservation. In the first, in Act III, scene i, Moll outspokenly defends her honor and defies male slander; in the second, which comes at the end of the play in Act V, scene ii, she responds to questions about marriage plans with cryptic, quasi-utopian words. Each of these examples gestures distinctly to the problematic space between words or representation and truth. The extra-marital intrigues of the sub-plot rely upon the potential of this space for deception and connotation; Moll's transgressive commentaries more implicitly tease us with it. It would be inaccurate to describe these two elements of 'social language' in *The Roaring Girl* as a defined semiotic in the manner of apparel and the 'dialect' of cant. Such social language nevertheless functions in the play as a third component of figuring the city in discursive terms that both structure and fragment it.

The play's double-talk is most vivid in the citizen-plot that makes up its sub-plot. Moll plays a minimal role in this plot, but its resolution near the play's overall conclusion must nonetheless be seen as part of the larger comedic harmony she orchestrates. The conservative, middle-class values of marriage and familial reconciliation that Moll upholds in the main plot are also vivid in the citizen-plot's final reunions, all of the latter's potentially destructive and darker plotting ultimately revised as salutary exercisings of sturdy marital bonds. As we will see, in the final scene, suspicions of dishonesty or infidelity are admitted and dismissed; the bawdy innuendo and deception that have been pervasive all but cease and the dialogue shifts from being primarily between men and women to being between men. The implications are that double-talk is the language of desire and that domestic and linguistic unruliness are interconnected and inevitable. By this, double-talk is linked to women and their speech, both in the citizen-wives who are as bawdy as their roving suitors, as well as more generally in this linkage of language with unruly desire.[27] In the lengthy resolution-scene in Act IV, desire is re-framed in terms of homo-social bonds that pointedly exclude women almost altogether, and social language concomitantly is re-constituted without women as genuine participants. Such a 'solution' to the innuendo produced and provoked by women is compelling, in part for its by now familiar incomplete and temporary nature.

The citizen-plot resolution in Act IV, scene ii reaffirms citizen to citizen (and citizen to citizen-wife) allegiance and nullifies the lascivious influence of young, aimless gallants like Laxton and Goshawk. However, while the main work of the scene is the reunion of Master Gallipot with his wife and the accompanying implication of restored social and marital coherence, the treatment of the gallants signals a very different project than such a straightforward emphasis of class boundaries and domestic loyalties. Both Goshawk and Laxton, clearly up to no good for much of the play in their dogged, self-serving pursuit of Mistresses Openwork and Gallipot, end up forgiven and even embraced by the women's husbands. Master Openwork derives a homely domestic wisdom from the revelation of purposed foul play by Goshawk towards his wife and himself. He responds to Goshawk's apparent contrition:

> *Openwork*:   No more, he's stung.
> Who'd think that in one body there could dwell
> Deformity and beauty, heaven and hell?. . . .
>   We all set
> In rings of gold, stones that be counterfeit:
> I thought you none.
> *Goshawk*:   Pardon me.
> *Openwork*:   Truth, I do.
>   This blemish grows in nature, not in you . . .
>   Wife, nothing is perfect born.
>   (IV.ii.211–219 passim)

Openwork reflects philosophically and quaintly, here, his rhymed couplets reinforcing his imagery's expression of a new-found proverbial wisdom. His commentary also reveals Openwork's own plot to test Goshawk's, not his wife's, fidelity as a friend. Goshawk is let off with a brief moral lesson from both Openworks that encompasses his reform as well as a kind of ode to citizen-marriage:

> *Openwork*: Come, come, a trick of youth, and 'tis forgiven;
>   This rub put by, our love shall run more even.
>
> *Mrs. Openwork*: You'll deal upon men's wives no more?
>
> *Goshawk*: No.—You teach me a trick for that! . . .
>
> *Openwork*: Make my house yours, sir, still.
>
> *Goshawk*: No.
>
> *Openwork*:   I say you shall:
>   Seeing, thus besieged, it holds out, 'twill never fall!
>   (IV.ii.229–234)

Despite Openwork's final comment, this resolution leaves some ambiguity as to where his loyalties lie. That is, the love and allegiance between

Openwork and Goshawk features at least as importantly in this passage as that between the citizen and his wife. If, as I am arguing, *The Roaring Girl* attempts to present a fable of a more semiotically cohered city, this dynamic between Openwork and Goshawk has compelling implications as a potential solution to the social and linguistic instability of relations with women, in this world. But such overtures as Openwork gives Goshawk and, as we will see, Gallipot gives Laxton, also problematically challenge social and especially domestic coherence in a manner that is not in keeping with the play's socially conservative values. The two citizens' gracious forgiveness of the gallants also signals a gullibility that does not seem altered by resolution, any more than it ensures true domestic or civic coherence. They are magnanimous towards these gallants at the expense of their wives; their marriages are 'saved,' but what is most vividly shored up is the bond between the men and their very unresolved distrust of women, an enigmatic vision of coherence.

This is particularly clear in the Gallipot-Laxton portion of the subplot, and its odd conclusion. Laxton's advances to a receptive Mistress Gallipot having evolved to an elaborate extortion-scheme, the affable and credulous Gallipot complies until Laxton's boldness and greed finally appal Mistress Gallipot herself, who admits the plot. Once his accomplice admits her role in the extortion, Laxton unfolds an explanation to the initially furious Gallipot that cagily allies him with men, especially Gallipot, against women's tacit frailty:

> *Laxton*: The first hour that your wife was in my eye,
>   Myself with other gentlemen sitting by
>   In your shop tasting smoke, and speech being used
>   That men who have fairest wives are most abused . . .
>   Your wife maintained . . .
>   For her own part,
>   She vowed that you had so much of her heart,
>   No man by all his wit, by any wile
>   Never so fine spun, should yourself beguile
>   Of what in her was yours . . .
>   I scorned one woman, thus, should brave all men . . .
>   Therefore I laid siege to her . . .   But sir, I swear
>   By heaven and by those hopes men lay up there,
>   I neither have nor had a base intent
>   To wrong your bed. What's done is merriment;
>   (IV.ii.303–335)

Laxton's soothing couplets in this speech differ distinctly from the crude, innuendo-laden prose he ably demonstrates elsewhere: "Tis one of Hercules' labors to tread one of these city hens, because their cocks are still crowing over them" (III.ii.217–209). Gallipot's response is precisely Laxton's aim: "Then, sir, I am beholden—not to you, wife—But Master Laxton, to your want of doing ill" (337–338). The entire scene of denouement ends with the clear integration of Goshawk and Laxton into this society, and a reinforcing of male, homosocial bonds:

> *Gallipot*:   Gentlemen,
>   Tarry and dine here all.
>
> *Openwork*:   Brother, we have a jest
>   As good as yours to furnish out a feast.
>
> *Gallipot*: We'll furnish out our table with it.—Wife, brag no more
>   Of holding out: who most brags is most whore.
>
>   (IV.ii.339–343)

The scene's, and the subplot's, final line is Gallipot's admonishment of his wife: "Who most brags is most whore." He crudely warns her against outspokenness and its automatic counterpart, whoredom, with a misogynist commonplace that emphasizes the men's closure of their ranks. His wife's whoredom is almost assured by her sex; what Gallipot does not want to lose is male respect, and especially this male friend, Laxton. Marriage seems incidental to this more privileged, male bond, an effect that trumps the affirmation of male-female relations that has also appeared to occur.

The sub-plot's resolution—its unstable combination of domestic harmony with the homosocial—raises more questions about coherence than it answers. Its solving of the instability of the social language of double-talk seems primarily to involve the absenting of women from such discourse, a solution which is no solution in its suggestion of dissolved class boundaries (between citizen and gallant) and undermined domestic institutions. The shift from double-talk to the loyal and denotative language of IV, ii proposes a solution that is not sustainable. Much like the play's treatment of the sartorial and of cant, an initial fantasy of semiotic coherence via an increased or new transparency is complicated when such transparency disallows the fantasy. It is a quite striking mechanism where what I read as a genuine idealism is systematically and realistically compromised. The play's staging of several fantasy solutions to the incoherent city is in earnest, as is its enacting of the insufficiency of the fantasy. I conclude this chapter with a final example of this action via another aspect of 'social language.' Fittingly, this concluding example involves Moll herself and two moments of highly self-conscious speech that embody and address women, women's speech, and the social.

Much of Moll's speech in *The Roaring Girl* could be described as "social" language by virtue of its preoccupation with different social rules, some of which she upholds and some of which she openly defies. The two particular speeches that are the focus of this discussion of social language in the play are distinct in their overt querying of women's position within society's organization, and in the very public (and socially condemned) outspoken-ness they enact in the process. In this latter sense, especially, these two speeches are vividly about women, speech, and the social, and in combination they both set forth and contain the anxious matter of the female transgressions they describe and enact.

The first speech, the well known retort in Act III, scene one, is often read in terms of its proto-feminist sentiments.[28] Moll has kept a clandestine appointment with the ne'er-do-well gallant, Laxton, only to thwart his advances and then verbally and physically berate him for his presumptions. She begins:

> Thou'rt one of those
> That thinks each woman thy fond flexible whore:
> If she but cast a liberal eye upon thee,
> Turn back her head, she's thine; or amongst company,
> By chance drink first to thee, then she's quite gone,
> There's no means to help her; . . .
> How many of our sex by such as thou
> Have their good thoughts paid with a blasted name
> That never deserved loosely or did trip
> In path of whoredom beyond cup and lip? (III.i.72–84)

Moll takes aim at Laxton's arrogance, disrespect for women, and slanderous deceit, condemning the use he makes of the slippery distance between words and the truth in both his misinterpretation of women's actions and his slanders. Her last remark in the passage above figures marital betrothal—"cup and lip"—as a "path of whoredom," a suggestive detail in a larger speech detailing women's victimization by less institutional means. Moll continues:

> But for the stain of conscience and of soul,
> Better had women fall into the hands
> Of an act silent than a bragging nothing: . . .
> In thee I defy all men, their worst hates

> And their best flatteries, all their golden witchcrafts
> With which they entangle the poor spirits of fools:
> Distressed needlewomen and trade-fallen wives–
> Fish that must needs bite, or themselves be bitten—
> Such hungry things as these may soon be took
> With a worm fastened on a golden hook:
> Those are the lecher's food, his prey. (III.i.85–87; 92–99)

For all her indignation, Moll is not simply defensive; this speech is the occasion for astute dissection of women's vulnerability and men's predatory advantage—a vulnerability that vividly links the bodily with the economic, as Jean Howard has observed.[29] The forthright and incisive analysis Moll articulates is a direct challenge, not just to actual cads like Laxton, but to patriarchal society—"all men"—in which women are thus vulnerable. Part of this vulnerability stems from being denied the kind of public, authoritative voice and speech that Moll performs and insists upon. Both the socially authorized and the socially aberrant are described in this speech, and are figured in the terms of public speech.

Moll's plaintive speech in Act III, scene i, is part of a contemporary apologist trend concerning women's state whose best known iterations were prose tracts like *Hic Mulier* and Rachel Speght's and Esther Sowernam's refutations of the misogynist *An Arraignment of Lewd, Idle, Froward, and Unconstant Women* (1615).[30] As records of this extended prose-debate indicate, however, proto-feminist views were highly controversial in the challenge to patriarchal structures and ideologies they represented, and, to many, symptomatic of the profound disorderliness of London. Thus Moll's speech not only represents a social commentary, but it also must be understood as representing a particular kind of threatening social incoherence by the content of her words as well as their public conveyance. On one level, such threats are contained by the Moll who advances them—her overt moral uprightness, benevolence, and singularity are already clear, muting her challenging social language. And yet, by this same speech, Moll can be seen as de-marginalizing herself in a way that trumps any easy dismissal of her words. That is, in defying "all men," Moll implicitly joins all women. It will take a second speech, during the play's denouement in Act V, to return Moll's transgressions and transgressive speech safely to the margins.

The Act V speech is a utopian revision of the venerable social institution of marriage. In the midst of *The Roaring Girl's* comedic reordering via the marriage of Sebastian and Mary FitzAllard, Moll, who remains in women's attire throughout the final scene, is asked about her own intentions in that direction:

> *Lord Noland*: Thou hadst a suitor once, Jack; when wilt marry?
>
> *Moll*: Who, I, my lord? I'll tell you when, i'faith:
> When you shall hear
> Gallants void from sergeants' fear,
> Honesty and truth unslandered,
> Woman manned but never pandered,
> Cheaters booted but not coached,
> Vessels older ere they're broached;
> If my mind be then not varied,
> Next day following, I'll be married. (V.ii.214–223)

The sing-song tetrameter and rhyming couplets of this speech create the tone of a nursery-rhyme or ballad. Moll's pronouncements strikingly share their metrical and rhyming pattern and their sentential tone with the satiric prophecy of the Fool in *King Lear*:

> When every case in law is right,
> No squire in debt, nor no poor knight;
> When slanders do not live in tongues,
> Nor cutpurses come not to throngs;
> When usurers tell their gold i'th' field,
> And bawds and whores do churches build,
> Then comes the time, who lives to see't,
> That going shall be used with feet.[31] (III.ii.87–94)

The Fool's ironic conclusion differs from Moll's apparent sincerity, but *The Roaring Girl's* stylistic quotation from the earlier play compels us to question Moll's utopian vision. Similarly to the Fool's more obvious conclusion of impossibility, Moll describes a society that is unimaginable, as Lord Noland confirms in exclaiming, "This sounds like doomsday" (V.ii.224). Moll will never marry, is the upshot of this speech, the particulars of its ideal less important than its main purpose in signalling her unwillingness, ultimately, to join society. Moreover, in its evocation of that character's Chorus-like function, the gesture to *Lear's* Fool suggests the potency of her words and her chosen marginalization. I see these utopian words in Act V as importantly containing Moll's resisting, protesting speech in Act III, scene one. She embodies a threat of the city in its most outspoken form in that earlier speech, but then is safely (but ironically) domesticated at the end by the idealism of her final speech and by her contentment with the marginality such claims necessitate. Her outlandishness is made accessible by its distance; her gesturing to such a social never-never-land confirms her benign status—she will never be in a position truly to assert her ideals and meanwhile will shore up society from the margins.

In formulating a hypothesis regarding city comedy's generic project of querying its vernacular, one aim was to determine the potential diversity of approaches that existed. *The Roaring Girl's* inclusion in this study is based on the great differences in approach and solution it represents compared to the two Jonson plays (themselves diverse), as well as to other likely city-play candidates like Middleton's *A Chaste Maid in Cheapside*. *The Roaring Girl* is benevolent in a way that *Epicoene* is not, its fantasies of coherence reveal considerable fissures, but its approach to the chaotic city and the city's slippery vernacular is conservative and implicitly trusting of social orderings, even when they require some chastening. This awaits clearer revelation via the contrast of *Bartholomew Fair's* departure from both *The Roaring Girl* and *Epicoene* in its re-visiting of the city-comedy project. *The Roaring Girl's* combination of benevolence and conservatism is an important element of its contribution to city comedy, but the two are not inseparable. It will take Jonson and the unreal realism of an urban fairground to create a thoroughly inverted but benign world where nothing matters, including language.

Chapter Four

Fair Game: Jonson's *Bartholomew Fair*, Language, and Play

The first words of *Bartholomew Fair* are: "A pretty conceit, and worth the finding!" They refer to their speaker, John Littlewit's, delight at his own cunning wordplay. He continues to editorialize his own speech:

> When a quirk or a quiblin does 'scape thee, and thou dost not watch, and apprehend it, and bring it afore the constable of conceit (there now, I speak quib too), let 'em carry thee out o' the archdeacon's court into his kitchen, and make a Jack of thee, instead of a John (there I am again, la!).[1]

Littlewit is obsessed with wordplay, especially his own. This creates a certain inanity in him, coupled with the lack of sophistication that his name suggests. But his prominence as the play begins clues us in to much more. *Bartholomew Fair* depicts an urban world where words—language itself—are play.

Littlewit comically signals *Bartholomew Fair's* reprisal of the exploration of language and the city that Jonson undertook with *Epicoene*. Broadly related to *Epicoene*, also a prose comedy, as well as to *The Roaring Girl* in its staging of the city as a set of language conflicts, *Bartholomew Fair* signals an evolution of this generic concern in its anarchic but ultimately genial suggestion that language is a game people play with themselves and each other, and nothing more. This tone and treatment of the vernacular—elsewhere loaded with significance and anxiety for Jonson, as we have seen—corresponds with its setting of the eclectic and festive world of the Saint Bartholomew's Day fair. This same setting invests the playfulness of this treatment with a broadly existential quality. Unlike the specifically West End, social-hothouse London of *Epicoene*; or the contrasting, benign Londons of citizen-society and underworld rogues in *The Roaring Girl*, *Bartholomew Fair* claims no particular social milieu within the city because it is available to all of them. It is a society of happenstance, its denizens drawn to the fair by the promise of buying or selling the sorts of trivial and transient "gives," "trifles" and "traps" that Jonson elsewhere laments cannot legitimately order a society.[2] Its recreation of a fair encompasses all—the entire city of London, and all who frequent such a large and diverse event—and such a setting evokes the whole world, as does the play's notable lack of a clear trajectory, resolution, or other structures. It offers us life as simply a day at the Fair, and a world in which language is not productive or unifying. In *Discoveries*, Jonson writes "Speech is the instrument of society," and asserts the importance of appropriate speech and its decorous exchange for the structuring, ordering, and furthering of a civil society; yet in *Bartholomew Fair* when language is ordered at all it is only for play and self-regard, as Littlewit's words enact and additional examples will reveal. Characters' speech structures the play, speech is indeed an instrument of this society, but surprisingly without the objectives of productive transaction or coherence we expect and *Discoveries* implies.

This is radical doubt about language and an existential expression of human life and significance. But it is also whimsical and temporary—the play as much as the Fair—and the spirit is importantly festive, not nihilistic. Jonson's suggestion that language's meaningfulness extends only so far as the rules of a game seems a problematic conclusion for the author of *The Grammar*, or of *Discoveries*, of so many encomiastic poems, even of *Epicoene*, whose satire relies on how much the vernacular, and vernacular decorum, does *matter* in society. *Bartholomew Fair* is a departure not just in its extremity, but in the celebratory tone of this extremity. The play's trajectory-less staging of an experience more than a plot must have appealed as a dramatic challenge; no less appealing, perhaps was the notion of abandoning or lampooning earnest language-questions in favor of a parodic extreme where language is central to the ways that nothing matters.[3]

CRITICAL, CONTEMPORARY, AND STYLISTIC CONTEXTS

Brian Gibbons' now seminal identification of a distinct genre of early modern city comedy, characterized by "critical and satirical design . . . urban settings . . . exclusion of material appropriate to romance, fairy-tale, sentimental legend or patriotic chronicle" (7), and appearing between 1597 and 1616, collects *Bartholomew Fair* in its canon of "sordidly realis[tic]" drama.[4] Others, since, have questioned the play's status as a city comedy, as part of critical efforts to hone the genre's hallmarks ever more precisely. Theodore Leinwand most famously excluded the play in his redefinition of the genre, its era, and central concerns,[5] but most recent critical discussion of city comedy frankly acknowledges *Bartholomew Fair's* significance for the genre, including the generic challenges it poses. In the 2004 collection of new work on Jacobean city comedy, *Plotting Early Modern London*, editors Angela Stock and Anne-Julia Zwierlein describe *Bartholomew Fair* as one of city comedy's "masterpieces" and dismiss much critical quibbling over the delimiting of the genre's boundaries in the period: "All forms of London drama set the dramatic and ideological framework within which city comedy worked and achieved its effects in the playhouses . . . To narrow the genre of satiric city comedy . . . means, in a sense, to narrow its dramatic influence."[6] Stock and Zwierlein propose their volume's title, "Plotting Early Modern London," as a key to understanding the project of city comedy, including *Bartholomew Fair*. 'Plotting London' was "both the subject and the objective of these plays," they comment; city comedies surveyed the city on multiple levels in order to assert "control, some sort of mastery over this amorphous urban marketplace"(4). *Bartholomew Fair's* vivid and particular surveying of a London fair world affixes its identity as a city comedy, but it is its unsettling assertion of the impossibility of any resulting control that makes it a crucial component of the genre and any generic plotting project. By this, city comedy not only stages a central preoccupation with plotting the city but also the simultaneous futility of such a project for this "amorphous urban" world. *Bartholomew Fair* indeed should be seen as one of city comedy's greatest achievements, but most significantly because its urban surveying concludes—more playfully than darkly—that control is impossible and mastery unimportant, as we will explore in more depth, below.

Bartholomew Fair's length and notorious shapelessness always have presented critics with the problem of how to read and what to read within it as it unfolds the fortunes of a diverse group of visitors and purveyors during a single day-at-the-Fair.[7] We get Littlewit, his wife Win-the-fight, his mother-in-law Dame Purecraft, and her mentor the Puritan "Rabbi" Zeal-of-the-land Busy; the foolish young Esquire Bartholomew Cokes, his obstreperous tutor Wasp, and Cokes' unwilling betrothed, Grace Wellborn; the zealous Justice Adam Overdo and his wife; and two gallants, Winwife and Quarlous. Equally colorful are those whose livelihoods are the fair: Knockem, Whit the bawd, Ursula the pig woman, Edgeworth the cutpurse. There are a lot of characters to keep straight and very little plot—a significant challenge for any reader to encompass. John Enck has argued that structure in the play is, in fact, slight, and that it is the atmosphere that is truly important to notice (Enck 191). This view has been challenged by Richard Levin, among others, who locates a distinct structure built around four groupings of the many

characters and what he views as their highly ordered interactions ("Structure"173–174).

Somewhere between the polarities represented by Enck and Levin is
Mary Bledsoe's more recent argument for understanding *Bartholomew Fair's*
structure in terms of the very disorderliness that appears to disrupt it.[8] Commenting that it is "a difficult play to appreciate . . . [i]t has the apparent
shapeless-ness and chaos of the actual Smithfield Fair it purports to imitate"
(Bledsoe 149), Bledsoe traces a central role of "linguistic enormity" through
Bartholomew Fair and concludes that it is structured around the exposition
of a range of such "enormities"—whose seventeenth-century sense was of
"irregularities"—in characters' language. Bledsoe establishes language-use as
a key topos and structuring principle of the play and surveys the range of
uses and abuses found therein. While such cataloging of different characters'
"enormities" is a useful starting point for *Bartholomew Fair*, Bledsoe does not
push past this point and further interrogate Jonson's precise relationship—
one that includes celebration, prescription, and distrust—to the workings of
language more generally. Following from Bledsoe's observation of language's
importance in the play but also, I hope, pushing past her, I would propose
the importance of approaching *Bartholomew Fair* as an additional dramatic
site for interrogation of the vernacular, one that might enable different
questions or conclusions than *Epicoene* while nonetheless participating in a
generic staging of the city in terms of language.

Bledsoe references Jonas Barish's convictions about the centrality of language to Jonson, and some further details of Barish's findings are pertinent to
suggesting *Bartholomew Fair's* place amid Jonson's oeuvre and preoccupations.
In *Ben Jonson and the Language of Prose Comedy*, a book whose analysis of the
comedies altered the critical horizon of Jonson scholarship, Barish depends
on the familiarity of Shakespeare.[9] He continually locates Jonson in terms of
his diverse and distinct differences from Shakespeare in tone, texture, artistic intention, rhetorical style, and attitude toward language. Dissecting syntax and periods, or sentence-units, Barish makes extensive discussion of the
marked contrast between the Ciceronian roundness of Shakespeare's periods
and the "exploded periods" of Jonson. He also observes that Jonson's prose is
irregular on principle, preserving syntactic balance only to upset balance: "if
he deploys symmetrical patterns, he does so only to disrupt them" (76).

Such a predictable syntactic detail is suggestive of some sort of authorial
bent or intent, and Barish duly considers the relationship between a writer's
style and thought-process or attitude. He concludes that a writer who shuns
connectives as thoroughly as Jonson may be thinking in other terms besides
the harmonious 'cause and effect' so easily located in Shakespeare. These

other terms are "perhaps of a world . . . so bewildering and disintegrated that nothing in it seems causally related to anything else" (77). With this, Barish sets up a comparison that suggests the skepticism of Jonson towards ideals of communion in society; he also significantly locates this sensibility in Jonson's very syntax and style, proposing that we might think about the playwright's notorious world-weariness as rooted in conclusions about language itself.[10]

The centrality of language and its contrasting work in Jonson's and Shakespeare's dramatic worlds is further discussed by social historian Lawrence Manley, who considers *Pericles* alongside *Bartholomew Fair*.[11] Making the case for *Pericles* as Shakespeare's take on the city-comedy genre of the day, Manley focuses on the transforming power of Marina's language and the unifying, Romantic power of the truth, spoken, which ultimately trumps the atomized city and its atomizing languages. *Bartholomew Fair*, Manley argues, is also interested in the transforming power of truth-revealed, but only in so much that what is revealed is that all, including language itself by this comparison, is folly (*Literature* 465). Unlike in most of Shakespeare, including *Pericles*, where a moral center is disturbed but, crucially, recovered by play's end, Jonson rarely projects a stable, moral center that might be disturbed in the first place. *Bartholomew Fair*, like many of its fellow Jonsonian creations, will not offer a concluding coherence in social, moral, or linguistic terms.

Contrastive states of resolution in selected Shakespearean drama and in *Bartholomew Fair* have been instructively noted by others, as well. For Thomas Cartelli, the play is Jonson's provocative attempt at an "urban arcadia" alongside Shakespeare's diverse comedies of removal and return.[12] Cartelli reads *Bartholomew Fair* as a specific response to Shakespeare's late plays and their pastoralism, but notes the distinct difference in the kinds of communities achieved by the ends of these very different plays. The complete and permanent unifications in Shakespeare's *The Tempest* or *The Winter's Tale* contrast sharply with the only temporary communion (and also parodic communion in its vehicle of a puppet-play) that is achieved at the conclusion of *Bartholomew Fair*. In Jonson's version of an urban arcadia, temporary unity is all that can be hoped for in a far from idyllic setting (168). With such a contrast, the role of language is worth querying, as well. In *The Tempest*, Caliban's dubiously valuable literacy and the ambiguous benevolence of Prospero's mage-like rhetorical power certainly comprise a complex interrogation of language's role in human society. The play's comedic reordering nevertheless reflects a basic belief in the return to conventional social order and in the institutions, like an authoritative and coherent vernacular, that uphold and create it. Such a belief is neither apparent in *Bartholomew Fair*

nor in Jonson's public drama as a whole. In Jonson's world, language cannot lend coherence to a fragmented world nonetheless dependent on it for
meaning. The unity Cartelli notes as significantly missing at the end of his
Smithfield-Arcadia is thus impossible for Jonson, for whom language is most
often the enemy of productive, social unity.

These contrasts between Shakespeare and Jonson, and others' observations of their contrasts, line out some fundamental values or anti-values in
Jonson's explorations of language and of London in his city comedies. The
sharp contrasts between the two dramatists' outlook on many things implied
by their distinct dramatic forms and subjects aids in reading Jonson, I would
argue without hesitation. But some of the more nihilistic attitudes this suggests in Jonson are not as helpful in reading *Bartholomew Fair's* surprisingly
festive take on these same anti-values. Or rather, it is important, turning now
to the play, to recognize the transposing of many of Jonson's serious questions or doubts about language—whether as medium or discourse—into the
genial anarchy and absurdity of a world where language is purely a game, and
little more. It is this understanding and treatment of language that 'structures' the play, I would argue. The elusiveness of a satisfactory answer to the
question of what, if anything, structures *Bartholomew Fair*, is perhaps the
result of looking for something less fundamental, or treated more earnestly,
than language itself.[13]

Bartholomew Fair's particular playfulness begins in its meta-theatrical
Induction. Following some discussion of this opening, my reading will focus
on two scenes, both episodes of great disorder with language-games at the
center of their comedy and import. These scenes are Act IV, scene iv, the
"Vapors" scene; and Act V, scenes iv and v together, which depict the puppet-
show that will bring together every character from the previous four acts and
conclude the play. Each of these scenes revisits the whimsical existentialism
of the Induction. Each—like the rest of the play—is structured only by the
ways that language keeps resurfacing as a meaningless but irresistible game.

THEATER, REALITY AND LANGUAGE IN THE *INDUCTION*.

As the *Induction* begins we are simultaneously projected into the world of the
play and suspended from this move by the entrance of a stage-keeper who is
the first character on stage and not a listed member of the *dramatis personae*
at all. No doubt there was a stage-keeper at the Hope, Bankside, on October
31, 1614, the play's first performance,[14] but he was probably not the person
onstage acting the part of "Stage-keeper" in this induction to the play. Our
first experience with the play is thus meta-theatrical, further enhanced by the

keeper's first remarks that the play is delayed due to an actor's pulled stocking. Such meta-theatrical blurring in prologues or inductions was not atypical of plays at the time,[15] but this induction's immediate signaling of a desire to play both with playing and with the gap between representation and reality serves early notice of its self-reflective and existential interests. The homeliness and comedy of the Stagekeeper also signal the geniality of this interest.

The vividly lowbrow Stagekeeper's constant frame of reference is to the reliability of language and the importance of relying on the appropriate discourses his language constitutes. He complains, "But for the whole play, will you ha' the truth on't? (I am looking, lest the poet hear me, or his man, Master Brome, behind the arras) it is like to be a very conceited scurvy one, in plain English. . . . He has not hit the humors, he does not know 'em; he has not conversed with the Barthol'mew birds, as they say" (*Induction,* 6–13). The problem is discursive—the play lacks the insights of one who has literally spoken with the Fair and its denizens, who knows its 'lingo.' The Stagekeeper's own lingo adds to the irony of his desire for plain English and proper decorum. His apposition of "scurvy" with the Latinate "conceited" renames the play and implies a distrust of his own "plain English" in concert with his doubts about the play.

Language is not a game for the Stagekeeper, but he quickly becomes part of the *Induction's*, and Jonson's, intention to make it one. This is clear when the *Prologue* he has been providing is interrupted by the Book-holder, who offers a "new one" of "articles drawn out in haste between the author and you" (58–60):

> It is further covenanted, concluded, and agreed that how great soever the expectation be, no person here is to expect more than he knows, or better ware than a Fair will afford . . . but content himself with the present. Instead of a little Davy to take toll o' the bawds, the author doth promise a strutting horse-courser with a leer drunkard, two or three to attend him in as good equipage as you would wish . . . A wise justice of peace *meditant*, instead of a juggler with an ape. A civil cutpurse *searchant*. A sweet singer of new ballads *allurant*; and as fresh an hypocrite as ever was broached *rampant*. (113–127)

Here is a new discursive mode of legalese as well as the language of heraldry used to pretentious effect with words like "searchant" and "allurant." As many have observed, Jonson also literalizes the tacit in a spectator's relationship to a performance here, the concretizing of which renders the entire enterprise absurd, as when the contract concludes by observing: "In witness whereof, as you have preposterously put to your seal already (which is your money), you will now add the other part of suffrage, your hands" (152–155). This last, of course, is an idiosyncratic truth about playgoing, but its earnest explicitness and precise diction combine to present the play as well as this 'reality' of attending a play as a linguistic, discursive, and transactional game. It is a joke on everyone, but perhaps especially the smug Book-holder, whose apparent stature as an arbiter disintegrates (though he doesn't know it) when what he is attempting to dictate is diminished as arbitrary. The *Induction* playfully asks us 'What is the office of the theater?' 'What are we agreeing to when we interact?' and 'What is language for?' What authority does language give us over truth, fiction, or negotiating between them? Answer: none that is serious, a playful statement to make as the play proper begins that has some quite serious implications.[16]

A DAY AT THE FAIR

The first half of *Bartholomew Fair* does not move so much as it accumulates towards the climactic Acts IV and V and the two scenes considered below. We arrive at the fair itself in Act II, having spent Act I meeting the two primary fair-going parties whose subsequent misadventures will form our entertainment, though never a clear arc of dramatic development. With these two parties we experience the Fair—and the city world it emblematizes, I would suggest—as a series of encounters with speech characteristics. Jonson clearly delights in the windy and repetitive rhetoric of the Puritan 'Rabbi' Busy, the angry obscenity of the demoralized tutor, Wasp, and the almost incomprehensible vehemence of the bawd, Whit, not to mention the satiric correspondence between their speech and their names. Critics note the degree to which *Bartholomew Fair's* characters each represent a different breach of decorum or speech eccentricity.[17] This creates a topography of speech styles and idioms that accomplish nothing but, importantly, are not meant to; the play's most absurd characters are those, like Wasp and Busy, with a desire for language to matter beyond performance. All of these speech tics mean that dialogue is largely without transaction—characters speech out of a fixation on their own words or speech. Littlewit, for example, speaks to his wife, Win, in Act I, scene iii, but his incantation-like repetition of her name is inimical to communication and to understanding much beyond this tic: "Oh Win, fie, what do you mean, Win? Be womanly, Win? Make an outcry to your mother, Win? . . . And Master Winwife comes a suitor to your mother, Win, as I told you before, Win, and may perhaps be our father, Win" (I.iii.40–46). Ursula, the pig-woman, offers a different dimension of this treatment of language. Her language's colloquial earthiness is distinctive, as others have noted,[18] but as important is her constant renaming of people and situations. She speaks to her servant, Mooncalf, early in the play: "My chair, you false faucet you . . . and a bottle of ale to quench me, rascal . . . Come, sir, set it here. Did not I bid you should get this chair let out o' the sides for me? . . . 'Tis well, changeling; because it can take in your grasshopper's thighs you care for no more . . . Fill, stote, fill . . . Fill again, you unlucky vermin" (II.ii.48–75 *passim*). Ursula continuously insults Mooncalf, each time with a new invention till Mooncalf becomes an array of arbitrary signs more than anything else. But Ursula is without malice—her renaming is good-natured play, and in her oft-remarked role as fleshly emblem of the Fair-world, it is important to note her colorful, indecorous language and her vivid use of words to create texture, not meaning.

The arbitrariness of words evident in speech like Littlewit's and Ursula's factors into the treatment of social institutions in the play, as well: in Act IV the young ward Grace Wellborn uses randomly selected words and the mere preference of a passerby to choose between Quarlous and Winwife for her husband:

> *Grace*: You shall
> write, either of you, here, a word or a name—what you like
> best—but of two or three syllables at most; and the next person
> that comes this way (because destiny has a high hand in business of this
> nature) I'll demand which of the two words he or she doth
> approve; and according to that sentence fix my resolution and
> affection without change. (IV.iii.48–55)

A marriage contract is turned into a merry word-game by this strategy, and Quarlous and Winwife agree to Grace's terms, both choosing names out of pastoral romances—for Quarlous, "Argalus" from Sidney's *Arcadia*; for Winwife, "Palamon" from *The Two Noble Kinsmen*—that enhance the sense of frivolity.[19] The entrance of Trouble-all—the needed, random arbiter of the word game—intensifies the scene's anarchic treatment of words and society. Trouble-all is the Fair's recognized lunatic, his dementia centered on Justice Overdo's jurisdiction and the word "warrant," an obsessive feature of his speech. This game of Grace's marriage thus will turn on the word-preference of a madman who already prefers one word above all others. A transaction takes place, but its inanity is playfully assured by its executor, Trouble-all, even beyond Grace's original plan. In Act IV, in the "Vapors" scene, we will get another, more communal, word-game, which will take questions of meaning and transaction to an ever more absurdly logical extreme.

LOGIC, LINGUISTIC CHAOS, AND "THE VAPORS"

The word "vapors" features in the speech of Dan Knockem much as "warrant" in that of Trouble-all: it dominates his expression, becoming by its repetition meaningless. Knockem uses "vapors" to signify almost anything, but increasingly signifies nothing by his giddy, verbal tic. In Act IV, scene iv, Knockem leads a small, drunken company in a round of "the Vapors," a game at first no less ambiguous than the word itself. Edgworth the cutpurse sketches the scenario. Speaking to Quarlous and Winwife, he describes what they will witness inside Ursula's booth, which doubles as an ale-house:

> . . . Yonder he is . . . fall'n into the finest company, and so transported with vapors; they ha' got in a northern clothier and one Puppy, a western man, that's come to wrestle before my Lord Mayor anon, and Captain Whit, and one Val Cutting, that helps Captain Jordan to roar, a circling boy; with whom your Numps [Humphrey Wasp, the tutor, whom the gentlemen seek] is so taken that you may strip him of his clothes, if you will. (IV.iii.111–118)

Edgworth describes a motley company gathered in the booth, Wasp among them, captivated by these "vapors," which seem to refer to ale or the drinking of ale as well as to the apparent game of contradiction the men play over their ale. Wasp is transported as much by the word-game as by the ale; both are intoxicating and neither serves any greater purpose beyond pleasure.

In the scene our disorientation is immediate as characters speak, but not clearly to each other, and almost every one features a distinct dialect or idiom, whether regional (Northern, Puppy, Captain Whit), trade-related (Knockem), or simply furiously choleric and illogical (Wasp):

> *Knockem*: Whit, bid Val Cutting continue the vapors for a lift, Whit, for a lift.
>
> *Northern*: I'll ne mare, I'll ne mare, the eale's too meeghty.
>
> *Knockem*: How now! My Galloway Nag, the staggers? Ha! Whit, gi' him a slit I'the forehead. Cheer up, man; a needle and thread to stitch his ears. I'd cure him now, an' I had it, with a little butter an garlic, long-pepper and grains . . .

> *Puppy*: Why, where are you, zurs? Do you vlinch and leave us i' the zuds, now?
>
> *Northern*: I'll ne mare, I in e'en as vull as a paiper's bag, by my troth, I.
>
> (IV.iv.1–13)

The actual vapors game is not yet afoot, but already the effect is faintly anar- chic as each man speaks but none truly converses with anyone else. Following this 'exchange,' the game begins in earnest. In his stage direction within the game, Jonson described the Vapors as *"nonsense: every man to oppose the last man that spoke, whether it concerned him or no"* (IV.iv), and the meaningless- ness of a game of punning and contradiction is obvious.[20] But this neglects the play's festive postulation of all language as play, as inherently a game, at least in the temporary, carnival world of the Bartholomew's Day Fair. More- over, the Vapors is not nonsense at all—studied carefully, the game proceeds via a logic that relies on, and delights in, the highly polysemic nature of many English words. The game operates according to an extreme logic at least in part based on this polysemic property of the English lexicon, an aspect of the vernacular both celebrated and deplored in the period. Language's object here is that it has no object beyond the game; exigencies of productive com- munication or significance are beside the point.

The game begins and progresses via retorts over a series of words: first "tire," then "know," then "pardon," and on through "reason," "sense," "vapor" itself, and finally "mind." In each case a striking disjunction is created, for a word will hold what seems like meaning and resonance until characters change the use of it or shift to another word with little productive rationale. As mentioned above, the logic of polysemy is at work here—the game, which at first appears bewilderingly incoherent, operates via rules of wordplay that trump other signifying expectations:

> *Knockem*: Why, well said, old flea-bitten, thou'lt never *tire*, I see.
>
> *Cutting*: No, sir, but he may *tire*, if it please him.
>
> *Whit*: Who told dee sho? That he vuld never *teer*, man?
>
> *Cutting*: No matter who told him so, so long as he *knows*.
>
> *Knockem*: Nay, I *know* nothing, sir, pardon me there.
>
> (IV.iv.16–21, italics mine)

This is both more slippery and more deliberate than simple contrariness, as each response redirects a word's meaning toward another valence. Knockem uses "tire" in the sense of "to cease or give out," but Cutting's reply, though possibly relying on the same definition, also suggests several other contemporary senses of the verb "tire": "to bore" or become bored by; "to prey upon;" and "to dress."[21] Whit's surprised querying of Cutting's words underlines a shift, perhaps to a less common usage. The game continues as Cutting rejoins in line 18 with "knows" in the conventional sense of "to be acquainted with a thing." Knockem's reply could rely on the same definition, but it is worth reviewing the *Oxford English Dictionary's* record for meanings of "know" during this period and find senses like "to recognize," "to distinguish," and "to confess" among many others.[22] "Know" is an enormously variable word, the play of which in a phrase like "I know nothing" is practically endless, a slippery prodigality that is part of this explicit word-game, but also projects this sense of a game beyond Act IV, scene iv, to the final scenes of the play, where matters of recognition, distinguishing, and confession all, confusedly, are factors.

With the word "reason," like "know" a word with diverse significations at the time, we observe a similar phenomenon a few lines later:

> *Knockem:* If he have *reason*, he may like it, sir.
>
> *Whit:* By no meansh, Captain, upon *reason*; he may like nothing upon reason.
>
> *Wasp*: I have no *reason*, nor I will hear of no *reason*, nor I will look for no *reason*, and he is an ass that either knows any or looks for't from me.
>
> *Cutting*: Yes, in some sense you may have *reason*, sir.
>
> (IV.iv.39–45 italics mine)

Defining and dating uses of "reason," *The Oxford English Dictionary* lists some familiar definitions which also were current in early modern English: a noun referring to human rationale, one of the fundamental principles of humanity; an explanation or account. But current also in Jonson's day were other senses that define reason as "a narrative, saying, or speech," and also as a synonym for "sentence," as in a syntactical unit. The dictionary also reveals that the phrase "Part of Speech" was also commonly described as a "Part of Reason," a striking conflation for the way Jonson seems to subvert both aspects of it throughout *Bartholomew Fair,* but especially in the pointed use of the word "reason" in this scene.

The Vapors' adherence to the polysemically literal takes precedence over any other level of sense, and the characters' intercourse is ruled by the game's genial but strict rules. The game's and the scene's anarchy is inevitable, too, as signaled by the fate of any who attempt to stand outside its playful imperatives. Quarlous, who has been watching and listening the while, comments, "Call you this vapors? This is such belching of quarrel as I never heard" (IV. iv.78–80). Using disdain to distance himself, Quarlous attempts to dismiss the game but only briefly maintains detachment. He swiftly is sucked into the game, as well, an outsider's stance clearly impossible:

> *Wasp*: Why do you laugh, sir?
>
> *Quarlous*: Sir, you'll allow me my Christian liberty. I may laugh, I hope.
>
> *Cutting*: In some sort you may, and in some sort you may not, sir.
>
> Knockem: Nay, in some sort, sir, he may neither laugh nor hope in this
> company.
>
> *Wasp*: Yes, then he may both laugh and hope in any sort, an't please him.
>
> *Quarlous*: Faith, and I will then, for it does please me exceedingly.
>
> *Wasp*: No exceeding, neither, sir.
>
> *Knockem*: No, that vapor is too lofty.
>
> *Quarlous*: Gentlemen, I do not play well at your game of vapors; I am not
> very good at it, but— (IV.iv.121–135)

Quarlous' attempt to extricate himself by appealing to a logic outside the game fails: nothing can signify when the game's object makes coherence outside its rules irrelevant. Jonson is also collapsing the distance between Quarlous and the folly he critiques as the critic finds his own language an untrustworthy medium and his fastest way into the game. He now participates by brawling instead of speaking, an extreme comment on the irrelevance of words and speech, finally.

The Vapors game disintegrates into quarrel and, finally, violence as everyone is drawn into a drunken brawl over nothing of consequence. Wordplay dissolves into physical violence and true anarchy, but these are also part of the game, Knockem hints, when he and Captain Whit use the chaos of the brawl to steal the others' cloaks, saying: "Gather up, Whit, gather up, Whit, Good vapors!" (IV.iv.147). This violent conclusion of the game appears to inject a more serious note into the anarchy which the scene and the game have treated with a light touch. Yet Knockem's suggestion that the fight and the theft are part of the game lessen their seriousness and situate them, as well, within the Fair's existential experience. This is all a part of the day at the Fair that all present implicitly signed on for when they arrived, much like the audience in the *Induction*. Part of being there is accepting and celebrating that all is a game.

What else is served by this game and its effects? The plot is served by
Edgworth's opportunity to steal Wasp's closely-guarded marriage-license during the mêlée into which the vapors disintegrates, certainly. The sheer texture
of atmosphere and off-beat characters offered is remarkable, recalling John
Enck's location of the play's entire meaning in its rendering of ethos.[23] More
thematically, this scene and its not-so-nonsensical Vapours game vividly foreground the nature of language, emphasizing its irresistible possibilities while
down-playing any serious consequences. The Vapors' hyper-logical object
opposes productive language and places language and signification at the
center of the scene as a whole. It thereby calls into question the meaningfulness of dialogue elsewhere in the play: a subsequent exchange between Wasp
and Mistress Overdo becomes strongly reminiscent of the game's logical contradiction. Beyond the game's boundaries, it seems, characters' interactions
remain Vapor-like:

> *Mistress Overdo*: What mean you? Are you rebels, gentlemen? Shall I
> send out a sergeant-at-arms or a writ o' rebellion against you?
> I'll *commit* you, upon my woman-hood, for a riot, upon my
> justice-hood, if you persist.
>
> *Wasp*: Upon your justice-hood? Marry, shit o' your hood; you'll
> commit? . . . Turd i' your teeth for a fee, now.
>
> (IV.iv.148–155 italics mine)

The justice's wife, scandalized by the violence of the brawl, uses "commit"
in its sense of consignment or explicitly placing in confinement. Wasp's
obscene retort pounces on the word for its more colloquial meaning and
makes the vulgar suggestion of fornication. The word-play that continues
here is markedly less genial, and the slippage of sense is more concrete than
during the game, and more barbed. Wasp's character is notably choleric, and
his speech typically disintegrates to this level of venom. That this particular
venom derives from the preceding vapors does not diminish its sting; but it
more importantly enacts a sense of uncontrollability as the game's challenge
to productive or transactional language spills over into the remainder of the
scene, affecting even Bristle the Majesty's watchman, who arrives to arrest
Wasp well after the game-proper has ended: "*Bristle*: Down? Yes, we will
down, I warrant you; down with him in his Majesty's name, down, down
with him, and carry him away to the pigeon-holes" (177–179). All speech in
this holiday world seems destined to become a game of Vapors.

Jonson pronounces didactically in his *Discoveries*, that "In all speech,
words and sense are as the body and the soul. The sense is as the life and

soul of language, without which all words are dead."[24] This is a serious concern for Jonson, as we have seen, in whose works matters of linguistic Custom, of decorum, of license, and of eloquence feature, often in the anxious mode of satire.[25] With *Bartholomew Fair* words and sense remain in the foreground, but satire is reserved, ironically, for those who take their connection too seriously. This perhaps surprising leniency from Jonson in fact coexists naturally, I would contend, with anxieties over the vernacular's shifting capabilities within society. The flip side of more anxious questioning is *Bartholomew Fair's* genial and existential experiment of a carnivalesque city where all language is folly, is play, and the game of the Vapors literalizes a dominant thematic principle of the play. This is an anarchic, but, ironically, utopian vision of linguistic and discursive freedom from an author so concerned with language and society. *Bartholomew Fair* and its holiday world, where nothing matters, not even language, offer one kind of solution to these concerns. In looking broadly at Jonson's dramatic works, Jonas Barish, as we have seen, identifies a marked stylistic feature of avoiding or minimizing syntactic connectives.[26] The resultant dramatic world is one in which characters are isolated from each other, society is a collection of disconnected atoms, and each character speaks a private language of his own (83). Viewed in such terms, *Bartholomew Fair* is in many ways Jonson's most complete realization of this technique and perspective; the Vapours-scene, however, somewhat refutes the last part of Barish's claim, for its characters do come together in speaking a language of play. Communion does occur, though differently than *Discoveries* suggests—it's fun, it's playful, it's unimportant.

"BY PLAIN DEMONSTRATION": THE PUPPET PLAY'S DEFEAT OF EARNESTNESS

The play's final scenes will take this to an even more anarchic extreme in Act V via the Puppet-Play that is their focal point. Here, two commonplaces of early modern popular entertainment—the play-within-a-play and the puppet-play—intersect, to layered discursive and satiric effect.[27] The difference in *Bartholomew Fair* is that its play is 'acted' by puppets, not human players, an absurdist difference that allows for mischievous reflection as the meta-discursive questions "What is truth, What is fiction?" and "Does it matter?" are rendered over-earnest when puppets are the players. It is all instead the most simplistic kind of fiction, it seems, and of very little matter. If, as in *Hamlet*, the players 'hold the mirror up to nature,' here in Act V of *Bartholomew Fair*, the puppet-players and their play hold the mirror up to playing, including the audience's rapt attention to the speech of these obviously fake and conventionally crude 'players.'

The inclusion of a puppet-play in *Bartholomew Fair* is contextualized helpfully by historian Nicholas Zwager.[28] Motions—the term referred both to puppet plays and to the individual puppets themselves—were a popular and ubiquitous entertainment in Jacobean London. A host of period texts refer to motions in varied contexts, but Jonson's plays are the most important source of information about motions and contemporary attitudes towards them. Popular motions derived from Biblical, classical, legendary, and sometimes contemporary history sources, and the farcical, even obscene, characteristics evident in *Bartholomew Fair's* motion of "Hero and Leander" were fairly standard, as were absurd violations of historical truth: Julius Caesar brawling with the Devil, or with Guy Fawkes.[29] The localization of the "Hero and Leander" story to a Thames-side wharf, for greater 'intelligibility,' was also not uncommon, for motions pandered to the most lowbrow tastes. These were not entertainments aimed at impressing or educating their audience through beauty, gravity, or eloquence.

Jonson is known to have detested puppet-plays. In *Discoveries* he laments the popular taste for their debased foolishness, commenting: "A man cannot imagine that thing so foolish or rude, but will find . . . an Admirer . . . The puppets are seene now, in despight of the players."[30] Given such disdain for motions and their popularity, we might question his inclusion of the device in his own play except as a gesture of verisimilitude. The puppet-play indeed does provide local color, but it also forms an integral part of *Bartholomew Fair's* relaxed and festive society-of-no-consequence. With its degraded doggerel- verse[31] and its mock-serious presentation of a well-known plot, Act V's motion giddily emphasizes its irrelevance on several levels. In so doing it satirizes desires for discursive perfection and coherence—the real preposterousness of characters like Cokes and Busy, we will see, is their inclination to take the puppets at their word.

As with the vapors scene, we are prepared for the puppet-play in the preceding scene, which foregrounds a similar playfulness towards linguistic degradation. Cokes discusses the imminent production with Leatherhead, the puppet-master, and John Littlewit, who has written the play-script for Leatherhead. The puppet-play will present the classical tale of the lovers Hero and Leander, combined with the legend of Damon and Pythias, but with some alterations made:

> *Cokes*: But do you play it according to the printed book? I have read that.
> *Leatherhead*: By no means, sir.

Cokes: No? How then?

Leatherhead: A better way, sir; that is too learned and poetical for our
    audience. What do they know what Hellespont is? "Guilty of
    true love's blood"? Or what Abydos is? Or "the other Sestos
    hight"?

Cokes: Th' art i' the right. I do not know myself.

Leatherhead: No, I have entreated Master Littlewit to take a little pains
    to reduce it to a more familiar strain for our people. . . .

Littlewit: It pleases him to make a matter of it, sir. But there is no such
    matter I assure you. I have only made it a little easy and modern
    for the times, sir, that's all; as, for the Hellespont, I imagine our
    Thames here; and then Leander I make a dyer's son, about Pud-
    dle Wharf; and Hero a wench o' the Bankside, who going over
    one morning to Old Fish Street, Leander spies her land at Trig
    stairs, and falls in love with her. Now do I introduce Cupid, hav-
    ing metamorphosed himself into a drawer, and he strikes Hero in
    love with a pint of sherry; and other pretty passages there are o'
    the friendship, that will delight you sir, and please you of judg-
    ment.

                                        (V.iii.106–130)

Leatherhead's cheerful dismissal of the eloquence and craft of Christopher
Marlowe's original poetry for his own, "easy and modern" version is the kind
of boorish disrespect for linguistic decorum and style that Jonson—and his
critic-creations like Truewit, in *Epicoene*—would have deplored. But we sense
only the absurdity of Leatherhead's argument and its product. In these puppet-play scenes, poetic barbarism is parodic, and Jonson's choice of Marlowe
as the victim of Littlewit's and Leatherhead's labors is satiric of all three—
Jonson was no fan of Marlowe's grandiloquence.[32] The spirit of this parody
and satire is good natured, however; the daftness is funny, not anxious.
Jonson's *English Grammar* purports to counteract perceptions of the "bar-
barisme . . . with which [English] is mistaken to be diseas'd," but in the
same text he also reveals a less anxious enthusiasm for English's rougher edges
that is useful for reading *Bartholomew Fair's* shift in temperament. He writes,
"Not that I would have the vulgar, and practis'd way of making, abolish'd
and abdicated (being both sweet and delightful, and much taking the eare)
but, to the end our Tongue may be made equal to those of the renowned
countries, Italy and Greece, touching this particular."[33] The delight in the
idiosyncrasies and poetic crudities of English evidenced in the first half of

this remark is let loose in *Bartholomew Fair* and combined with the color and crudities of the city. The puppet-play constitutes the play's most vivid expression of this delight, unencumbered by the anxieties that equally attend the *Grammar*.

The motion begins with a verse-prologue spoken by Leatherhead that introduces the 4-beat, sing-song meter and couplet-rhyme of the puppet-play within the prose of the larger play. These effects as well as the crude expression; the relocation along the wharves of contemporary London; the puppet's version of the "Hero and Leander" legend—all these elements turn the original poem as well as the puppet play, poetry, even London itself into a comic joke whose pure silliness outweighs how dark a statement this degradation could create:

> *Leatherhead*: This while young Leander with fair Hero is drinking,
>   And Hero grown drunk, to any man's thinking!
>   Yet was not three pints of sherry could flaw her,
>   Till Cupid, distinguished like Jonas the drawer,
>   From under his apron, where his lechery lurks,
>   Put love in her sack. Now mark how it works.
>
> *Puppet Hero*: O Leander, Leander, my dear, my dear Leander,
>   I'll forever be thy goose, so thou'lt be my gander . . .
>
> *Puppet Leander*: And sweetest of geese, before I go to bed,
>   I'll swim over the Thames, my goose, thee to tread . . .
>   But lest the Thames should be dark, my goose, my dear
>   friend, Let thy window be provided of a candle's end.
>
> *Pup. Hero*: Fear not, my gander, I protest I should handle
>   My matters very ill, if I had not a whole candle.
>
> *Pup. Leander:* Well then, look to't, and kiss me to boot.
>
>   (V.iv.288–312)

These lines read more like a drinking-song than dramatic verse, as romantic and epic love-plot conventions are tossed aside, one after the other: the revised scene is a tavern, Cupid's arrow is the lecherous thrust of a city drawer, love is bestial copulation, and Hero's noble lines are drunken and crude.

Such thorough flouting of the parameters of genre, discourse, and language is difficult not to read as gleeful here. For Jonson the puppet-play offers a heightened opportunity to destabilize our sense of the coherence offered by such parameters. There are ongoing exchanges between Leatherhead and Puppet Leander, for example, which are part of the performance but not part of the "Hero and Leander" story. This blurring underscores our expectations of boundaries, logic, and decorum, and their absence and irrelevance, here. The puppets abuse and assault Leatherhead throughout, further collapsing dramatic boundaries as well as logical boundaries, since Leatherhead himself is the puppeteer. The whole point is that such logic is unimportant; all import is trumped by play.

Language is very much a game amid this silliness—further into the puppet-play, the puppets' dialogue becomes dominated by words repeated as occasions for Punch-and-Judy style poundings on Leatherhead and each other:

> *Leatherhead*: Who chances to come by but fair Hero in a sculler?
> And seeing Leander's naked leg and goodly calf,
> Cast at him, from the boat, a sheep's eye and a half.
> Now she is landed, and the sculler come back;
> By and by you shall see what Leander doth lack.
>
> *Pup. Leander*: Cole, Cole, old Cole.
>
> *Leatherhead*:   That is the sculler's name
> Without control.
>
> *Pup. Leander*: Cole, Cole, I say, Cole. . . . Old Cole. . . .
> Why Cole, I say, Cole.   (V.iv.123–132, 137)

All of Puppet Leander's "replies" become verbal and, most likely, physical repetitions in this slapstick game, and the words cease to mean anything, especially as violence takes over:

> *Pup. Leander*: Row apace, row apace, row, row, row, row, row.
>
> *Leatherhead:* You are knavishly loaden, sculler, take heed where you go.
>
> *Puppet Cole*: Knave i' your face, Goodman rogue.
>
> *Pup. Leander*:   Row, row, row, row, row, row.
>   (V.iv.183–187)
>
> *Pup. Jonas*: A pint of sack, score a pint of sack i' the coney.
>
> *Cokes*: Sack? You said but e'en now it should be sherry.
>
> *Pup. Jonas*: Why, so it is: sherry, sherry, sherry.
>
> *Cokes*: Sherry, sherry, sherry. By my troth he makes me merry.
> (205–210)

As Cokes' interjections remind us, we are not the only audience of the puppet-play, and not the only ones lampooned for some type of over-earnestness. Cokes is transported by the language of the play, and follows it with obtuse enthusiasm—his responses to the puppets suggest he hardly recognizes that they are puppets and not actors. Cokes' dim-witted grasp of life matches the puppet-play's inanity; his comedy in the scene chiefly derives from the suitability of the motion's meaninglessness and his own. The other over-earnest observer is Zeal-of-the-Land Busy, the profuse and polemical Puritan "Rabbi." Cokes' earnestness is moronic, while Busy's is humorless and sanctimonious. His utter lack of perspective concerning the puppets augments the sense of language as a game he cannot or, hypocritically, will not play.

Busy loudly interrupts the puppet-play in Act V, scene v, outraged by its immorality. A satiric portrayal of Puritan opprobrium in this setting is conventional—Puritan disapproval of theatrics of any kind was notorious, and as frequently a target in the playhouses as the playhouses themselves were targets of pious condemnations.[34] But Busy responds to the motion as real, not as crude theatrics, confronting the puppets and initiating a "disputation" with them that underscores his inability to treat language as anything but deadly serious, an over-earnestness which in this setting is far more ludicrous than the motion itself. This irony is heightened by the meaninglessness of Busy's own rantings, and by the fact that the disputation becomes its own game of contradiction:

> *Busy:* . . . Yet, I say, his calling, his profession is profane, it is profane, idol.
>
> *Puppet D.:* It is not profane!
>
> *Leatherhead:* It is not profane, he says.
>
> *Busy:* It is profane.
>
> *Puppet D.:* It is not profane.
>
> *Busy:* It is profane.
>
> *Puppet D.:* It is not profane.
>
> *Leatherhead:* (to Puppet Dionysius) Well said, confute him with "not," still. (V.v.67–75)

This is much less of a word-game than the Vapors—it is simply furious and futile contradiction that sends up the contemporary, learned practice of *disputatio* and mocks Busy for his utter humorlessness as well as for the obliviousness with which he participates in a game of disputing with a profane puppet over profanity.

Unlike the generative movement of the Vapors' word-play, V, v's disputation is markedly static—stuck in potentially endless rebuttal, language becomes fully meaningless in an entirely different way than heretofore in the play. This is taken to a comical and provocatively epistemological extreme with Busy's final condemnation of the puppets and their defiance of him on the basis of signification. As his "main argument," Busy levels the period's most infamous, anti-theatrical argument against the puppet-players, that, "you are an abomination; for the male among you putteth on the apparel of the female, and the female of the male."[35] His condemnation is defied by Puppet Dionysius, and then conclusively trumped by a quite literal instance where *nothing* matters:

> Puppet D.: It is your old stale argument against the players, but it will not
> hold against the puppets; for we have neither male nor female amongst
> us. And that thou may'st see, if thou wilt, like a
> malicious purblind zeal as thou art!
> *The puppet takes up his garment.*
> (V.v.103–106)

There is nothing under the puppet's garment, an absence that matters in its confirmation of the puppet's claim and its confutation of Busy's suspicion that there existed 'something' concrete that mattered. What signifies is not language but unambiguous, physical truth, for language always is contestable and we are most absurd when we cannot imagine its inherent gaps. Peter Womack's comments on Jonson's exposure of semiotic instability in a different text apply here in *Bartholomew Fair*, as well, suggesting something characteristic for Jonson in staging such exposures as well as in the questions about language that underlie them:

> The point in this *coup de theatre* is that it releases truth from language
> altogether: the characters concerned are struck dumb, and not merely by
> a verbal representation which is more convincing than their own, but by a
> demonstration which is incontestable because it is wordless.[36]

Language's instabilities are most appropriate for play, and one who resists or defies this understanding is appropriately silenced, as is Busy by this physical 'punch-line' of a moment.

The puppet-play's work as part of the play's ending is not resolution, however. A reading concerned with character or dramatic structure can observe some elements of denouement and reordering as the entire, motley crew of both fairgoers and fair-folk are brought together by the puppet-play and characters like Busy are provoked and chastened. But any larger conclusion importantly is denied by virtue of the motion's projected continuation back at Justice Overdo's house, beyond the limits of the play's final scene:

> *Quarlous:* . . . and remember you are but Adam, flesh and blood! You
> have your frailty; forget your other name of Overdo and invite us
> all to supper . . .
> *Overdo*: I invite you home with me to my house, to supper. I will have
> none fear to go along . . . So lead on.
> *Cokes:* Yes, and bring the actors along, we'll ha' the rest o' the play at
> home. (V.v.96–115 passim)

These last lines, in their invitation to "the actors," strikingly conflate the puppet-play and its stage-Smithfield audience with the larger theater and audience of which it is a mischievous microcosm. This blurring of puppets with actors with audiences with, ultimately, the larger city, extends the Fair's holiday-world and its simultaneously anarchic and utopian insistence that language is play, beyond the bounds of the playhouse. If there is a hint of resignation in this idea, there is also tolerance and generosity.[37] Quarlous' last lines, above, encompass this larger world almost pastorally, while the action's proposed continuation implies that none of this is containable. Playing, of all things, whether onstage or with words, is unpredictable, an uneasy concept which *Bartholomew Fair* re-imagines as humane, festive, and without grave consequence.

BARTHOLOMEW FAIR'S EPILOGUE: A CONCLUSION

The play's outward-looking, un-contained ending is reinforced by the details of its *Epilogue*. The original text and performance were not given one, according to Leah Marcus.[38] For Marcus, this absence means that the play ends with "no reminder of the need to bring the play's license to a close" (175), a reading that attends to *Bartholomew Fair's* incoherence but not to its more interesting existentialism and the ideas about language its "license" compels. Marcus also makes no suggestion about intention, which seems crucial—I contend that the missing *Epilogue* was a deliberate aspect of Jonson's project in the play. Given this distinct choice, the *Epilogue* added for the play's court performance must be read as a re-framing of the play's deliberately inconclusive conclusion. This *Epilogue's* function is not just ceremonious but stabilizing of the play's ambivalence. That is, without changing the plot's ending, the added *Epilogue* does alter the play's gesture toward indefinite play by a dual appeal to sources of authority, one explicit and one implicit:

> You majesty hath seen the play, and you
>> Can best allow it from your ear and view.
> You know the scope of writers, and what store
>> Of leave is given them, if they take not more,
> And turn it into licence. You can tell
>> If we have used that leave you gave us well;
> Or whether we to rage or licence break,
>> Or be profane, or make profane men speak.
> This is your power to judge, great sir, and not
>> The envy of a few. Which if we have got,
> We value less what their dislikes can bring,
>> If it so happy be, t'have pleased the King. (*Epilogue* 1–12)

These lines directly address the King's power as arbiter and tastemaker, and to please the King was an important objective from a political and commercial standpoint, of course. But it is also crucial based on the King's ideological potency as the source of political, religious, and social coherence, a symbolic role the Stuarts' Absolutist doctrine took quite seriously.[39] James' judgment—James himself—returns us to a meaning-full world; to imply incoherence in his presence would be almost treasonous.[40]

More implicitly, the authority of language itself appears to be reinstated by this ceremonial epilogue, with its graceful iambic pentameter lines and encomiastic tone and trajectory. Words like "licence" and "profane," so recently vivid elements of word-games and anarchic defeats of meaning, are now stabilized in the poetic lines of verse and by their implicit connection to the king's solidifying judgment. The conventional appeal to the King or patron for approbation, in the aftermath of this particular play, takes on a heightened sense of such redemption.

Or of disingenuousness. Does the play's deconstructive whimsy in fact extend to the reaches of this *Epilogue*? For the poem also can be seen as an ironic joke on these same conventional sensibilities. Required as a courtly formality (the rules of which Jonson was well aware as a regular producer of masques for the court), the *Epilogue* obediently asserts the necessity of the King's regulating presence even while the play and its ending make clear that such containment is impossible or at least ineffective. There can be no cohering epilogues in a world where language is a game—no words, not even words for or by the King, matter. Looked at closely again, words like "scope" resonate with multiple meanings and connotations, and the "scope of writers" is not so easily pinned down, even in this period of severe censorship. Such an anarchic reading of *Bartholomew Fair's Epilogue* is verified by the very quality of play dominant throughout, I would argue. Ultimately, it can and should be read and interpreted either way, in a final playfulness that seems strangely appropriate: the epilogue serves both as a sincere appeal to containment and as an appealing final joke and final type of word-game to play on everyone, including the King himself. Along with language, everything becomes fair game.

Conclusion

At the end of *Bartholomew Fair*, Rabbi Busy's furious condemnation of the players' gender-bending "abomination" is silenced by the puppet's lifting of his own robe to expose the absence of any distinguishing genitalia, male or female. The scene offers a hilarious demonstration of Busy's zealous absurdity, but it also constitutes an unmasking of the discursive as well as the linguistic, as both the importance of gendered distinctions and of words themselves are defeated by the absolute and wordless signifying of nothing at all beneath the puppet's robe. If Jonson's staging of this moment using puppets seems to trivialize any significance, it is just as possible to view this choice as a way to heighten the grotesqueness and parodic import of this potent comment on the arbitrariness of language.

The centrality of women to early modern confrontations with language questions is a contention underlying my reading of three city comedies' staging and organizing of London. At a time when the city, the vernacular, and the public and private roles of women all were perceived as changing and expanding, city comedy is a key literary form for exploring the linkage of language and gender in early modern culture. As we have observed, both *Epicoene*'s and *The Roaring Girl*'s depictions of London hinge on women and their relationship to vernacular speech as well as urban languages such as the sartorial and the underworld dialect of cant. Where, then, does *Bartholomew Fair* belong in this generic hypothesis, with its playful but nonetheless radical critique, particularly via Busy and the puppets at the end of the play? As discussed at length in chapter four, above, *Bartholomew Fair*'s most important contribution to city comedy's nexus of language and the city is its surprisingly relaxed postulation of language as a game, and when all language is a game, the speech of both men and women, as well as social discourse between them, also is only a game. The result is a diminution of gender as a critical and problematic element of parsing the city. Grace Wellborn's selection of a husband, discussed above in chapter four, serves emblematically on this point, as the match between Grace and Winwife is dispatched by a contest of arbitrary words. Grace is the least egregious linguistic offender in *Bartholomew Fair*, but this does not exclude her, a member of the fair-world for the day, from participating fully in the language this world rests upon, nor is she any more or less authoritative in her participation than anyone else. Men and women all play these games, and there can be no serious concerns at the heart of language that does not matter. *Bartholomew Fair*, it seems, takes city comedy's generic concern for language and the city to a parodic extreme where this concern, and indeed any stable category of meaning, evaporates.

But if *Bartholomew Fair* defuses the centrality of gender to a thesis regarding city comedy's engagement with the city and the vernacular, its reveling in the arbitrariness of language, including the stark defeat of linguistic signification, helps illuminate the extent to which its fellows in this study also toy with this more radical critique. My study concludes by revisiting these plays in order to bring out the significant recurrence of unmasking moments analogous to *Bartholomew Fair*'s with Rabbi Busy, each of which depends upon gender discourse to expose the limits of such discourse as well as of language itself. A brief consideration, finally, of Jonson's late play, *The Staple of News* (1626), weighs the question of whether such preoccupation with and distinctive staging of the city in terms of the linguistic were a Jacobean phenomenon or belong to a broader slice of seventeenth-century dramatic sensibilities.

Unmasking onstage traditionally signals the revelation of a true identity to an assembled company ignorant of this truth up till now. A commonplace of comedy, the unmasking that typically occurs near the end of a play plays a crucial role in the reordering—often including a return to properly gendered social coherence—that must conclude the action. It is striking, then, to note Jonson's unmasking of a puppet in *Bartholomew Fair*, and its effect not simply of disrupting re-order but of interrogating the very linguistic and discursive bases of order and re-order. In *Epicoene* and *The Roaring Girl*, distinct as these plays are from each other and from their later fellow in this study, we also find unmasking scenes which challenge re-order on several levels.

The notorious unmasking at the end of *Epicoene* complexly confronts discursive gender, only to ultimately suggest its insignificance in the face of other factors of apparent coherence. Morose's objections to his new bride, the ideal "silent woman," stem from her equally stereotypical loquacity once married, and he first seeks to annul this disastrous union via a claim of impotence: "Morose: 'Ladies, I must crave all your pardons—for a wrong I have done to your whole sex . . . being guilty of an infirmity which . . . I thought I might have concealed—I am no man, ladies" (V.iv.29–38). Morose's explicit unmanning of himself, here, and the subsequent attempt to disallow the marriage based on Epicoene's apparent promiscuity both signal the preeminence of discourses of male and female sexuality and roles in marriage. The very constructed nature of what it is to be a man or a woman, hinted at in Morose's "I am no man," is made strikingly clear in the next moment, as Epicoene is revealed to be a boy, his womanhood literally a performance. With the removal of the boy's "peruke," or wig, and the unambiguous physical display of a young boy's head and features, "woman" (and "man") is revealed as purely discursive, but words also are suddenly irrelevant in the face, literally, of this concrete signification. Indeed, the dialogue and apparent plot of the entire play are rendered shockingly superfluous with the exposure of Dauphine's/Jonson's super-plot. J.A. Jackson has described *Epicoene* as Jonson's deconstruction of the traditional comedy of humors via its conclusion's revelations to the audience both onstage and off: "This tearing apart of illusion . . . is . . . a reminder of the illusion in which the audience participates" (J.A. Jackson 3). This unmasking moment is a naming of illusion as illusion, and equally a revelation of words, names, language, and the discourses by which we think we know what to expect, as illusive and arbitrary. We are given a "staging and unraveling of manifold expectations—from gender roles to Jonsonian theatrical construction to language in general" (J.A. Jackson 13), according to Jackson, a claim which buttresses my reading of the play's deep concern for women's role in shaping the vernacular and urban life, but points the way, as well, to a more deconstructive appraisal of the play's interests. *Epicoene*'s unmasking moment and its implications render the play's final critique of language as radical as *Bartholomew Fair*'s.

The Roaring Girl confronts the inconsistency, the instability, and the injustice of contemporary, urban, gender discourse throughout its action, but it too, upon re-visiting, stages a final unmasking scene where more than just a true identity is revealed. As with *Epicoene*, and typically for the comedic plot conventions of the play, the unmasking takes place in the final scene, when Moll first is presented in women's clothing and a mask as Sebastian's choice of bride. Welcomed heartily by all based on this appearance, especially Sebastian's snobbish father, this bride is then revealed to be the notorious Moll and immediately rejected by Sir Alexander as a result of this unmasking. This moment's comedy and function in the play's love-plot are straightforward, but the unmasking offers a nuanced comment regarding semiotic instability, gender roles, and discursive/dramatic expectations very near the end of the play.

The primary butt of this unmasking moment is Sir Alexander, whose priggish snobbery and self-regarding judgments of others, especially Moll, have served as foil to Moll's individualism and the lovers' plot throughout the play. The narrow-minded condemnation of Moll by Sir Alexander in this scene is nothing new. What is new is the way Moll is presented several different ways over the course of the scene and the resulting comment on appearance and identity created by more than one level of masking and unmasking. For example, and as noted in chapter three, when Moll enters in women's clothing and masked, she both is and is not truly in disguise. She is, after all, female, thus appearing in women's clothes is in an important sense no mask at all for her. What is masked, here, is her personal identity in favor of the social identity of a young, marriageable woman, the latter immediately and enthusiastically accepted by all present, based on what Moll displays sartorially. Moll is thus in disguise as what she explicitly has chosen not to be up till now: a female cipher whose only pertinent signification is the social identity awarded her by others, especially men. That this social identity entirely concerns display—the sartorial—and seems importantly anonymous is made clear by Sir Alexander's pleased comment upon seeing Moll enter in this disguise: "Now has [Sebastian] pleased me right. I always counseled him/ To choose a goodly personable creature: / Just of her pitch was my first wife, his mother (V.ii.130–132). Moll's unmasking, then, operates on several levels, as her revealed personal identity immediately will destroy this anonymous but privileged social identity, and we are given another opportunity to consider the slippery disjunctions between sartorial as well as discursive representation and identity. The scene concludes as a moralizing commentary concerning the judgmental self-regard of figures like Sir Alexander, but such a conventional resolution cannot fully disrupt the implications of the scene's unmasking, not just of Moll, but of the instability of the sartorial and the discursive as signifiers, and of the problem of trust in such signifiers as absolute truths.

In addition to this concluding scene's work, *The Roaring Girl* includes another scene that is provocatively overt as an unmasking of linguistic indeterminacy. Midway through Act V, scene i, the play's famous canting scene (discussed above in chapter three), Moll's swaggering confidence as a translator and teacher of cant to her gentlemen companions is momentarily but importantly shaken by some of Trapdoor's words:

Moll: [*To Trapdoor*] Come, you rogue, cant with me . . .

Trapdoor: I'll have a bout if she please.

Moll: Come on, sirrah.

Trapdoor: Ben mort, shall you and I heave a booth, mill a ken, or nip
     a bung?

> And then you'll couch a hogshead under the ruffmans, and there you shall wap with me, and I'll niggle with you.

Moll: Out, you damned impudent rascal! [*Hits and kicks him.*] . . .

Lord Noland: Nay, nay, Moll, why art thou angry? What was his gibberish?

Moll: Marry, this, my lord, says he: 'Ben mort'—good wench—'shall you and I heave a booth, mill a ken, or nip a bung?'—shall you and I rob a house, or cut a purse? . . . 'And then we'll couch a hogshead under the ruffmans,'—and then we'll lie under a hedge . . . 'And there you shall wap with me, and I'll niggle with you.'—and that's all.

Sir Beauteous: Nay, nay, Moll, what's that wap?

Dapper: Nay, teach me what niggling is; I'd fain be niggling.
(V.i.182–208)

Trapdoor outrages Moll by mentioning "wapping" and "niggling," two canting words she bashfully refuses to translate. William West comments on this moment in which cant, for all its apparent otherness, serves as a tool for Moll's re-inscription into the binary of gender roles, her refusal to translate prurient words a feminine demurring in the company of men (West 244–245). Moll is momentarily unmasked, then, but so is cant's purported threat to vernacular and social coherence as it functions, here, as hegemonically as any discourse. Even more significant an unmasking operates in the way Trapdoor finally offers a definition for wapping and niggling as "fadoodling." West explains: "So obvious seems the sexual meaning of the terms wapping, niggling, and fadoodling that it is startling to learn that it is illusory. Wapping is not in fact fadoodling, since fadoodling means "nothing"" (245). The scene—and the dynamic between both Trapdoor and Moll and Moll and the gentlemen—shifts in meaning depending on whether or not they, and we ourselves, recognize the joke that "fadoodling" is not a word at all. The word functions as a marker of distinction between people, dividing them according to how they understand it; the fact that it is a nonsense word which serves in this capacity further underlines the arbitrariness of all language.

While limiting its reading of city comedies to three important works, this study has raised the question of a generic project of staging the city as a set of linguistic or semiotic problems. Further work remains, certainly, to establish this reading as an authoritative hypothesis. One pertinent question for such a task is where the boundary lies, in time and mood, marking the conclusion of the era and the concerns of city comedy. One recent scholar has chosen to focus exclusively on the decade from 1603–1613 for his reading of the genre. Theodore Leinwand argues that it is within these years that we see not only a preponderance of Jacobean city comedies, but also a group of plays all self-consciously concerned with status or class differences. Leinwand admits the relative arbitrariness of his timeline; it rests mainly on his decision to exclude *Bartholomew Fair* (1614) from his consideration and thesis. But if this relatively late and unique play is included, as I would argue it must be, where might city comedy's generic project conclude? In city comedy I am suggesting the convergence of setting and a topicality of broad linguistic interrogation, including of the metaphysical and semiotic, that demands some further testing as to its status as a Jacobean phenomenon.[1] Jonson's *The Staple of News*, a Caroline-era play that marked the playwright's return to the public stage as well as to an urban London scene, on both counts after a lengthy hiatus, provides the means for such a test.[2]

Critics find a clear link between Jonson's 1620 masque at court, *News from the New World*, and *The Staple of News*, the latter play returning to and expanding upon the masque's mention of a "staple of news . . . /whither all shall be brought, and thence again/ vented under the name of Staple-news" (45–47).[3] The masque's setting is the moon, in keeping with the Jacobean court's appetite for the fantastic, but when Jonson takes up the burgeoning new discourse of "news" a second time, he seems pointedly to have chosen a cityscape in order to, once again, stage a language-scape. This reprisal makes a suggestive link to the Jacobean plays, however *The Staple* possesses other qualities which at first appear to distance it not only from other city comedies but even from much of the rest of Jonson's comedic works. The play long has puzzled and dissatisfied critics by what has been seen as an awkward mixture of dramatic modes and an atypical sentimentality and didacticism in its denouement.[4] Jonson introduces a moral allegory into a New Comedy plot set in quotidian London, as, with little subtlety, a young heir and his disguised and disapproving father, a group of upstart newsmen, trades-people, and a miser are joined by an elaborate depiction of money in the desired and vulnerable figure of Lady Aurelia Clara Pecunia Do-all. Distinct from the vertiginous irony that concludes *Epicoene* or the anarchic dilation at the end of *Bartholomew Fair*, *The Staple of News* concludes with a conventional paean to the virtues and rewards of moderation, with the chastened and reformed prodigal heir, Pennyboy Junior, now equipped to treat his bride, Pecunia, decorously and wisely:

Pennyboy Senior: And lastly, to my Nephew,
                    I give my house, goods, lands, all but my vices,

> And those I go to cleanse; kissing this Lady,
> Whom I do give him too, and joyne their hands.

Pennyboy Canter: If the spectators will joyne theirs, we thank 'hem.

Pennyboy Junior: And wish they may, as I, enjoy Pecunia.

Pecunia: And so Pecunia her self doth wish,
> That she may still be aid unto their uses,
> Not slave unto their pleasures, or a Tyrant
> Over their fair desires; but teach them all
> The golden mean: the Prodigal how to live,
> The sordid, and the covetous, how to die:

> That with sound mind; this, safe frugality.[5] (V.vi.54–66)

Though in other literary contexts Jonson is famously attentive to decorum and the judicious, as the final lines of one of his comedies these are surprisingly conventional. The play makes explicit use of an unmasking, but with none of the complexity with which, as we have seen, the three Jacobean city comedies address gender, identity, and language. Pennyboy Canter, father to the prodigal and disguised until Act IV in order to observe his son's behavior, finally is provoked by his son's indiscretions into revealing his true identity and rectifying the abuses he incredulously has witnessed. While the unmaskings surveyed above toy with the new coherence their revelations conventionally should offer, if anything signaling further incoherence, the unmasking of Pennyboy Canter, by contrast, appears neatly to defeat the excesses of the news-Staple, the "jeerers" who run it, and the proposed "Canter's College" Junior wishes to found. In these ways *The Staple of News* appears to diverge widely from the earlier comedies, suggesting that they and their concerns are indeed part of a relatively brief, Jacobean moment that did not extend into the 1620's. And yet, while this later play's apparent omissions and diminutions suggest a delimiting of city comedy and the particular nexus of city and vernacular as a Jacobean phenomenon, *The Staple of News* offers important evidence of an abiding, connected concern for urban coherence and linguistic coherence for Ben Jonson, in a later moment still prompting him to reprise these imbrications with a play whose range of disjunctions in fact constitute his most totalized query of language, discourse, and coherence in the city.

Amid the play's allegory and prodigal plot, its most vivid feature is its concern with the "varying ramifications of language" (Sanders "Republics" 136), as depicted in the trio of the Staple of news itself, the society of jeerers who also serve as Staple reporters, and the proposed Canter's College. Commenting on past critical querying of the play's incongruencies, Richard

Levin has argued for the central importance of these three linguistic institutions to the main plot's emphasis on the perils of excess. In a sequence from the news-Staple to the jeerers' meaningless noise to the proposal of the college, each represents a further expression of Pennyboy Junior's prodigality (R. Levin, "Staple" 450). Levin is keen to see these language features as coherently united with the less critically-regarded allegory in the play (445), but it is equally important to note the constant threat to both dramatic and linguistic coherence they pose. As Julie Sanders has argued concerning the play's treatment of language: "Language carries the potential of unifying but also of disunifying and Jonson appears fascinated by the factions of language that occur in any number of different and disparate communities" (Sanders, "Republics" 137). This claim could be made for all of Jonson's comedies, but with *The Staple's* focus on "news," language—in all its ambiguities—finally has become a sheer commodity in a completely superficial market.

The action of the play is, in fact, completely fragmented by different "factions of language," both from within and from without. Not only do we have the superficial and utterly new discourse of news, the vapors-like noise of the jeerers, and the projected institutionalization of a college for content-less city jargons, but throughout all five acts of the play the action is interrupted by a group of "Gossips," older women whose unsophisticated and highly colloquial responses constitute yet another language-texture of the play's London scene. The gossips' role most vividly illustrates an aspect of all of these urban languages in the play: they go on practically simultaneously, competing for our attention and contacting one another almost not at all. Thus the city is a texture of languages, but the only unifying they do is to commonly underline this competitive and commodity-driven urban world where everything, especially language, is a thing. The first scenes of the play accordingly depict the progress of Pennyboy Junior's excessive spending on a new suit, cloak, hat, boots, spurs, and, finally, the news. Pennyboy's visit to the Staple-office is that of a customer to a market, where he can choose among news "Authenticall," "Apocryphal," "Barber news," "Taylors news, Porters, and Watermens news," "Vacation news, Terme news, and Christmas news," "news o'the faction," "Reformed news, Protestant news, and Pontifical news" (I.v.8–15). Critics' attention to *The Staple's* allegory of Lady Pecunia has emphasized its awkward distance from the urban, quasi-realism of commodification described above, or, as in Levin's argument, attempted to view the play's treatment of language as a component of the allegory's peremptory message regarding excess. The play's language and its allegory indeed are linked in the play, but rather in the way that the allegory additionally functions as part of the play's reduction of the city to things. Karen Newman points out, for example, that in *The Staple of News*, allegorical characters such as Lady Pecunia and her retinue symbolize things instead of the moral values and psychological states more typical of allegory (Newman, "Engendering" 60). Newman articulates *The Staple's* distinction:

> Whereas the pressure of allegory is always towards abstraction, in Jonson's play there is a continual slippage from the intangible or general to the material and concrete . . . Jonson's allegorical figures are material—reifications, things, part and parcel of the growing commodity culture of early seventeenth-century London. (Newman, "Engendering" 60–61)

The manifold significance of this difference involves not only a further commodified portrayal of the play's London setting, but also a meta-discursive suggestion that allegory itself is but another thing. Jonson's inclusion of allegory in *The Staple* should be seen not as the anxious and questionable move of a poet faltering in his confidence, but as the resonant choice of an artist-critic intent on depicting the utter commodification of his urban world.

Critic Raphael Shargel reads *The Staple of News* as a crucial extension of Jonson's interests and practices in the better-known and respected middle comedies. According to Shargel, Jonson's first Caroline production offers not yet a departure from earlier work, but, "for the last time in his career," a continuation of the experiments of the Jacobean plays (Shargel 68), in particular "the depiction of conflict without resolution" (Shargel 47). Such a recurring aesthetic for staging the city is most importantly linguistic, I have argued. And in *The Staple of News* we are offered perhaps Jonson's most complete depiction of the city as a contention of linguistic practices, indeed as a contentious market of linguistic commodities, whose irresolution emphasizes an indeterminacy, by now familiar, which is social, discursive, and linguistic.

The dramatic content of the play—with the Staple office; the news and jeering scenes in acts three and four, particularly; and the proposal of the canter's college—offers a bounty of language battles and signals *The Staple's* affinity with the middle comedies. Jonson goes one better with *The Staple,* however, extending the expansiveness and contention beyond content to form. Shargel takes on others' attempts to make sense of or dismiss *The Staple's* aesthetic disjointedness by arguing that in the play's very shape and structure Jonson intentionally is creating contradiction: "[H]ere is an equally tense conflict between dramatic traditions, as if the generic character of the play were in sympathy with its chaotic action. Realism and allegory lock horns, but like other figures of contention in Jonson's ungovernable city, each fails to triumph over or fully to extricate itself from the world of its adversary" (Shargel 47). The play's figuring of society as a competition of sheer words is thus doubled on the discursive level: the real significance of Jonson's allegory or New Comedy plot or satirical realism lies in the unresolved dialectic created between these distinct modes, throughout, with the Gossips' Intermeans providing even further, structural, contention that is both within and without the play. The play's final scene appears to effect a unifying and conventional recuperation of the prodigal, as discussed above, but even this feels oddly superimposed on the other culminations, which include Pennyboy Senior's furious, oral examination of his dogs and the return of the Jeerers/news-emissaries, whose noise and news-mongering now are explicitly and cheerfully collapsed:

> Almanac: Let's upon him,
>   And if we cannot jeer him down in wit,
> Madrigal: Let's do't in noise. (V.v.21–23)

The jeerers disperse at the end of this penultimate scene, but the odd, artificiality of the final scene's moralizing only adds to the underlying sense that news and noise still will proliferate and, in any case, that the main point is the disjunction here enacted. Shargel describes the play's "representational extremes" and shifting of "generic cloaks," which push inconsistency, as well as the audience's expectations, vividly into the foreground (Shargel 47), finding this extreme featuring of contradiction a triumph of a dramatic inconclusiveness he traces through Jonson's Jacobean middle period. But it is crucial to recognize, as well, the discursive nature of these generic contradictions, and the linguistic inconclusiveness played out as part of dramatic incoherence. *The Staple of News'* rendering of contradiction on the structural, discursive, and linguistic level enacts an inconclusiveness that is the ultimate unmasking in its deconstructive inclusion of the author himself in contentions which he may not arbitrate from a position outside. All, including the play and its author, are caught up in an inconclusiveness that perhaps is city comedy's most potent emblem of language and city.

    The Staple of News thus is a provocative iteration of the nexus of concerns and expression identified here with Jacobean city comedy, but perhaps the play serves most importantly as a key to an updated understanding of Jonson himself. Shargel avers that *The Staple of News* should be "recognize[d] . . . as a linchpin in the Jonson canon" (Shargel 48), underlining the value of reassessing the play's (and Jonson's) continuities and discontinuities. As surveyed here, even the play's radical departures in fact participate in the further exploration of the role and possibilities for language in society that is crucial to recognize. Jonson was an active theorist of language-and-society whose range of works, including his popular city comedies, all were occasions for distinct but connected theoretical expositions. The understandable but misguided tradition of treating Jonson the neoclassical poet and rhetorical stylist separately from Jonson the Juvenalian satirist, Jonson the courtly masque-poet, and Jonson the minutely observant city critic, may be corrected by the realization of Jonson's all-encompassing and lifelong interest—sophisticatedly, enthusiastically, and anxiously—in one of the central concerns of his time and place: the English vernacular's place in an ever more diffuse, urban society.

Notes

NOTES TO THE INTRODUCTION

1. Ben Jonson, *Ben Jonson*, ed. C.H. Herford and Percy and Evelyn Simpson, vol. 8 (Oxford: Clarendon Press, 1966) 465, 504. All subsequent references to *The English Grammar* and *Discoveries* will be to this edition, and will be parenthetical.

2. This view of London is shared by a wide range of literary, historical, and cultural studies critics. See Susan Wells, *The Dialectics of Representation* (Baltimore and London: Johns Hopkins University Press, 1985) 102–132; Lawrence Manley, "From Matron to Monster: Tudor-Stuart London and the Languages of Urban Description," *The Historical Renaissance: New Essays on Tudor and Stuart Literature and Culture,* ed. Heather Dubrow and Richard Strier (Chicago and London: University of Chicago Press, 1988) 347–374. For a collection of essays predicated on London's urban materialism and complexity at the turn of the sixteenth century, see Lena Cowen Orlin, ed. *Material London, ca. 1600* (Philadephia: University of Pennsylvania Press, 2000. For more strictly historical studies of the period, see Joseph Ward, *Metropolitan Communities: Trade Guilds, Identity, and Change in Early Modern London* (Palo Alto, CA: Stanford University Press, 1997); Keith Wrightson, *English Society 1580–1680* (London: Hutchinson and Co., 1982).

3. See Richard Foster Jones, *The Triumph of the English Language: A Survey of Opinions Concerning the Vernacular from the Introduction of Printing to the Restoration* (Palo Alto, CA: Stanford University Press, 1953) for an early and influential study from which subsequent work derives. More recently, see Richard Bailey, *Images of English: A Cultural History of the Language* (Ann Arbor: University of Michigan Press, 1991); Charles Laurence Barber, *Early Modern English* (1977) (Edinburgh: Edinburgh University Press, 1997); John Earl Joseph, *Eloquence and Power: The Rise of Language Standards and Standard Languages* (London: Frances Pinter, 1987); James Milroy and Lesley Milroy, *Authority in Language: Investigating Language Prescription and Standardization* (London, Boston: Routledge and K.Paul, 1985). For a

recent literary treatment of this question of the language in transition, see
Paula Blank, *Broken English:Dialects and the Politics of Language in Renaissance Writings* (London and New York: Routledge, 1996).

4. Ben Jonson, *Ben Jonson*, ed. C.H. Herford and Percy and Evelyn Simpson, 11
    volumes (Oxford: Clarendon Press, 1966). Thomas Middleton and Thomas
    Dekker, *The Roaring Girl*, ed. Paul Mulholland (Manchester: Manchester Uni-
    versity Press, 1987). For additional dramatic works of Middleton and Dekker,
    respectively, see Thomas Middleton, *The Works of Thomas Middleton*, ed. A.H.
    Bullen, 8 volumes (Boston:Houghton-Mifflin, 1885–1886); Thomas Dekker,
    The Dramatic Works of Thomas Dekker, ed. Fredson Bowers, 4 volumes (Cam-
    bridge: Cambridge University Press, 1953–1961).

5. That literary works are complex artifacts of culture is today a commonplace,
    due to the influence of New Historicist/Cultural Poetics theory and criticism.
    Steven Mullaney, writing when this materialist turn was gaining momentum,
    describes a shift in his approach to literature's function. In the introduction to
    The Place of the Stage: License, Play, and Power in Renaissance England (1988),
    he explains: "I have sought to view the popular stage not merely . . . as a
    literary phenomenon but as one of a diverse body of cultural practices." And,
    he asserts, "Literature itself is conceived neither as a separate and separable aes-
    thetic realm nor as a mere product of culture, but as one realm among many for
    the negotiation and production of . . . meaning" (5). Mullaney is interested
    in the various discursive and non-discursive ways in which a society 'makes
    sense of itself, to itself,' and argues that the stage was a crucial and crucially
    discursive site for this.

    Karen Newman poses the question "How was femininity fashioned and
    deployed in early modern England?"(xvii), and homes in on drama, explaining
    her focus, "because I argue that drama, as spectacle, provided a peculiarly use-
    ful locus for analyzing the production and management of femininity in early
    modern England" (xx). The theater as a locus of discursive production works
    on a range of levels. In *The Stage and Social Struggle in Early Modern England*
    (1994), Jean Howard examines the appearance, role and significance of "the-
    atricality" in the period, what she describes as a "discourse of theatricality" that
    did ideological work in its society. Explaining her specific focus on the theater,
    Howard notes "the unique role of the public theater in ideological production
    in Renaissance England" (3), and goes on to consider some of the implications
    of thinking about the institution in this way. In a comment that to me points
    to why language in drama should be re-considered, she adds, "The secular pub-
    lic theater was a relatively new institution in Renaissance culture, and the plays
    produced for that theater reflect a heightened self-consciousness about what it
    means to create fictions, to manipulate audiences, and to negotiate between
    the lived world and discursive representation of it" (10).

    See Steven Mullaney, *The Place of the Stage: License, Play and Power in
    Renaissance England*, 2nd edition (Ann Arbor: University of Michigan

Press, 1995); Karen Newman, *Fashioning Femininity and English Renaissance Drama* (Chicago and London: University of Chicago Press, 1991); *The Stage and Social Struggle in Early Modern England* (London: Routledge, 1994). See also Louis Adrian Montrose, *The Purpose of Playing: Shakespeare and the Cultural Politics of the Elizabethan Theatre.* (Chicago: University of Chicago Press, 1996); Montrose has been one of the more influential proponents and theorists of the New Historicism.

6. Blank, *Broken English* 1. Lynda Mugglestone's work on attitudes toward accent in spoken English is also relevant here on the subject of "attitudes toward English," which draws attention from literary project's like Blank's as well as the fields of historical-linguistics, socio-linguistics, and critical linguistics, with its focus on ideologies of language. See Lynda Mugglestone, *'Talking Proper': The Rise of Accent as Social Symbol*, 2nd edition (Oxford and New York: Oxford University Press, 2003).

7. Crowley and Taylor provide a series description page in the prefatory pages of Blank's book, which is a volume in "The Politics of Language" series from Routledge. On the series title-page, Crowley and Taylor caption the series with an unidentified passage from Saussure: "In the lives of individuals and societies, language is a factor of greater importance than any other. For the study of language to remain solely the business of a handful of specialists would be a quite unacceptable state of affairs."

8. The tension Greene characterizes between the calibrated and the shifting self Peter Womack has re-considered from the perspective of the linguistic. Womack proceeds from the Bakhtinian concepts of monologism, dialogism, and the phenomenon of Renaissance heteroglossia to characterize the tension evident in Jonson as a desire for monologism in the face of a dialogical world. Blank has since challenged Bakhtin's notion of heteroglossia as overly romantic, but Womack's argument nevertheless offers an additional lens by which to consider the contradictions between *Discoveries* and the comedies. See Peter Womack, *Ben Jonson* (New York: B. Blackwell, 1987) "Introduction" and 79–85.

9. *The Grammar* and *Discoveries* both were published in the 1640 *Works* of Jonson, a second volume following the 1616 *Works.* As such, they appear significantly later than the major plays and might be considered extraneous, however the *Grammar* was probably composed much earlier, its first version destroyed in a catastrophic fire in Jonson's house in 1623. *Discoveries*, a kind of commonplace book of accumulated adages, can be seen to span Jonson's career in the background of his more public iterations.

10. Jonas Barish, *Ben Jonson and the Language of Prose Comedy* (Cambridge: Harvard University Press, 1960) especially 41–89; L.C. Knights, *Drama and Society in the Age of Jonson* (London: Chatto & Windus, 1937).

11. Douglas Lanier, "Masculine Silence: *Epicoene* and Jonsonian Stylistics," *College Literature* 21.2 (June 1994):1–18. Lanier references earlier work by Stanley

Fish that signals the evolution in Jonsonian criticism made even more vivid in Lanier. See Stanley Fish, "Authors-Readers: Jonson's Community of the Same." *Representations* 7 (Summer 1984): 26–58.

12. Many critics have been interested in comparing Shakespeare with city comedy; Barish's landmark study includes a lengthy and detailed comparison. The reliable result has often been a reduction of city comedy's purview to the narrowly local or simply satirical next to Shakespeare's Ciceronian fullness and expansive scope beyond the local and the commercial. Jean Howard addresses this problem: "The continuing monumental presence of Shakespeare within our curriculum and our culture function both as an incitement and a prohibition to scholarly work . . . If he does not deal with an issue, too often it gets ignored, leading to a partial picture of the field we study. . . . If we want to study dramatic depictions of London's shopkeepers and their wives, we need to look elsewhere [than Shakespeare.] If we want to explore mappings of city space and the complex social relations within the city, again, we need to look elsewhere" (15–16). See Jean Howard, "Shakespeare and the London of City Comedy." *Shakespeare Studies* 39 (2001): 1–21. The resurgence of critical interest in city comedy has created a turn within Shakespeare studies toward seeking traces of city comedy's urban sensibilities in Shakespeare's works, heretofore seen as almost entirely distant from any kind of specifically local ethos. For one recent study in this vein, see John Michael Archer, *Citizen Shakespeare: Freemen and Aliens in the Language of the Plays* (London: Palgrave/Macmillan, 2005).

13. Brian Gibbons, *Jacobean City Comedy. A Study of Satiric Plays by Jonson, Marston and Middleton* (London: Methuen, 1968, rev. ed. 1980) 11. Gibbons' seminal status for contemporary thought about city comedy is described in the introduction to a recent anthology of new work on city comedy, in which the authors and co-editors memorably use the phrase "sordid realism" to characterize city comedies' urban depictions. See Dieter Mehl, Angela Stock, and Anne-Julie Zwierlein, eds., "Introduction," *Plotting Early Modern London: New Essays on Jacobean City Comedy* (Aldershot, Hants. And Burlington, VT: Ashgate Press, 2004) 3.

14. Major studies include Gibbons (1968); Lawrence Manley, *Literature and Culture in Early Modern London* (Cambridge: Cambridge University Press, 1995); Matthew R. Martin, *Between Theater and Philosophy: Skepticism in the Major City Comedies of Ben Jonson and Thomas Middleton* (Newark, DE: University of Delaware Press, 2001); and Gail Kern Paster, *The Idea of the City in the Age of Shakespeare* (Athens, GA: University of Georgia Press, 1985). Recent dissertations include: Carol Lise Hayes, *Mapping City Comedy: Topographies of London and the Anomalous Woman*, diss., University of California—Irvine, 2000 (Ann Arbor: UMI, 2002); Juana Irene Greene, *Desired Properties: Materializing and Managing Social Relations in Early Modern City Comedy*, diss., Columbia University, 1999 (Ann Arbor: UMI,

2002); Judith Kovacs Mandy, *City Women: Daughters, Wives, Widows and Whores in Jacobean and Restoration City Comedy*, diss., Lehigh University, 1996 (Ann Arbor: UMI, 2002); Virginia Lee Larsen, *Thomas Middleton as Social Critic: A Study of Three Plays*, diss., University of California—Santa Cruz, 1995 (Ann Arbor: UMI, 2002); Herbert Jack Heller, *Penitent Brothellers: Grace, Sexuality, and Genre in Thomas Middleton's City Comedies*, diss., Louisiana State University, 1997 (Ann Arbor: UMI, 2002).

15. Wells 105, 106–118 passim.

16. Jean Howard, "Women, Foreigners, and the Regulation of Space in *Westward Ho*," *Material London, ca. 1600*, ed. Lena Cowen Orlin (Philadelphia: University of Pennsylvania Press, 2000) 152.

17. Edmund Spenser, *The Works of Edmund Spenser: A Variorum Edition*, ed. Edwin Greenlaw et al., 11 vols. (Baltimore: Johns Hopkins Press, 1932–57) 10.16. Richard Helgerson, in *Forms of Nationhood*, famously seized upon this phrase of Spenser's as one emblem of the generational, nationalist project his book hypothesizes. Helgerson's interest is in tracing a distinctly nationalistic, literary impulse among a group of Elizabethans, and while his focus suggests interest in the profound implications of English standardization for this purportedly national project, Helgerson never actually confronts the nuances of vernacular debates. Richard Helgerson, *Forms of Nationhood: The Elizabethan Writing of England* (Chicago: University of Chicago Press, 1992).

18. This value is implicit, for example, in Hardin Aasand's recent review of Martin, in which he describes critical interest in city comedy as "a product of a Jacobean London in the throes of emergent capitalism that challenged social order and stability" (947). See Aasand, Rev. 947–948.

19. See note 3, above. Milroy and Milroy's focus continues to be aspects of linguistic prescription and related matters of linguistic authority. Jones and, currently, Bailey, as historians of perceptions, or "images of English," provide the most relevant historical-linguistic discussions to a project such as mine.

20. Jones quoted in Juliet Fleming, "Dictionary English and the Female Tongue," *Privileging Gender in Early Modern England*, ed. Jean R. Brink. *Sixteenth-Century Essays and Studies* 23: 175–204.

21. Paula Blank, "Languages of early modern literature in Britain," *The Cambridge History of Early Modern English Literature*, ed. David Loewenstein and Janel Mueller (Cambridge University Press, 2002) 141. Blank's work, beginning in 1996 with the publication of *Broken English* (see note 3 above), has offered a valuable corrective to earlier critical celebrations of Renaissance linguistic "exuberance." For an example of this earlier stance, see Jane Donaworth, *Shakespeare and the 16ᵗʰ Century Study of Language* (Urbana, IL: University of Illinois Press, 1984).

22. Helene Cixous, *The Laugh of the Medusa*, transl. Keith Cohen and Paula Cohen *Signs* 1, No. 4 (1976 Summer): 875–893; Luce Irigaray, *This Sex Which is Not One*, transl. Catherine Porter with Carolyn Burke (Ithaca, NY:

Cornell University Press, 1985); Julia Kristeva, "The Semiotic and the Symbolic" (1984) *The Women and Language Debate: A Sourcebook*, eds. Camille Roman, Suzanne Juhasz, and Christianne Miller (New Brunswick: Rutgers University Press, 1994). In addition to Kristeva's essay, both Cixous' and Irigaray's works, listed above, are anthologized in this sourcebook, compiled by gender and language scholars Roman, Juhasz, and Miller in the mid-1990s and indicative of gender and language studies' emergence as a field.

23. On systems of gender in grammar, see Suzanne Romaine, *Communicating Gender* (New Jersey, London: Erlbaum, 1999); George Lakoff, *Women, Fire, and Dangerous Things: What Categories Reveal about the Mind* (Chicago, London: University of Chicago Press, 1987). On gender and language, including the lexicon, see Dale Spender, *Man Made Language* (London: Routledge & Kegan Paul 1980); Anne Curzan, "Gender Categories in Early English Grammars: Their Message to the Modern Grammarian" in B. Unterbeck and M. Rissanen, eds. *Gender in Grammar and Cognition*, Volume 2 (Berlin: Mouton de Gruyter, 1999) 561–576.

24. Deborah Cameron is the most well-known scholar among sociolinguists working on gender and language, though her interests are not limited to the sociolinguistic. She is the editor of the most influential and widely used published work in gender and language studies, to date, now in a second edition. See Deborah Cameron, ed., *The Feminist Critique of Language: A Reader* (London, New York: Routledge, 1990). See also: Mugglestone 1995; Robin Lakoff, *Language and Women's Place* (New York: Harper & Row, 1975); Mary Crawford, *Talking Difference: On Gender and Language* (London: Sage, 1995).

25. Mugglestone 206. See also note 6 above.

26. Mugglestone 168. For earlier work on this subject, see Diana Bornstein, "As Meek as a Maid: A Historical Perspective on Language for Women in Courtesy Books from the Middle Ages to *Seventeen* Magazine," *Women's Language and Style*, eds. Douglas Butturff and Edmund Epstein (Akron, OH: LRS Books, 1978)132–138.

27. Fleming 141. With this notion, Fleming implicitly gestures to the sophisticated materialism of Raymond Williams, whose work Margaret Ferguson directly indicates as central to her work on the imbrications of imperialism and literacy (see note 41 above). Ferguson offers a usefully succinct encapsulation of Williams' ideas and their significance to work on language and literacy debates:

> Many scholars . . . understand standardization in language as a self-evident notion, a reference . . . to a set of facts about language . . . Other theorists, however, hold with Raymond Williams that a standard language occurs when "a selected usage becomes authoritative," providing a model of "correctness, which, widely backed by educational institutions," works to "convict a

majority of native speakers . . . of speaking their own language 'incorrectly.'" . . . In many discursive contexts . . . the standard becomes a metaphysical fiction defining language as "existing in other than its actual variations" (*Keywords*, 106). (Ferguson 83) Raymond Williams, *Keywords: A Vocabulary of Culture and Society* (New York: Oxford University Press, 1976), quoted in Ferguson, *Dido's Daughters: Literacy, Gender, and Empire in Early Modern England and France* (University of Chicago Press, 2003) 83–84.

28. David Richter writes comprehensively about both philosophical practices. Structuralism he describes first in terms of the special insight that, "though language may not be everything, practically everything we do that is specifically human is expressed in language" (809). Turning specifically to the linguistic theory of Ferdinand de Saussure, Richter discusses his establishment that "the special symbol systems of the natural languages are systems based on differences" (810, and then goes on to detail Saussure's influential general principles. Describing the post-structuralism of Deconstruction, Richter focuses on the significance of Derrida and his central notion that "all thought is necessarily inscribed in language, and that language itself is fraught with intractable paradoxes. We can repress or ignore these paradoxes, but we cannot escape from them or solve them" (818). One of the central paradoxes of language is its reliance on "absence" for its presence. Richter glosses Derridean theorizing:

> Ultimate meaning, genuine presence, is always deferred—just as looking up one word in a dictionary leads to another and so on indefinitely. Between signifier and signified, therefore, there is not the rigid relationship of container and contained. Rather, there is always "freeplay" (*jeu*), which suggests that language can never be pinned down to meaning, that it is always already indeterminate. (820)

See David Richter, ed. *The Critical Tradition: Classic Texts and Contemporary Trends,* 2nd ed. (Boston: Bedford Books, 1998) 809–827. For primary texts, see Ferdinand de Saussure, *Course in General Linguistics*. 1923. (New York: Philosophical Library, 1959); Jacques Derrida, "Structure, Sign, and Play in the Discourse of the Human Sciences." 1966. transl. Richard Macksey and Eugenio Donato *The Structuralist Controversy: The Languages of Criticism and the Sciences of Man* (Baltimore: Johns Hopkins University Press, 1970); Jacques Derrida, *Of Grammatology*. 1967. (Baltimore: Johns Hopkins University Press, 1976).

29. Keir Elam argues: "our own age, like Shakespeare's, is one of intense linguistic awareness. The central importance of language in contemporary thought, manifested most directly in the growth of linguistics, of semiotics, of the philosophy of language and of language-oriented sociology, raises the problem of how to approach . . . the language and linguistic culture produced in other ages." See Elam, *Shakespeare's Universe of Discouse: Language Games in the Comedies* (Cambridge University Press, 1984) 2.

30. See note 14 above. For other recent work attentive to such discursive complexity and contingency, see especially Patricia Fumerton, "Homely Accents: Ben Jonson Speaking Low" *Renaissance Culture and the Everyday*, eds. Patricia Fumerton and Simon Hunt (Philadelphia, PA: University of Pennsylvania Press, 1999) 92–111. Chapter three of the present study references similarly nuanced work that focuses on the politics of "cant" both on the early modern stage and in the broader society.

31. Susan Wells postulates a growing disjunction between such traditional civic institutions and structures of order as the guilds; see Wells, 107–108. See also Ward for a historian's challenge to such a view in his study of the early modern guilds. Ward asserts that the guilds in fact did adapt to the times and were not mere holdovers of an earlier, more bounded city and age.

32. This is a widely accepted view, though other plays have recently gained increased critical attention, especially the late plays. See Julie Sanders, "'Wardrobe Stuffe': Clothes, Costume and the Politics of Dress in Ben Jonson's *The New Inn*," *Renaissance Forum*, 6.1 (Winter 2002): 1–15. 12 September 2003

33. Barish discusses Jonson's use of both prose and verse throughout his dramatic works, and postulates a relationship for Jonson between vice and verse, and prose and folly, 142–144. See also Larry D. Bradfield, "Prose Decorum and the Anatomy of Folly in *Bartholomew Fair*," *Emporia State Research Studies*, 32.2 (Fall 1983): 14.

34. *The Shoemaker's Holiday* is included in at least one recent anthology of "City Comedy": James Knowles, ed., *The Roaring Girl and Other City Comedies* (New York: Oxford University Press, 2001). The play's London setting certainly qualifies it, however it is an historical London—the scene is London in the 15th century, not contemporary London. The play's date, 1599, also places it just a little too early to be a true Jacobean city comedy. *The Shoemaker's Holiday* notably is anthologized in volume 1 of the *Drama of the English Renaissance* series co-edited by Russell and Rabkin; volume II is where city comedy is substantially anthologized. See Russell A. Fraser and Norman Rabkin, eds., *Drama of the English Renaissance, Volume I: The Tudor Period* (New York: MacMillan Publishing Co. Inc., 1976); Fraser and Rabkin, *Drama of the English Renaissance, Volume II: The Stuart Period* (Upper Saddle River, NJ: Prentice-Hall, Inc., 1976). The play's distance from the satiric flavor of later city comedy also is suggested by William Tydeman's description of its "overwhelming vote of confidence in London, its lifestyle, its moral code, its respectability, its positively benevolent tendency to encourage citizens to good works and good behavior" (42), in a survey of sixteenth-century drama. William Tydeman, "The Image of the City in English Renaissance Drama" *Essays and Studies* 38 (1985): 29–44.

35. Dekker, *Dramatic Works* (see note 4 above).

36. Thomas Dekker, *The Wonderful Year; The Gull's Horn-Book; Penny-Wise, Pound-Foolish; English Villainies Discovered by Lantern and Candlelight, and Selected Writings*. ed. E.D. Pendry (Cambridge, MA: Harvard University Press, 1968) 65–109. Pendry's "Introduction" to this collection of Dekker's prose works discusses his turning to the pamphlet trade at first during times of plague (theaters being closed), and the sustenance this work provided over an uncertain and debt-plagued career. See Dekker, *Wonderful Year* 5.
37. Middleton, *Works* (see note 4 above).
38. See Martin 13–16, 115. Martin's study of Middleton's skepticism begins from the classical antecedents of the Renaissance tradition of skepticism; he detects a consistent dualism in Middleton's major comedies that prevents overly sentimental (or overly nihilistic) conclusions.

NOTES TO CHAPTER ONE

1. Richard Foster Jones, *The Triumph of the English Language: A Survey of Opinions Concerning the Vernacular from the Introduction of Printing to the Restoration* (Palo Alto, CA: Stanford University Press, 1953); Richard Bailey, *Images of English: A Cultural History of the Language* (Ann Arbor: University of Michigan Press, 1991).
2. Jean E. Howard, "Westward Ho" 152. Howard takes up a city comedy co-authored by Dekker and John Webster in 1604, but her opening discussion of city comedy's generic properties is of value to my consideration of the genre.
3. For historical discussion of this era of change, see Wrightson 128–155 passim. See Ward for more specific discussion of the changing city in terms of its traditional economic and social structures. See also Theodore B. Leinwand, *The City Staged: Jacobean City Comedy, 1603–1613* (Madison, WI: University of Wisconsin Press, 1986) 83, on Jacobean London as a "centre of conspicuous consumption."
4. William Camden, *Britain [Britannia]*, tr. Philemon Holland (London, 1610) (Ann Arbor, MI: University Microfilms) 421.
5. Wrightson, 155, 149. In addition to the work of historians, listed in Note 3 above, see Lena Cowen Orlin, ed., *Material London, ca. 1600* (Philadelphia, PA: University of Pennsylvania Press, 2000) for a wide-ranging group of essays focusing on different aspects of the city at the turn of the century. The collection's title suggests its premise of examining elements of London life and culture at a moment of material proliferation and, implicitly, growing awareness of such proliferation.
6. Helgerson 1.
7. William Camden, *Remaines Concerning Britain*, ed. R.D. Dunn (Toronto and London: University of Toronto Press, 1984) xxii.

8. William Bullokar, *Booke at Large, for the Amendment of Orthographie for English Speeche* (1580) (Ann Arbor, MI: University Microfilms); Richard Mulcaster, *The Elementarie* (1582) (Ann Arbor, I: University Microfilms); Robert Cawdrey, *A Table Alphabetical* (1604) (Ann Arbor, MI: University Microfilms). For extensive discussion of early modern dictionaries and orthographies and the significance of their appearance between approximately 1550 and 1650, see Paula Blank, "Broken English" 7–32. See also Fleming.

9. Fleming 182. Fleming works from John Earl Joseph 48–60. The ideas Fleming is interested in, of the process of language standardization and the perceived need for such standardization, are also explored in both historical and contemporary contexts by Milroy and Milroy.

10. John Bullokar, *An English Expositor* (1616) (Ann Arbor, MI: University Microfilms); Henry Cockeram, *The English Dictionary: or an Interpreter of hard English words* (1623) (Ann Arbor, MI: University Microfilms); Thomas Blount, *Glossographia* (1656) (Ann Arbor, MI: University Microfilms). Also see Blank 7–32.

11. See Ferguson 272–275, for a related discussion on word-play in early modern English speech, and contemporary attitudes towards this, quite different from our own. Punning and wordplay were part of a range of what we might call ambiguous linguistic practices that were not considered eccentric in an era in which vernacular language was so variable and un-standardized.

12. For a related but slightly different take on the subject of language and women, see Bornstein 132–138 on the history of prescribing proper language for women and "women's language" as a sociological phenomenon of conditioning, not a biological one. Though this differs markedly from Fleming's focus, there is a shared interest in uncovering the history of women's relationship to language.

13. There is a considerable range of scholarship exploring early modern drama and discourses of gender and femininity. The sartorial and the cosmetic, both related and unrelated to the stage, have also been considered recently. See Newman, "Fashioning Femininity"; Jean E. Howard, "Crossdressing, The Theatre, and Gender Struggle in Early Modern England," *Shakespeare Quarterly* 39:4 (Winter 1988): 418–440; Frances Dolan, "Taking the Pencil out of God's Hand: Art, Nature, and the Face-Painting Debate in Early Modern England," *PMLA* 108.2 (1993): 224–239; Annette Drew-Bear, "Face-Painting Scenes in Ben Jonson's Plays," *Studies in Philology* 77:4 (Fall 1980): 388–401; Sanders, "Wardrobe Stuffe."

14. Fleming 188. John Florio, *A Worlde of Words, or Most Copious and Exact Dictionarie in Italian and English.* 1598. (Ann Arbor, MI: University Microfilms).

15. Walter Ong, "Latin Language Study as a Renaissance Puberty Rite," *Studies in Philology* 56:2 (1959) 103–124.

16. John Stow, *The Survey of London*, ed. Henry B Wheatley (London: J. M. Dent & Sons, Ltd., 1945) 3. Stow references John Norden, *Speculum Britanniae pars: The Description of Hertfordshire* (1598) (Ann Arbor, MI: University of Michigan: University Microfilms); and William Lambert [Lambarde], *A Perambulation of Kent* (1570) (Ann Arbor, MI: University Microfilms). See Helgerson, 131–132 on Stow's Survey as one of a number of chorographies or "descriptions"—including Drayton's *Poly-Olbion*, Speed's *Theater of the Empire of Great Britain*, Camden's *Britannia*, and Saxton's maps of English shires—that must be considered a collective product. Helgerson's interest in these works' common political/ideological project is not sufficient enough a reason for him to miss acknowledging the uniquely urban character of Stow.

17. Manley, "Matron to Monster" 347–374.

18. Newman, "Fashioning Femininity" 132.

19. Newman, "Fashioning Femininity" 131. Newman quotes from a later edition of Stow, according to her note, which is not included in the earliest editions of the *Survey*. The passage has been dated as a c. 1619 addition based on its use of terms like "agglet." See Newman 172, note 3.

20. Philip Stubbes, *The Anatomie of Abuses*. 1583. ed. Margaret Jane Kidnie (Tempe, AZ: Renaissance English Text Society, 2002); Stephen Gosson, *The Schoole of Abuse, Early Treatises on the Stage* (London: The Shakespeare Society, 1853).

21. Howard, "Crossdressing" 422.

22. Ralph Lever, *The Arte of Reason, Rightly Termed, Witcraft*, London, 1573, image 7, column 1, *Early English Books Online*. University of Washington Libraries. 11 March 2004 http://eebo.chadwyck.com/eebo/image/15541/.

23. Martin 43.

24. Stephen Gosson, *Pleasant Quippes for Upstart Newfangled Gentlewomen* (1596) (Ann Arbor, MI: University Microfilms). Gosson's tract, appearing almost fifteen years after Stubbes' *Anatomie*'s first printing, is significant in suggesting no waning of the popular appetite for fashion, or of popular concern for fashion's corrupting effects.

25. Fumerton, "Homely Accents."

26. Fumerton finds the postmodern language-theorizing of Gilles Deleuze and Felix Guattari useful in countering the pervasive but overly Romantic Bakhtinian notion of Renaissance "heteroglossia." Fumerton works from Deleuze and Guattari's *A Thousand Plateaus: Capitalism and Schizophrenia,* tr. Brian Massumi (Minneapolis, MN: University of Minnesota Press, 1987), and uses their questioning of the concept of "major" languages to suggest that "every major language—and especially a language as unstable as English in the Renaissance—was from the start a 'becoming minoritarian' or 'becoming-minor of the major language'" (93). According to Fumerton, this concept enables new consideration of Scots-English and English at the

court of James I, and representations of dialects like Jonson's depictions in masques like *For the Honour of Wales.*

27. C.J. Sisson, "King James the First of England as Poet and Political Writer," *Seventeenth Century Studies Presented to Herbert Grierson* (Oxford: Clarendon Press, 1938) 61.

28. William N. West, "Talking the Talk: Cant on the Jacobean Stage," *English Literary Renaissance* (Spring 2003) 250.

29. With the term "perlocutionary," West gestures to the Speech-Act theory of language developed most famously by J.L. Austin in 1962. Speech-Act theory's emphasis on language as action, as a mode not just of expression but of doing has made it valuable to scholars and critics of dramatic literature, including early modern drama. Speech-Act theory distinguishes between "illocutionary" and "perlocutionary" acts. "Illocution" can be defined as what we bring about *in* saying something; "perlocution" as "what we bring about or achieve *by* saying something" (Elam 6–7). For a useful, working description of Speech-Act theory, both generally as and applied to Shakespearean drama, see Elam, "Introduction," esp. p.6–11. See also J.L. Austin, *How to Do Things With Words* (1962), 2nd ed. (London: Oxford University Press, 1976).

30. Ben Jonson, *Ben Jonson*, eds. C.H. Herford and Percy and Evelyn Simpson, vol. 8 (Oxford: Clarendon Press, 1966). All subsequent references to the *English Grammar* and *Discoveries* will be taken from Herford and Simpson, volume 8, and will be parenthetical.

31. Julie Sanders, Kate Chedzgoy, Susan Wiseman, "Introduction," *Refashioning Ben Jonson: Gender, Politics, and the Jonsonian Canon*, eds. Sanders et al (New York: St. Martin's Press, 1998) 4–5.

32. For discussion of Lever and other contemporaries and the debate about the best mode of shoring up English as an authoritative and articulate vernacular, see R.F. Jones, Chapters III and IV: "The Inadequate Language, Part I," 68–93; and "The Inadequate Language, Part II," 94–141.

33. Ian Donaldson, ed., *Ben Jonson* (Oxford: Oxford University Press, 1985) xiii. Donaldson cites A.C. Swinburne's (1888) early critical take on *Discoveries*. On literary imitation, see also G.W. Pigman, "Versions of Imitation in the Renaissance," *Renaissance Quarterly* 33 (1980): 1–32. Pigman emphasizes the Renaissance concept of *imitatio* in terms of its roots in a Latin rhetorical tradition. Imitation was central to Humanist Latin language and textual study; Jonson—writing in English—transposes this practice, endowing English with this authoritative Latinate practice.

34. John Creaser, "Enigmatic Ben Jonson," *English Comedy*, eds. Michael Cordner, Peter Holland, and John Kerrigan (Cambridge: Cambridge University Press, 1995) 105.

35. Thomas Dekker, ed. E.D. Pendry; Thomas Middleton, *Works,* ed. A.H. Bullen.

36. E.D. Pendry, "Introduction," Thomas Dekker, *Wonderful Year, etc.* 5. Pendry's introduction to his edited volume of Dekker's prose works provides a detailed description and consideration of Dekker's troubled career and the London climate within which he sought (and often failed) to succeed.

37. Robert Greene, *A Notable Discussion of Coosenage* [sic], *now daily practiced by sundry lewd persons, called connie-catchers, and crosse-byters* (1591); *A Disputation between a Hee conny-catcher and a Shee conny-catcher* (1592); *The Blacke Bookes Messenger* (1592) All: (Ann Arbor: University Microfilms). Thomas Nashe, *Pierce Penniless, His Supplication to the Devil* (1592) (Ann Arbor, MI: University Microfilms).

38. Thomas Harman, *A Caveat for Common Cursitors Vulgarly Called Vagabonds* (1567) (Ann Arbor, MI: University Microfilms). For additional discussion of cant's role in London's life and imagination, see Blank, 52–67; see also John L. McMullan, *The Canting Crew: London's Criminal Underworld 1550–1700* (New Brunswick, NJ: Rutgers University Press, 1984) 95–116.

39. In particular, see Blank, "Broken English," 33–68 on Renaissance notions of "coining" words and words as commodities in both a playful and serious sense. See also Newman, "fashioning" 129–143 on words and commoditization.

40. Middleton, *Works* vol. VIII, 1–45.

41. Middleton, *Works* vol. VII.

42. Covatta 54, 142. For a different perspective on Middleton's dramatic career against the backdrop of the growing Puritan revolution, see Margo Heinemann, *Puritanism and Theatre: Thomas Middleton and Opposition Drama Under the Early Stuarts* (Cambridge: Cambridge University Press, 1980).

43. Middleton, *Works* vol. V, *A Chaste Maid in Cheapside* V, iv, 112–116.

NOTES TO CHAPTER TWO

1. Ben Jonson, *Epicoene, Ben Jonson*, ed. C.H. Herford and Percy and Evelyn Simpson, vol. 5 (Oxford: Clarendon Press, 1966) 3.2.66–77. All subsequent references to this edition of the play will be parenthetical.

2. Ben Jonson, *Epicoene*, ed. R.V. Holdsworth (New York: The New Mermaids—W.W. Norton & Co., Inc., 1979) 68, n. 68.

3. Jane Schneider, "Fantastical Colors in Foggy London: The New Fashion Potential of the Late Sixteenth Century," *Material London, ca. 1600*, ed. Lena Cowen Orlin (Philadelphia: University of Pennsylvania Press, 2000) 122. The growth of Cultural Studies has fueled attention to the material factors of early modern culture and ideologies, such as the sartorial. Sumptuary and attempts at sumptuary regulation have attracted significant critical interest from the fields of literature and history, but also law. See Peter Goodrich, "Signs Taken for Wonders: Community, Identiy, and a History of Sumptuary Law," *Law and Social Inquiry* 23 (1998) 707–728, a review of Alan Hunt, *Governance of the Consuming Passions: A History of Sumptuary*

Law (New York: St. Martin's Press, 1996). In the realm of literary/cultural studies, see Ann Rosalind Jones and Peter Stallybrass, *Renaissance Clothing and the Materials of Memory* (Cambridge: Cambridge University Press, 2000) 187–188, for discussion of the ineffectuality of sumptuary legislation and the simultaneous anxiety surrounding the sartorial license of the theaters. See also Sanders, "Wardrobe Stuffey," which connects the sartorial directly to city drama in a reading of Jonson's late play "The New Inn."

4. Huston Hallahan identifies this triad of utterances in *Epicoene* but does not explore its gender dynamics. Hallahan cites Renaissance attitudes toward the tongue in establishing the opposition between silence/eloquence and chatter in his reading of *Epicoene*. See Huston Hallhan, "Silence, Eloquence, and Chatter in Jonson's *Epicoene*," *Huntington Library Quarterly: A Journal for the History and Interpretation of English and American Civilization* 40 (1977) 117–127. For an excellent discussion of attitudes toward and treatments of the tongue in the period, see Carla Mazzio, "Sins of the Tongue," *The Body in Parts: Fantasies of Corporeality in Early Modern Europe*, ed. Carla Mazzio and David Hillman (New York: Routledge, 1997) 53–79.

5. An earlier play, *Every Man In His Humour* (1605), was originally set in Italy but its scene and characters were transferred to England when the play was revised for inclusion in the 1616 *Works*. See Jonas Barish 130–141.

6. Barish's influential attention to Jonsonian language and stylistics is evident in much of the criticism that follows *Prose Comedy*, even when it diverges or differs from the original's reading. See Hallahan; William Slights, "*Epicoene* and the Prose Paradox," *Philological Quarterly* 49 (1970): 178–187; more recently, see Lanier, "Masculine Silence."

7. Among other sources, Lanier cites Stanley Fish's provocative work on Jonson's shorter poetry and its idiosyncratic stylistics which eschews decorative, even mildly representative language. Stanley Fish finds in Jonson's poetry a consistent resistance to using language for representation, based on an understanding of language—words—as ornamental, superficially appareling (and thus also concealing) the real underneath. In much of Jonson's encomiastic poetry, the whole point of the poem often becomes a discussion of the impossibility of describing the person of merit, specifically because of the speciousness of words that are merely ornament, and because such a noble person should need no ornamentation. Jonson spends his poems deliberately representing the failure of representation. Douglas Lanier cites Fish's work on the poetry to discuss this distrust of linguistic representation in Jonson as a central component in the poet's ideals of a masculine stylistics that, once again, shuns representation in the form of ornament or reliance on anything outside the thing or self itself. According to Lanier, the ideal of masculine stylistics becomes a "strategic silence" (3) whose impossibility, especially on the stage, Jonson must confront again and again. Taken together, the work of Lanier and Fish suggests a stylistics ironically

opposed to language altogether in its most extreme form, a notion to which *Epicoene*'s conclusion perhaps also alludes. J.A. Jackson takes up this question regarding the play's conclusion and extends this trend of reading Jonson deconstructively by reading *Epicoene* as both literature and literary criticism, a play that "thoroughly manipulates and deconstructs" itself (2) by a surprise ending which forces its audience to reflect on their own role in constructing the plot they expected to see.

Also helpful on representation as a problem is Christy Desmet's work on feminine rhetoric in Shakespeare, in which she first describes the Ancient and Renaissance rhetorical commonplace associating rhetorical ornament with women. Ornate speech becomes associated with pleasure and with clothing—both distorting of the truth. Ornament is wanton, and despite Ancient associations of the ornate with the effeminate man, by the early modern period this had shifted to women, although there was some disagreement about the relative good of elegant rhetoric.

Lastly, it is worth citing the work of Martin Elsky on the subject of Jonson and representation in language. Elsky considers Jonson's connection to the Philosophical Grammar movement, a Medieval holdover in many ways that gained new traction in Jonson's time because of shifting concerns about the vernacular. Philosophical Grammar was the belief in a stable, referential relationship between words and things: words name things in accordance with their metaphysical natures, and there are no uneasy distances between signifier and signified. The view of many has been that Humanism scoured Philosophical Grammar's principles from curricula and grammar textbooks, but men like Juan Luis Vives continued the tradition, and Jonson's knowledge of Vives is evidenced by the numerous references to him in *Discoveries* and *The English Grammar*. Elsky aligns Jonson's concern for eloquent language with Philosophical Grammar's belief in referential language, language that inherently embodies the qualities of what it names—language that is therefore not representative, but transparent. See Fish; Lanier, "Masculine Silence"; J.A. Jackson, "'On forfeit of your selves, think nothing true': Self-Deception in Ben Jonson's Epicoene," *Early Modern Literary Studies* 10.1 (May 2004): 28 pars. 29 June 2006 ; Christy Desmet, "Speaking Sensibly: Feminine Rhetoric in *Measure for Measure* and *All's Well that Ends Well*," *Renaissance Papers* 1986, eds. Dale B.J. Randall and Joseph A. Porter (Durham, NC: The Southeastern Renaissance Conference, 1986): 43–51; Martin Elsky, "Words, Things, and Names: Jonson's Poetry and Philosophical Grammar," *Classic and Cavalier: Essays on Jonson and the Sons of Ben*, ed. Claude J. Summers and Ted-Larry Pebworth (Pittsburgh, PA: University of Pittsburgh Press, 1982): 91–104.

8. See Fleming; Fleming's work belongs to a group of studies in recent years which re-insert women as critical but often latent cultural and political actors: see Suzanne Gossett, "'Man-maid, begone!': Women in Masques," *English Literary Renaissance* 18.1 (Winter 1988) 96–97, 112–113.

9. Feminist scholars in particular have been forthright about turning to other fields or critical approaches in their research and scholarship. In an early

version of an essay on *Epicoene* and commodification, Karen Newman explicitly announces the new mode of inquiry she is attempting: "My reading of *Epicoene* willfully shifts its focus away from Morose and the gallants, away from Jonsonian satire and classical allusion, away from the exclusively literary, and gestures toward, in Althusser's terms, the production of a different theoretical problematic . . . [that is,]changing the terms of reading" (516). Margaret Ferguson and Eve Rachele Sanders similarly situate their critical stance and the determined interdisciplinarity of their approach to early modern language and literature: "From where we stand, from our positions as teachers in department of English, we believe that literacy studies matter . . . because of the new perspectives they bring to our understanding of familiar subjects (writers, readers) and objects (books, manuscripts) of literary studies" (4). See Karen Newman, "City Talk: Women and Commodification in Jonson's *Epicoene*" *English Literary Renaissance* 53 (1989): 503–518; Eve Rachele Sanders and Margaret W. Ferguson, "Literacies in Early Modern England" *Critical Survey* 14.1 (2002): 1–8.

10. Though there is some dispute amongst scholars regarding the origins of the oldest English ballads, all agree that the ballad as a form originated around or prior to the medieval period as an oral compositional mode. The ballad of the battle of Chevy Chase, considered old by the late 16th century, is used by historian Adam Fox as an example of the fluidity and persistence of oral culture in early modern England. The madrigal, by contrast, was a new musical form in the period. It was a polyphonic composition that originated in Italy and reached England in the 1530s, but developed into a mature, native style by the 1580s and has a strong and legitimate association with the last decades of the 16th century as the period of "the flowering of the English madrigal" (606). See Adam Fox, *Oral and Literate Culture in England, 1500–1700* (Oxford: Clarendon Press, 2000) 1–3; "Madrigal" *The Oxford Companion to English Literature*, Fifth Ed., ed. Margaret Drabble (Oxford University Press, 1985) 605–606.

11. See Anne Barton, *Ben Jonson, dramatist* (Cambridge: Cambridge University Press, 1984) 177. See also Genevieve Love, "A Circle in the Water: Theatricality, Embodiment, and Absence in Early Modern Drama" Diss. Cornell University, 2002, on the relationship between plays as simultaneous performed events and printed texts in the period, and many playwrights' efforts to theorize and manipulate this relationship.

12. See Sara van den Berg, "Reading Dora Reading: Freud's 'Fragment of an Analysis of a Case of Hysteria,'" *Literature and Psychology* 32.3 (1986): 27–35, for connection of the sensual with the male, voyeuristic pleasure of reading a text that becomes female in its implicitly objectified state.

13. This inclination to polarities in Jonson has become a critical commonplace, and it is true that Jonson is easiest to approach in terms of extremes. See Gabriele Bernhard Jackson, *Vision and Judgment in Ben Jonson's Drama*

(New Haven: Yale University Press, 1968) 4, on the Jonsonian tension between "what ought to be and the mundane reality of what could be." See also Womack 6, 103. Womack reads Jonsonian polarity via Bakhtin and the problem of linguistic monologism vs. dialogism.

14. Patricia Parker writes at length on the pervasive dynamic of dilation versus restraint in the Renaissance, and dilation's frequent association with the feminine, both bodily and discursively. Parker sees this dynamic in Renaissance poetics, whereby the poet or playwright struggles to restrain or maintain control over the wayward, implicitly female, body of the text. She also describes the issue of the dilation of discourse itself as a major preoccupation, citing Erasmus' interest in the expansion of discourse and simultaneous anxiety over controlling such expansion. Less abstractly, women frequently were figured as "unflappable talkers" in texts whose focus is the question of how to master or contain such excessive feminine speech, how to bring closure to potentially endless dilation. See Patricia Parker, *Literary Fat Ladies: Rhetoric, Gender, Property* (London: Methuen, 1987) 9–14, 26–27.

15. See Dolan 229–231, which traces early modern attitudes toward cosmetics in terms of anxiety over a new female agency of self-transformation. For specific discussion of cosmetics and "painting" in Jonson, see Drew-Bear.

16. Hallahan surveys a range of examples from the period which posit silence as eloquence itself, not its opposite. In particular, he includes illustrations of popular contemporary emblems of the eloquent virtue of silence. See Hallahan, 119, and 118, 122.

17. On the period concern for "inkhornism," see R.F. Jones 94–141. See also Blank, "Broken English" 40–52.

18. Robert Greene, *Greene's Groat's Worth of Wit* (1592) (Ann Arbor, MI: University Microfilms); Thomas Becon, *The Syckmans'* [sic] *Salve* (1560) (Ann Arbor, MI: University Microfilms). The full title of Greene continues, "*bought with a million of repentence: Describing the follie of youth, the falshoode of makeshift flatterers, the miserie of the negligent, and mischiefs of deceiving courtesans. Written before his death, and published as his dyeing request,*" its 'last testament' implication perhaps suggests its morally curative properties, though Jonson's use of it with the Collegiates is no less ludicrous.

19. See Tessa Watt, *Cheap Print and Popular Piety 1550–1640* (Cambridge: Cambridge University Press, 1991) 4, for introductory discussion of her study: early modern cheap print and the relationship, often symbolic, its consumers developed with it; Watt wants to look not at popular print itself so much as the role of print in culture, both high-brow and low-brow.

20. See Newman, "Fashioning Femininity" 129–143, a chapter focused particularly on *Epicoene*.

21. See Edward B. Partridge, *The Broken Compass: A Study of the Major Comedies of Ben Jonson* (London: Chatto & Windus, 1958) 168–169; also more recent consideration of the same issue in Hallahan, 123; see also Philip

Mirabelli, "Silence, Wit, and Wisdom in *The Silent Woman*" *SEL: Studies in English Literature, 1500–1900* 29.2 (Spring 1989): 320.

22. Newman, "Fashioning Femininity" 3–12, delineates the powerful conflation of women's speech and sexuality, of the oral and the genital, of a public voice with a transgressively public body. Newman cites contemporary tracts on proper behavior such as Thomas Becon's *Catechisme* (1564) and Henry Smith's *A Preparation for Marriage* (1598 and 1630), both of which feature an obsession with the always potentially transgressive female mouth. Other texts from the period equally reflect and, more rarely, comment upon this view. Elizabeth Cary's 1613 closet-drama, *The Tragedie of Mariam* offers an unrelenting view of the consequences of this conflation for both sexes: men are tyrannized by it, and women ignore it at their peril. Newman details the phenomenon:

> Women frequently were figured synechdochically as mouths, open and voracious . . . the obsession with the female mouth is not always focused literally on the genitals only [as in Becon] but on the mouth as a source of speech, as well . . . disallowed speech is a sign throughout the period of sexual transgression . . . An open mouth and immodest speech are tantamount to open genitals and immodest acts" (10–11).

Carla Mazzio's work on early modern representations of the tongue also suggests the perceived threat of female speech. Mazzio traces a relationship between speech and the tongue that was complicated by understandings of the tongue both as an organ coded-male for its 'member' status; and as an unstable, female-coded organ by virtue of its simultaneous vulnerability and need for disciplining. The tongue is associated with a monstrous orality and, in at least one important example, is explicitly gendered female. In Thomas Tomkiss's 1607 play, *Lingua: Or the Combat of the Tongue and the Five Senses for Superiority*, Lingua is female. Her actions and portrayal encompass all the previous associations with female transgression, rendered explicitly in this personification of the speech-organ. Mazzio remarks that "of all the inhabitants of Microcosmus, Lingua is the one who does not seem to know her place" (65), and notes Lingua's visual spectacle, on-stage, as she enters, "appareled in a Crimson Satin gowne." Lingua's "endlessly protean" quality is both generative and threatening (66). The unruliness of the female tongue—or in this concretizing inversion, the tongue as female—magnifies the problem of female speech. Indeed, the view of the tongue as an additional male member suggests one problematic dimension of female speech as a masculinity that was *un*-anatomically correct. See Mazzio. *Epicoene*, then, by virtue of its subtitle "the silent woman," immediately signals its central concern for women and their language, if not explicitly their tongues, and also gestures distinctly to an oral-literate dynamic by evoking the powerful association of women and an unruly orality.

23. Howard, "Shakespeare" 8–9, 16–18. See also Barish for a book-length reading of Jonson's dramatic language with many comparisons to Shakespeare's.

Much has been written, of course, on Shakespeare's dramatic language. Both William Carroll and Keir Elam make *Love's Labours' Lost* the focal point of their investigations of Shakespearean language, Elam in particular using speech-act theory to analyze what he sees as language-games in the plays (see Introduction, above, for fuller discussion of this work). Jane Donawerth approaches Shakespeare's language as part of the so-called "linguistic exuberance" of the Elizabethan period, now often questioned. Recently Shakespeare scholarship has sought to resituate Shakespeare amongst his peers and cultural milieu, notably considering his dramatic language, for example, in terms of its traces of the city and the citizens so prevalent in the works of his fellow playwrights. See: William C. Carroll, *The Great Feast of Language in* Love's Labours' Lost (Princeton University Press, 1976); Elam, "Universe of Discourse"; Donawerth; John Michael Archer.

24. Ian W. Archer, "Material Londoners?" *Material London, ca. 1600* ed. Lena Cowen Orlin (Philadephia: University of Pennsylvania Press, 2000) 174–175. *Material London, ca. 1600,* collects essays from a wide range of disciplines, all of which take as their central focus the city of London and its material, and burgeoningly commercial, reality.

25. Quoted in Lanier, "Masculine Silence" 7–8. See also Note 7, above, for a reference to Stanley Fish's study of Jonson's non-representational ideal in the stylistics of his poetry.

26. Kathleen McCluskie has remarked upon the degree to which Truewit's lengthy speeches in II, ii, are culled directly from Juvenalian satire. Translated into English and with details cleverly transposed to contemporary London, Truewit's discourses and invectives are nonetheless an explicit quotation of a favorite Classical, satirical source of Jonson's. Though this is by no means the only time Jonson gestures to or borrows from his satiric forbears, it is one of the most substantial and exact, according to McCluskie, and has several implications. First, such 'quotation' points to the Humanist tradition by which classical notions of satire, and of eloquence, infused early modern schooling and those, like Jonson, trained within it. The Juvenalian source becomes a kind of literate inside-joke for Jonson, and for Truewit, as well as for others 'Humanistically' familiar with Roman satire. Secondly, the fact that Truewit's deliberately over-long speeches are quotations from a Juvenalian tradition of jaundiced critique makes them perhaps most significant as simply copia. That is, as important as the content is simply the excess of language, the potential power of words and speech as sheer, if erudite, noise. See Kathleen McCluskie, *Renaissance Dramatists* (Atlantic Highlands, NJ: Humanities Press International, Inc., 1989) 164–165.

27. See note 16, above.

28. Ben Jonson, *The Alchemist, Ben Jonson*, ed. C.H. Herford and Percy and Evelyn Simpson vol. 5 (Oxford: Clarendon Press, 1966). All subsequent references will be to this edition and will be parenthetical.

29. Hugh Broughton, *The Concent of Scripture* (Ann Arbor, MI: University Microfilms). Norton editor Robert M. Adams here notes the speech's derivation from Broughton, but also argues that "It is neither necessary or possible to understand the gibberish she recites" (248).

Certainly the gibberish effect, alone, produces the desired chaotic effect in the scene without any contextual consideration. There is in fact great ironic significance in the particular text Dol is "quoting," however, and in the spectacle of a woman spouting the earnest scholarship of an illustrious linguist and the Elizabethan age's foremost Hebraist. Jonson's evocation of Broughton's text thus is interesting on several levels. *The Concent of Scripture* was a painstaking attempt at establishing a conclusive chronology of the Bible, and particularly the Old Testament, at a time when this was controversial. Broughton was well-known as an ardent Puritan in addition to being a Hebrew scholar, and Dol's ranting recitation also mimics a kind of Puritan zealotry and pious oratory stereotypical at the time, which Jonson will take to its illogical extreme with Rabbi Zeal-of-the-Land Busy in *Bartholomew Fair*. Also, though Dol speaks in English, Broughton's strong association with Hebrew and the speech's reliance on a scriptural tone and syntax evokes that learned and highly arcane language, employing it as a tool of deceit as vividly as Subtle and Face use the jargon of alchemy. Walter Ong has commented upon the "failure" of Renaissance Hebrew by comparison to the pervasive currency of Renaissance Latin in educated, male circles of the time. The categorical remoteness, then, of Broughton's text and the Hebrew with which it was associated, makes Dol's speeches in IV, v all the more incantatory and strange. See Robert M. Adams, ed. *Ben Jonson's Plays and Masques* (New York and London: W.W. Norton and Co., 1979) 248, n. 9; Ong, "Latin-Puberty" 104.

30. Truewit first objects to Otter's incorrect prefix in "omnipotentes," a basic error suggesting Otter's complete incomprehension of the Latin he so often tosses around. His second error, and particularly Truewit's adamant correction, emphasizes the significance of class as much as gender with literacy, as Otter makes a far more subtle mistake of noun declension that the gallant finds outrageous. It is class (and education) that stands between Otter and the complete, nuanced, Latin literacy Truewit possesses. The play makes this point vividly in this exchange, but for all its mockery of Otter's "Latin-ing," such show-literacy is also pervasive in the talking city. Truewit's outrage is as much an exposition as a condemnation of a fashionable city phenomenon.

NOTES TO CHAPTER THREE

1. Thomas Middleton and Thomas Dekker, *The Roaring Girl*, ed. Paul A. Mulholland (Manchester: Manchester University Press, 1987). All subsequent references will be to this edition and will be parenthetical.

2. I use the term "semiotics" deliberately, to signal the structuring (albeit imperfectly according to period anxieties) of early modern urban culture by several different but related (and regularly collapsed) sign systems, including language and the sartorial. Discussing attributes of early modern society via the theoretical, linguistic terms of semiotics is not my own innovation. See Sanders, "Wardrobe Stuffe," par. 2. Sanders describes her project as an "investigation of the resonance of costume. Metaphorical and material, in one specific Caroline play, Ben Jonson's *The New Inn* (1629), which deploys the semiotics of dress in a sustained fashion across its five acts." For a helpful overview of the structural-linguistic ideas behind the theory of Semiotics, see Richter 809–817.

3. Critical treatments which collectively discuss these three dramatists are not abundant, and those that exist tend to be comparative, with one of the three the main object of the study. The differences in their treatments of London and the venues of their dramatic output make easy comparisons unhelpful. There is valuable work on Jonson and Middleton as dramatist-, and 'realist'-peers: see Martin 13–22. Other discussions that bring together the three tend to be anecdotal: see Sara van den Berg, "The Passing of the Elizabethan Court," *Ben Jonson Journal* 1: 31–61. van den Berg focuses on the authorial roles of Dekker and Jonson in a discussion of James' installation versus Elizabethan civic pageants and the cultural change apparent by such a comparison.

4. Middleton, Dekker, and Jonson all had roles in the creation of the elaborate civic pageantry that accompanied James I's accessional journey through the city to his coronation. See van den Berg, "Elizabethan Court" 44–52. Middleton's substantial work for the city authorities all occurred during James I's reign.

5. See Leinwand 7, for a concise overview of the society and characters staged by Jacobean city comedy. Leinwand devotes individual chapters to "Merchant-Citizens" and "Gentleman-Gallants," both central types of the genre.

6. Nathan Field, *Amends for Ladies, Nero and other Plays*, ed. Herbert P. Horne, Havelock Ellis, Arthur Symons, and A. Wilson Verity (London: Vizetelly, 1888). Field's alternative use of Moll, and Middleton's and Dekker's innovation, are discussed in Lorraine Helms, "Roaring Girls and Silent Women: The Politics of Androgyny on the Jacobean Stage," *Women in Theatre: Themes in Drama* 11 (Cambridge: Cambridge University Press, 1989) 70.

7. The *Hic Mulier* and *Haec Vir* pamphlets appeared within a week of each other in February, 1620. *Hic Mulier* appeared first, condemning "mannish women." *Haec Vir* constitutes a response in the form of an imagined dialogue between the 'Womanish-Man' and the 'Mannish-Woman' that ultimately communicates a conservative message of the importance of proper gender distinction. This pamphlet exchange joined an already ongoing print-debate about the nature of woman and female propriety whose most

notorious components were Joseph Swetnam's *An Arraignment of Lewd, Idle, Froward, and Unconstant Women* (1615); and the pamphlet defenses Swetnam's misogyny elicited: Rachel Speght, *A Muzzle for Melastomus* (c. 1617), and Esther Sowernam, *Ester Hath Hanged Haman* (1617), all texts (Ann Arbor: University Microfilms). Swetnam's invective also inspired a play, *Swetnam the Woman-Hater, Arraigned by Women* (perf. 1617–18, publ. 1620), anthologized in Katherine Usher Henderson and Barbara F. McManus, eds., *Half-Humankind: Contexts and Texts of the Controversy about Women in England, 1540–1640* (Urbana: University of Illinois Press, 1985). Henderson and McManus provide some critical overview of the period and this phenomenon; see also Linda Woodbridge, *Women and the English Renaissance: Literature and the Nature of Womankind, 1540–1620* (Urbana: University of Illinois Press, 1984). For critical discussion explicitly linking the *Hic Mulier-Haec Vir* debate with the gender concerns of *The Roaring Girl*, see Mary Beth Rose, "Women in Men's Clothing: Apparel and Social Stability in *The Roaring Girl*," *English Literary Renaissance* 14.3 (Autumn 1984): 367–391.

8. See chapter one, notes 37 and 38, on cant and writings about cant in the period. For two recent treatments of cant as staged in the early modern theater, see: West 233–240, West's article opens with a comprehensive discussion of cant in Jacobean culture, outside the playhouse. See also Jodi Mikalachki, ""Gender, Cant, and Cross-Talking in *The Roaring Girl*," *Renaissance Drama* XXV (Evanston, IL: Northwestern University Press, 1994) 119–143. As her title indicates, Mikalachki discusses cant specifically in terms of *The Roaring Girl*.

9. Jones 172. Jones quotes Richard Flecknoe (*Miscellania*, 1653) on the state of the vernacular; Flecknoe uses terms strikingly similar to Middleton, discussing language in terms of apparel: "That of our Ancestors having been plain and simple: That of Queen Elizabeths dayes, flaunting and pufted like her Apparell" (172, n. 5). Jones goes on to quote William Webbe (*A Discourse of English Poesie*, 1586), who describes the rhetorical styling of a new play as "a new sute" (174).

10. See chapter two, note 3 on sumptuary laws and regulation, as well as the significance of dress in early modern culture. See also Mary E. Hazard, *Elizabethan Silent Language* (Lincoln, NE: University of Nebraska Press, 2000) 88, on the importance and number of functions of textiles and clothing in the period. Hazard quotes an Erasmian adage, popular in England at the time, that suggests the simultaneous importance and instability of the sartorial in this society: "Clothing is the body's body, and from this too one may infer the state of a man's character" (from *De Civitate, Works* 25: 278) 88.

11. Goodrich 2. "Imagined communities," by now a commonplace of cultural inquiry, is a phrase first coined by Benedict Anderson. See Benedict

Anderson, *Imagined Communities: Reflections on the Origin and Spread of Nationalism*, (London and New York: Verso, 1991).

12. Questions concerning the role of clothing/the sartorial in early modern culture drive much current conversation between critics from the fields of literature, history, and legal history, among others. Julie Sanders' "Wardrobe Stuffe" is emblematic of recent work addressing attempts at sumptuary regulation, apparel, costume in the early modern theater, and their explicit examination by city-engaged dramatists like Jonson. Sanders sets out the key elements to thinking about the sartorial in the period: clothing as a significant semiotic system, at least as important as spoken language, and arguably more important than written. Sanders writes, "Clothes were at various turns invested with the powers of magical transformation, the assertion of identities, personal and national, and the power to subvert hierarchies of rank and gender"("Wardrobe" 1). For a recent major study on clothing and the sartorial in the period, see Jones and Stallybrass. See also Goodrich on the legal history of sumptuary in the period; see Hazard on the "silent language" of dress; like Sanders, Hazard posits the importance of considering the diverse semiotics of early modern English culture, especially the cultures of the court and the crowded city.

Cross-dressing is also an aspect of preoccupations with the sartorial and social stability. For discussion of cross-dressing in terms of its relation to attempts at sartorial regulation, see Jean Howard, "Crossdressing," and "Sex and Social Conflict: The Erotics of *The Roaring Girl*," *Erotic Politics: Desire on the Renaissance Stage*, ed. Susan Zimmerman (New York: Routledge, 1992) 170–190. In "Crossdressing," Howard further emphasizes the notion of "Dress, as a highly regulated semiotic system" which became "a primary site where a struggle over the mutability of the social order was conducted." Howard cites Philip Stubbes' opening of *The Anatomie of Abuses* with an analysis of apparel: "For Stubbes, transgressions of the dress code don't just *signal* social disruption; they constitute social disruption" (422, italics original). Also on cross-dressing and apparel, see: Rose; Helms; also James Mardock, "Hermaphroditical Authority in Jonson's City Comedies," *Ben Jonson Journal* 9 (2002): 69–85.

13. "placket"; "codpiece" *The Oxford English Dictionary Online*, 2nd edition, 2004, September 2004 http://dictionary.oed.com/.

14. Mulholland 159–160, n.26, 27, 29. See also Stubbes 118.

15. Howard, "Crossdressing" 420. Jean Howard's role in re-introducing a modern critical readership to *The Roaring Girl* cannot be overestimated. See also Howard, "Sex and Social Conflict."

16. For an additional example of sartorial anxiety expressed in terms of foreign otherness, see Sanders, "Wardrobe" n.3. Sanders cites Henry Fitzgeoffrey's *Notes from the Blackfriars* (London 1617), sigs Fv-F2:

Knowest thou yon world of fashions now come in

> In Turkie colors carved to the skin,
> Mounted Polonianly until hee reeles,
> That scornes (so much) plaine dealing at his heeles.
> His Boote speakes Spanish to his Scottish spurres,
> His Sute cut Frenchly, round bestuck with Burres.
> Pure Holland is his Shirt, which proudly faire,
> Scornes to outface his Doublet everywhere.

17. Stephen Orgel takes up the issue of the boy-actor and the question of eroticism. See Orgel, "Why Did the English Stage Take Boys for Women?" *Teaching Shakespeare Through Performance,* ed. Milla Cizart Riggio (New York: Modern Language Association, 1999) 102–113.

18. On inkhornism, see chapter two, including note 17.

19. West 250. West borrows the term "perlocutionary force" from the speech-act theory work of J.L. Austin, and cites Austin's work on the effectivity of utterances in verbal performance (250, n. 37).

20. West 229. See also chapter one on the early modern vernacular and attitudes as well as critical treatments of it. Chapter one, notes 1, 8, 9 and 10 provide citations for contemporary language guides as well as several scholarly treatments of early modern English.

21. See chapter one, note 26, on Patricia Fumerton's reading of Deleuze and Guattari on major and minor languages and their relationship. See also Blank, "Broken English" 52–67 on cant dictionaries and cant's relationship to perceptions of the early modern vernacular.

22. Blank "Broken English" 18. Blank considers the first vernacular dictionaries in England to be the cant dictionaries of pamphlet-writers like Thomas Harman and, later, Thomas Dekker. See also Mikalachki 120–121, on canting-pamphlets as both titillating 'entertainments' as well as guides to the language.

23. Tearcat's language is reminiscent of that of the "voyages and discoveries" chronicled (and regularly updated) by Richard Hakluyt in the period. See Richard Hakluyt, *Voyages and Discoveries: The Principal Navigations, Voyages, Traffiques and Discoveries of the English Nation* (1598), ed. Jack Beeching (London: Penguin Books, 1972). For discussion of Hakluyt's chronicles and the related chorographic and topographical endeavors of Christopher Norden and John Speed—all part of a devoutly nationalistic project of the 1590s, see Helgerson 163–191 on Hakluyt; and 105–147 on Norden and Speed.

24. See Mikalachki on cant guides as sources of upper class titillation. Mikalachki discusses records of criminal-depositions regarding the supposed anti-society of vagrants. She notes that the vivid testimonials to canting—the only archival examples of thieves' cant—are all given by women, and that, "Women seem to be the chief purveyors of cant to a gentle male audience" (130). See also West on the dynamics of cant on the Jacobean stage: West describes

cant used as a vehicle of upper class "coloniz[ation]" of the lowest classes, instead of the more expected opposite (240); he also discusses the ways that cant on stage often reveals the "rhetorical erotics of language" (243).

25. West sees the significance here in terms of marks of class; I see the language question raised as equally as important.

26. See Camden, "Remaines" 45–55, for a period discussion of the matter of names as "significative [sic], and not vaine senseless sounds" (52).

27. See chapter two, note 23. See also chapter two, note 14, for reference to and discussion of Patricia Parker's work on Romance and the association of the feminine and dilation, both physiological and rhetorical.

28. See Helms 64–65; see also Rose 381–382. Simon Shepherd broadly surveys the phenomenon of the 'roaring girl' in a study whose title announces its interest in reading proto-feminism in unorthodox portrayals of women. He specifically discusses Moll's Act III speech in *The Roaring Girl* in Simon Shepherd, *Amazons and Warrior-Women: Varieties of Feminism in Seventeenth-Century Drama* (New York: St. Martin's, 1981) 80–83.

29. Howard, "Crossdressing" 437. Mary Beth Rose links the bodily with the social in this speech, but does not read this as the complaints of a victim; rather, Moll is appealing to women to take sexual responsibility for themselves. See Rose 382.

30. See note 5, above.

31. William Shakespeare, *King Lear, The Complete Works of Shakespeare,* 5th edition, ed. David Bevington (New York: Pearson/Longman, 2004) 3.2.87–94. Credit is due to Sara van den Berg for pointing out to me the suggestive echoing of Lear's Fool in Moll's final speech, here. I have found no other critical connection or consideration of the two in this context.

NOTES TO CHAPTER FOUR

1. Ben Jonson, *Bartholomew Fair, Ben Jonson*, ed. C.H. Herford and Percy and Evelyn Simpson, vol. 6 (Oxford: Clarendon Press, 1966) 1.1.13–18. All subsequent references to the play will be to this edition and will be parenthetical.

2. Fish 37. Fish describes Jonson's lyric poem "To the World, A Farewell" in terms of an intentional failure of representation: "Nets," "Gyves," etc. cannot order society. In *Discoveries* Jonson also makes similar judgments about the social and ephemeral. See *Timber, or Discoveries,* in *Ben Jonson*, ed. C.H. Herford and Percy and Evelyn Simpson, vol. 8 (Oxford: Clarendon Press, 1966) 537, 559.

3. Though my sense of *Bartholomew Fair's* geniality rests on reading its linguistic enormities as a parodic decision to invert critique by turning language explicitly into play, a notion of the play's resignation of more satiric impulses has been a dominant aspect of critical treatment of its thematics. Jonas

Barish's thesis of Jonson's growing tolerance as he approached *Bartholomew Fair* has been influential and provocative. Edward Partridge's major study challenges Barish in its argument that Jonson developed an increasingly jaundiced perspective over time. Gabriele Bernhard Jackson sees Jonson's increased optimism as responsible for artistic failures later in his career—key to Jonson's satiric (and most brilliant) vision was the ever-present tension between "the glory of what ought to be and the mundane reality of what could be" (4). J.A. Bryant, Jr., rehearses all of these positions in considering the recurrence of a Jonsonian figure in the plays—a figure through whom Jonson is continually working out the responsibility of the poet or critic towards society. See Barish; Partridge; Gabriele Bernhard Jackson; J.A. Bryant, Jr., *The Compassionate Satirist: Ben Jonson and his Imperfect World* (Athens, GA: University of Georgia Press, 1972).

4. Gibbons 11. In the introduction to their edited volume, *Plotting Early Modern London: New Essays on Jacobean City Comedy*, co-editors Stock and Zwierlein coin the phrase "sordid realism" to describe "the defining mode and spirit of the 'canonical' city comedies by Ben Jonson, John Marston and Thomas Middleton." See Mehl, Stock, and Zwierlein, 3.

5. Leinwand defines city comedy in terms of "intrigues and romances in which a particular configuration of the dramatic triangle formed by citizens, gallants, and wives, whores, widows, and maids is plotted," and accordingly narrows the period of true city comedy to the decade of 1603–1613. See Leinwand 7.

6. Angela Stock and Anne-Julia Zwierlein, "Introduction," Mehl et al. eds. 3.

7. *Bartholomew Fair* was not included in the 1616 *Works* and its critical fortunes have varied (perhaps accordingly). John Enck's description of it as an "eccentric product," and that "for literary history it becomes a side eddy, a dead end" (189) is not a condemnation by any means, but a recognition of the play's idiosyncratic design and erratic critical reception. Its complexities have attracted critics, but at the same time made the play difficult to treat. See John Enck, *Jonson and the Comic Truth* (Madison, WI: University of Wisconsin Press, 1957) 189–208. See also Barish, 187–239 on the play. Other early treatments of the play's problematic structure include Robert E. Knoll, *Ben Jonson's Plays; An Introduction* (Lincoln, NE: University of Nebraska Press, 1964); Richard Levin, "The Structure of Bartholomew Fair," *PMLA* 80.3 (June 1965): 172–179; Leo Salingar, "Crowd and Public in *Bartholomew Fair*," *Renaissance Drama* X (Evanston, IL: Northwestern University Press, 1979) 141–159; Frances Teague, *The Curious History of Bartholomew Fair* (Lewisburg, PA: Bucknell University Press, 1985).

8. Mary W. Bledsoe, "The Function of Linguistic Enormity in Ben Jonson's *Bartholomew Fair*," *Language and Style: An International Journal* 17.2 (Spring 1984): 149–160.

9. See especially Barish 45–89 for extensive comparison of passages from both.

10. See Elam's study of language and discourse in Shakespearean drama, in which he describes what he sees as a Baroque quality of self-reflection and the meta-linguistic in much drama of the period, including Jonson's. For Elam, the tendency to constantly place and replace language "en abyme" in drama of this period is remarkable, but he views this habitual reflexivity as mainly playful and technical and does not conjecture about what might have been at stake in this for writers. Elam, "Universe of Discourse" 23–24.

11. See Manley, "Literature and Culture" 463. For a different kind of discussion of Shakespeare versus city comedy (not exclusively Jonsonian), see Howard, "Shakespeare-City Comedy."

12. Thomas Cartelli, "*Bartholomew Fair* as Urban Arcadia: Jonson's Response to Shakespeare," *Renaissance Drama* XIV (Evanston, IL: Northwestern University Press, 1983) 151–172.

13. In recent years and in a materialist critical framework strongly influenced by a post-deconstructive moment open to linguistic indeterminacy, several critics have reframed Jonson and his stances on rhetoric, for example, in terms of more fundamental principles of language, identity, and epistemology. See: Lanier, "Masculine Silence"; West; Fumerton, "Homely Accents."

14. Herford and Simpson 9.245.

15. Salingar 156. Salingar emphasizes the extent to which *Bartholomew Fair* is a play about crowds and the theater and about the relationship between spectator and poet, including the effect of the meta-theatrical.

16. Peter Womack has approached Jonson specifically in terms of his attitudes toward language in a useful way for reading *Bartholomew Fair's* comparative geniality. Womack writes: "The comic corollary of Jonson's linguistic classicism is a hypersensitive consciousness of the anarchic and unverifiable plurality of the vernacular" (103). See Womack, "chapter three," especially p. 103.

17. See Barish 187/–195; Bledsoe 150. See also Bradfield for a specific discussion, following Barish, of the play's prose form and its examination of linguistic folly.

18. Many critics have focused on Ursula as an importantly central figure in a play which otherwise appears to lack a dramatic, thematic, or characterological center. Ursula is an earthy figure in her literally enormous humanity, and there is critical interest in what is figured concerning the feminine by Ursula, principally, as well as by other female characters in *Bartholomew Fair*. On the portrayal of women and their thematic function in *Bartholomew Fair*, particularly Ursula, compared with women-characters in Middleton and Shakespeare, see Gail Kern Paster, "Leaky Vessels: The Incontinent Women of City Comedy," *Renaissance Drama* XVIII (Evanston, IL: Northwestern University Press, 1987), 43–65; also Shannon Miller, "Consuming Mothers/Consuming Merchants: The Carnivalesque Economy of Jacobean City Comedy," *Modern Language Studies* 23.2–3 (Spring-Summer 1996): 73–97. For a reading focused solely on *Bartholomew Fair*, see Erin Roland-Leone, "Jonson's Vessels

Runneth Over: A Look at the Ladies of *Bartholomew Fair*," *English Language Notes* 33.1 (September 1995): 12–15.

19. Editor R.V. Holdsworth cites Jonson's disdain for Romances: "Jonson regarded [them] as frivolous entertainments." See Ben Jonson, *Epicoene* (1979) 92, n. 52.

20. Jonson coined the term "nonsense" for his stage direction, here in IV.iv. *The Oxford English Dictionary* lists as its first example for definition 1a, ("That which is not sense; spoken or written words which make no sense or convey absurd ideas; also, absurd or senseless action."): "1614 B. Jonson *Bart. Fair* IV.iv, Here they continue their game of vapours, which is Nonsense." See "Nonsense." Def. 1a. *The Oxford English Dictionary*. 2nd ed. 1989.

21. "Tire." *The Oxford English Dictionary*. 2nd ed. 1989.

22. "Know." *The Oxford English Dictionary*. 2nd ed. 1989. The *OED* devotes nearly five pages to the range of definitions for "know." Of the dozens of different definitions, only about ten date from later than 1620.

23. Enck 193. See also note 3 above.

24. Herford & Simpson 8. 621.

25. See Fish 28, 34, on Jonson's resistance to representation in his poetry and the connection of this resistance to notions of eloquence. See also Womack 79–85.

26. Barish 76–77.

27. Staging a play within a play was no innovation of Jonson's. If the most famous instance of this, and the meta-theatrical and existential responses it can evoke, is *Hamlet* (c.1600), there are numerous other examples both pre- and post-dating *Bartholomew Fair*: *The Spanish Tragedy* (printed 1592),*The Tragical History of Doctor Faustus* (c. 1590), *A Midsummer Night's Dream* (c. 1595), *The Tempest* (1611), and Jonson's own *Volpone* (1605) constitute only the most well-known contemporary productions which incorporated some version of a 'play-within-a-play.' William Shakespeare, *Hamlet, The Complete Works of Shakespeare*, 5th Edition, ed. David Bevington (New York: Pearson/Longman, 2004); Thomas Kyd, *The Spanish Tragedy, Drama of the English Renaissance I, The Tudor Period*, ed. Russell A. Fraser and Norman Rabkin (New York: Macmillan Publishing Co., Inc., 1976); Christopher Marlowe, *Doctor Faustus, Drama of the English Renaissance* I, The Tudor Period, ed. Russell A. Fraser and Norman Rabkin (New York: Macmillan Publishing Co., Inc., 1976); Shakespeare, *A Midsummer Night's Dream*, Bevington (2004); Shakespeare, *The Tempest*. Bevington (2004); Ben Jonson, *Volpone, Ben Jonson*, ed. C.H. Herford and Percy and Evelyn Simpson, vol. 5 (Oxford: Clarendon Press, 1966). Interest in the meta-theatrical in early modern drama has grown under the influence of the New Historicism and its interest in the potency of drama's cultural and political poetics. See, especially, Montrose; also Mullaney.

28. Nicolaas Zwager, *Glimpses of Ben Jonson's London* (Folcroft, PA: Folcroft Library Editions, 1976) 1–75 passim. Zwager discusses Jonson's importance to our modern knowledge of Renaissance puppet plays, and also describes the most popular plots.

29. George Speaght, *Punch and Judy, a History* (London: Studio Vista Ltd., 1970) 33–36.

30. Herford & Simpson 8.582.

31. Bradfield 14. Bradfield reads Jonson's use of verse or prose in his plays in terms of an intention to explore vice (verse—in *Volpone, The Alchemist*) or folly (prose—in *Epicoene, Bartholomew Fair*). Bradfield is most interested in *Bartholomew Fair's* inclusion of a puppet play as the only excursion into verse in the play as a whole. The jangling doggerel of this "poetry," serves mainly to undermine or pervert the critique of vice and immorality typically signaled by verse in plays such as *Volpone*. In this sense, too, there is the suggestion of a shifted attitude towards the significance of language, style, and what these index.

32. In *Discoveries*, Jonson wryly critiques "the Tamerlanes and Tamerchams of the late age, which had nothing in them but the scenical strutting and furious vociferation to warrant them to the ignorant gapers" (542), a sideways and judgmental glance at Marlowe's style. Recently, Jason Scott-Warren has argued that Marlowe himself comically undercuts the potential high-mindedness of his original poem's reliance on classical texts. Marlowe's poem in fact parodies the Humanist tradition out of which it derived. It is appealing to consider Jonson's own undercutting of Marlowe's poem in this light, with Jonson perhaps resenting Marlowe's parodic endeavor and thus utilizing "Hero and Leander," among many possible choices, to further parody decorum and call into question any stable judgment. See Jason Scott-Warren, *Early Modern English Literature* (Polity Press, 2005): 38–40.

33. Both passages quoted from Jonson's *The English Grammar*. See Herford & Simpson 8.465 and 8.501.

34. Margot Heinemann, *Puritanism and Theatre: Thomas Middleton and Opposition Drama Under the Early Stuarts* (Cambridge: Cambridge University Press, 1980) 18–47. Heinemann's larger subject is the question of Middleton's opposition to the crown and potential Puritan sympathies; part of her aim is to complicate the overly simplistic picture of Puritan anti-theatricalism in the period. Pages 18–47 (Chapter 2) nevertheless provide a useful overview of Puritan condemnation of the popular theaters.

35. For a thorough discussion of anti-theatricalism in the period, see Scott-Warren, 105–116. For contemporary sources on this topic, see Stephen Gosson, *Playes Confuted in Five Actions* (1582); Philip Stubbes, *The Anatomie of Abuses* (1583); William Prynne, *Histrio-Mastix. The Players Scourge, or, Actors Tragedies* (1633).

36. Womack 106–107.

37. Bryant 135–145. Bryant locates the role of Jonsonian 'spokesperson' in Tom Quarlous, but here we get a similar commentary-moment from Justice Overdo. He quotes proverbial Latin, explaining that his snooping intentions around the Fair were: "*Ad correctionem, non ad destructionem; ad aedificandum, non ad diruendam*": for correction, not destruction; for building, not ruining. Bryant sees Quarlous's spokesperson as importantly changing from satirist to compassionate observer of foibles—an important element of the play's greater geniality. With the final words quoted here, Overdo also seems to be acknowledging a more tolerant attitude towards the anarchic Fair-world now being extended outwards.

38. Leah Marcus, "Of Mire and Authorship," *The Theatrical City: Culture, Theatre and Politics in London, 1576–1649* eds. David L. Smith, Richard Strier, and David Bevington (Cambridge: Cambridge University Press, 1995) 170–182.

39. Jonathan Goldberg, *James I and the Politics of Literature: Jonson, Shakespeare, Donne, and their Contemporaries* (Baltimore, MD: Johns Hopkins University Press, 1983) is still the most authoritative text on the extent of Stuart Absolutism, even under the milder aegis of James I. See also Hardin Aasand, "'To blanch an Ethiop, and revive a corse': Queen Anne and *The Masque of Blackness*," *SEL: Studies in English Literature, 1500–1900* 32 (1992): 279–280. Aasand's focus is Jonson's *Masque of Blackness*, but part of his discussion helpfully outlines the patriarchal ideology of the Jacobean court.

40. In "Of Mire and Authorship," Marcus makes the suggestion that the unusually numerous amount of accompanying materials that surround the first printed edition of *Bartholomew Fair*—Prologue, Epistle, Epilogue, Induction—indicate the poet's uneasiness with the play's "sprawling license" (171) and are attempts to subject it to higher standards of decorum. Alternatively, she considers the *Prologue*'s and *Epilogue*'s appeals to the king as evidence that Jonson intended the play to serve as "a *tour de force* in defense of royal authority" (173). Marcus' hypothesizing about the significance of the play's ancillary materials is astute, though my reading of the *Epilogue*'s closing purpose is more anarchic.

NOTES TO THE CONCLUSION

1. Leinwand 7–9. In recent work on *Epicoene*, Adam Zucker proves the continued currency of this question of city comedy's boundaries. First listing the notable studies that have offered definitive characteristics—Gibbons (1968), Alexander Leggat (1973), and Leinwand (1986)—Zucker offers his own, intentionally capacious definition of the genre: "I will use the designation [of "city comedy"] in its broadest sense to denote a play obviously set in London that relies predominantly on comic narrative elements to produce and make sense of the complexities of an urban setting" (60, n.25). Zucker

is most interested in the economics of social relations as *Epicoene*'s way of "making sense of" the city; his description of city comedy's concern for the complexities of urban life suggests the value of reading the plays as a series of interrogations, and of determining where this specific objective changes.

2. *The Staple of News* is of worthy comparative value, despite its differences and distance from Jonson's middle period. The play's editor Anthony Parr, who overall does not draw provocative critical links between *The Staple* and earlier works, offers the somewhat faint assessment of the play's origins in "nothing less than Jonson's entire reading and previous literary endeavor," connecting the play's idiosyncrasies to "the fact that *The Staple* comes late in a consciously shaped career, so that Jonson is already aware of approaching 'the close, or shutting up of his circle,' recapitulating old concerns, and drawing on his past work for inspiration" (11). In discussing the play itself, Parr describes Jonson's linguistic preoccupations that importantly link the *The Staple* to earlier works, I would contend, though Parr himself does not note this. He describes "Jonson's awareness of the growing fragmentation of the learned and professional world . . . [which] Jonson clearly regard-ed . . . as a kind of Babel"; and "Jonson's sense of a world that is literally 'encoded,' its disparate activities each defined by the idiom it employs" (46). More recently Raphael Shargel has made an assertive case for linking *The Staple of News* with Jonson's earlier comedic works for the stage. Shargel comments: "[*The Staple*] tends to fall between the cracks of Jonson studies, where scholars are reluctant to consider it either as a work of the "middle period" or . . . in the style of the late Jonson. In fact, although it belongs properly to the later era, it holds greater affinities with Jonson's Jacobean dramas" (47). See Anthony Parr, ed. *The Staple of News* by Ben Jonson (Manchester: Revels Plays—Manchester University Press, 1988); Raphael Shargel, "A Stewed Comedy: Chaos and Authority in *The Staple of News*" *Ben Jonson Journal* 12 (2005):45–72.

3. Ben Jonson, *News from the New World*, *Ben Jonson*, eds. C.H. Herford and Percy and Evelyn Simpson, vol. 7 (Oxford: Clarendon Press, 1966) 511–525.

4. Critics famously have struggled to offer a satisfactory reading of *The Staple of News*'s place in Jonson's oeuvre, and Shargel notes a pattern of omitting *The Staple* altogether from studies of both "middle" and "late" Jonson (Shargel 70, n.8). Both Richard Levin and Barish focus on the play's linguistic satire, with Barish reading it as a resurgence of Jonson's earlier satiric interests. Levin argues that language-excesses unify the play but concludes by noting "failures in execution of the overall design" (453) that signal a decline in artistic power. Parr, as well, ultimately finds the play too disjointed. Devra Rowland Kifer takes a different approach, arguing that the play's disparate elements are not as important as its status as a festive comedy, and pointing out its numerous references to Shrovetide, Lent, and holiday. Recent

criticism has tended to sidestep the question of the play's aesthetic quality or unity and to focus on the vivid materiality of the news-Staple and the allegorical figure of money. Both Karen Newman and Julie Sanders make materialist-critical readings which focus on "the news" as part of the growing commodity-culture of seventeenth-century London. See Shargel 70; Barish 240–241, 257; Richard Levin," *The Staple of News*, The Society of Jeerers, and Canter's College" *Philological Quarterly* XLIV (Oct. 1965): 447–450, 453; Devra Rowland Kifer, "*The Staple of News*: Jonson's Festive Comedy." *SEL* 12 (1972): 337; Karen Newman, "Engendering the News" *The Elizabethan Theatre* 14 (1996): 50–51, 59–60; Julie Sanders, *Ben Jonson's Theatrical Republics* (New York: St. Martin's Press; London: Macmillan Press,1998) chapter on *The Staple of News*: "The Commonwealth of Paper: Print, News and *The Staple of News*" 123–143, especially pp. 123–125.

5. Parr, *The Staple of News*. All subsequent references will be to this edition of the play, and will be parenthetical. Besides the play's inclusion in Herford and Simpson's complete works edition of Jonson [see: Ben Jonson, *The Staple of News, Ben Jonson*, ed. C.H. Herford and Percy and Evelyn Simpson, vol. 6 (Oxford: Clarendon Press, 1966)], it is worth nothing the relative lateness of this first critical edition in England (1988) of the play. See also Herford and Simpson, vol. 2, 169–186, for a useful and thorough introduction to the play.

Bibliography

Aasand, Hardin. Review of *Between Theater and Philosophy: Skepticism in the Major City Comedies of Ben Jonson and Thomas Middleton*, by Matthew R. Martin. *Renaissance Quarterly* 56.3 (Autumn 2003): 947–948.

———. "'To Blanch an Ethiop, and Revive a Corse': Queen Anne and *The Masque of Blackness*." *SEL: Studies in English Literature, 1500–1900*. 32 (1992): 271–285.

Anderson, Benedict. *Imagined Communities: Reflections on the Origin and Spread of Nationalism*. London and New York: Verso, 1991.

Archer, Ian W. "Material Londoners?" in *Material London, ca. 1600*. ed. Lena Cowen Orlin. Philadelphia, PA: University of Pennsylvania Press, 2000. 174–192.

Austin, J.L. *How to Do Things with Words*, 2nd edition. London: Oxford University Press, 1976.

Ayers, P.K. "Dreams of the City: The Urban and the Urbane in Jonson's *Epicoene*." *Philological Quarterly*. 66.1 (Winter 1987): 73–86.

Bailey, Richard W. *Images of English: A Cultural History of the Language*. Ann Arbor: University of Michigan Press, 1991.

Barber, Charles Laurence. *Early Modern English*. 1977. Edinburgh: Edinburgh University Press, 1997.

Barton, Anne. *Ben Jonson, dramatist*. Cambridge: Cambridge University Press, 1984.

———. "London Comedy and the Ethos of the City." *The London Journal*. 4.2 (1978):158–180.

Barish, Jonas A. *Ben Jonson and the Language of Prose Comedy*. Cambridge, MA: Harvard University Press, 1960.

Blank, Paula. *Broken English: Dialects and the Politics of Language in Renaissance Writings*. London and New York: Routledge, 1996.

———. "Languages of Early Modern Literature in Britain." The Cambridge History of Early Modern English Literature. eds. David Loewenstein and Janel Mueller. Cambridge and New York: Cambridge University Press, 2002. 141–169.

Bledsoe, Mary W. "The Function of Linguistic Enormity in Ben Jonson's *Bartholomew Fair*." *Language and Style: An International Journal*. 17.2 (Spring 1984): 149–160.

Blount, Thomas. *Glossographia, or a Dictionary, Interpreting all such hard words . . . (1656)*. Ann Arbor: University Microfilms.

Bornstein, Diana. "As Meek as a Maid: A Historical Perspective on Language for Women in Courtesy Books from the Middle Ages to *Seventeen* Magazine." *Women's Language and Style*. eds. Douglas Butturff and Edmund Epstein. Akron, OH: LRS Books, 1978. 132–138.

Bradfield, Larry D. "Prose Decorum and the Anatomy of Folly in *Bartholomew Fair.*" *Emporia State Research Studies*. 32.2 (Fall 1983): 5–53.

Brady, Jennifer and W.H. Herendeen, eds. *Ben Jonson's 1616 Folio*. Newark, DE: University of Delaware Press, 1991.

Breitenberg, Mark. *Anxious Masculinity in Early Modern England*. Cambridge: Cambridge University Press, 1996.

Broughton, Hugh. *The Concent of Scripture* (1590). Ann Arbor, MI: University Microfilms.

Bruster, Douglas. "The New Materialism in Renaissance Studies." *Material Culture and Cultural Materialisms in the Middle Ages and Renaissance*. ed. Curtis Perry. Arizona Studies in the Middle Ages and the Renaissance, vol. 5. Turnhout: Brepols, 2001. 225–238.

Bryant, Jr., J.A. *The Compassionate Satirist: Ben Jonson and his Imperfect World*. Athens, GA: University of Georgia Press, 1972.

Bullokar, John. *An English Expositor: Teaching the Interpretation of the Hardest Words Used in our Language* (1616). Ann Arbor, MI: University Microfilms.

Bullokar, William. *Booke at Large, for the Amendment of Orthographie for English Speeche* (1580). Ann Arbor, MI: University Microfilms.

Burke, Lucy, Tony Crowley and Alan Girvin, eds. *The Routledge Language and Cultural Theory Reader*. London and New York: Routledge, 2000.

Camden, William. *Britain [Britannia]*. tr. Philemon Holland. London 1610. Ann Arbor, MI: University Microfilms.

———. *Remaines Concerning Britain*. ed. R.D. Dunn. Toronto and London: University of Toronto Press, 1984.

Cameron, Deborah. *Feminism and Linguistic Theory*, 2nd edition. New York: St. Martin's, 1992.

———, ed. *The Feminist Critique of Language: A Reader*. London, New York: Routledge, 1990.

Carew, Richard. *The Excellencie of the English Tongue*. In *Remaines Concerning Britain*. by William Camden. Ed. R.D. Dunn. Toronto and London: University of Toronto Press, 1984. 37–44.

Carrithers, Jr., Gale H. "City-Comedy's Sardonic Hierarchy of Literacy." *SEL: Studies in English Literature, 1500–1900*. 29 (1989):337–355.

Carroll, William C. *The Great Feast of Language in* Love's Labour's Lost. Princeton, NJ: Princeton University Press, 1976.

Cartelli, Thomas. "*Bartholomew Fair* as Urban Arcadia: Jonson Responds to Shakespeare." *Renaissance Drama XIV*. Evanston, IL: Northwestern University Press, 1983. 151–172.

Cawdrey, Robert. *A Table Alphabetical* (1604). Ann Arbor, MI: University Microfilms.

Cockeram, Henry. *The English Dictionarie* (1623). Ann Arbor, MI:University Microfilms.

Covatta, Anthony. *Thomas Middleton's City Comedies.* Lewisburg, PA: Bucknell University Press, 1973.

Creaser, John. "Enigmatic Ben Jonson." *English Comedy*. eds. Michael Cordner, Peter Holland, and John Kerrigan. Cambridge: Cambridge University Press, 1995. 100–118.

Cressy, David. *Literacy and the Social Order: Reading and Writing in Tudor and Stuart England.* Cambridge: Cambridge University Press, 1980.

Curzan, Anne. "Gender Categories in Early English Grammars: Their Message to the Modern Grammarian." *Gender in Grammar and Cognition*, volume 2. eds. B. Unterbeck and M. Rissanen. Berlin: Mouton de Gruyter, 1999.

———. "The Study of Language and Gender." Unpublished essay, 2001.

Dekker, Thomas. *The Dramatic Works of Thomas Dekker*. ed. Fredson Bowers. 4 vol. Cambridge: Cambridge University Press, 1953–1961

———. *The Wonderful Year, The Gull's Horn Book, Penny-Wise, Pound-Foolish, English Villainies Discovered by Lantern and Candlelight and Selected Writings*. ed. E.D. Pendry. Cambridge, MA: Harvard University Press, 1968.

Deleuze, Jacques, and Felix Guattari. *A Thousand Plateaus: Capitalism and Schizophrenia*. tr. Brian Massumi. Minneapolis, MN: University of Minnesota Press, 1987.

Desmet, Christy. "Speaking Sensibly: Feminine Rhetoric in *Measure for Measure* and *All's Well that Ends Well*." *Renaissance Papers* 1986. eds. Dale B.J. Randall and Joseph A. Porter. Durham, NC: The Southeastern Renaissance Conference, 1986.43–51.

Dillon, Janette. *Theatre, Court and City, 1595–1610: Drama and Social Space in London*. Cambridge: Cambridge University Press, 2000.

Dolan, Frances E. "Taking the Pencil out of God's Hand: Art, Nature, and the Face-Painting Debate in Early Modern England." *PMLA* 108.2 (1993): 229–231

———. "Reading, Writing, and other Crimes." in *Emerging Subjects: Feminist Readings of Early Modern Culture*. eds. Valerie Traub, M. Lindsay Kaplan, Dympna Callaghan. Cambridge: Cambridge University Press, 1996. 142–167.

Dolan, Frances and Georgianna Ziegler, with Jeanne Addison Roberts. *Shakespeare's Unruly Women*. Washington, DC: Folger Library, 1997.

Donaldson, Ian. "Language, Noise, and Nonsense: *The Alchemist.*" *Seventeenth-Century Imagery: Essays on the Uses of Figurative Language from Donne to Farquhar*. ed. Earl Miner. Berkeley, CA: University of California Press, 1971. 69–82.

———. *The World Upside Down: Comedy from Jonson to Fielding.* Oxford: Clarendon Press, 1970.

Donawerth, Jane. *Shakespeare and the 16ᵗʰ Century Study of Language.* Urbana, IL: University of Illinois Press, 1984.

Drabble, Margaret, ed. *The Oxford Companion to English Literature,* 5ᵗʰ edition. Oxford: Oxford University Press, 1985.

Drew-Bear, Annette. "Face-Painting Scenes in Jonson's Plays." *Studies in Philology* 77.4 (Fall 1980): 388–401.

Dubrow, Heather and Richard Strier. "Introduction: The Historical Renaissance." *The Historical Renaissance: New Essays on Tudor and Stuart Literature and Culture.* eds. Heather Dubrow and Richard Strier. Chicago: University of Chicago Press, 1988. 1–12.

Elam, Keir. *Shakespeare's Universe of Discourse: Language-Games in the Comedies.* Cambridge and New York: Cambridge University Press, 1984.

Elsky, Martin. "Words, Things, and Names: Jonson's Poetry and Philosophical Grammar." *Classic and Cavalier: Essays on Jonson and the Sons of Ben.* eds. Claude J. Summers and Ted-Larry Pebworth. Pittsburgh, PA: University of Pittsburgh Press, 1982. 91–104.

Enck, John J. *Jonson and the Comic Truth.* Madison, WI: University of Wisconsin Press, 1957.

Ferguson, Margaret W. *Dido's Daughters: Literacy, Gender, and Empire in Early Modern England and France.* Chicago and London: University of Chicago Press, 2003.

Field, Nathan. *Amends for Ladies.* in *Nero and Other Plays.* eds. Herbert P. Horne, Havelock Ellis, Arthur Symons, and A. Wilson Verity. London: Vizetelly, 1888.

Fish, Stanley. "Authors-Readers: Jonson's Community of the Same." *Representations.* 7 (Summer 1984): 26–58.

Fleming, Juliet. "Dictionary English and the Female Tongue." *Privileging Gender in Early Modern England.* ed. Jean R. Brink. *Sixteenth Century Essays and Studies* 23. 175–204.

Fox, Adam. *Oral and Literate Culture in England, 1500–1700.* Oxford: Clarendon Press, 2000.

Fraser, Russell A. and Norman Rabkin, eds. *Drama of the English Renaissance, Volume I: The Tudor Period.* New York: MacMillan Publishing Co. Inc., 1976.

———. *Drama of the English Renaissance, Volume II: The Stuart Period.* Upper Saddle River, NJ: Prentice-Hall, Inc., 1976.

Fumerton, Patricia. "Homely Accents: Ben Jonson Speaking Low." *Renaissance Culture and the Everyday.* eds. Patricia Fumerton and Simon Hunt. Philadephia, PA: University of Pennsylvania Press, 1999. 92–111.

Garner, Shirley Nelson. "'Let Her Paint an Inch Thick': Painted Ladies in Renaissance Drama and Society." *Renaissance Drama XX.* Evanston, IL: Northwestern University Press, 1989. 123–139.

Gibbons, Brian. *Jacobean City Comedy*. London: Methuen, 1980.

Gill, Roma. "The World of Thomas Middleton." *'Accompaninge the players': Essays Celebrating Thomas Middleton, 1580–1980*. ed. Kenneth Friedenreich. New York: AMS Press, 1983. 15–38.

Goldberg, Jonathan. *James I and the Politics of Literature: Jonson, Shakespeare, Donne, and their Contemporaries*. Baltimore: Johns Hopkins University Press, 1983.

Goodrich, Peter. "'Signs Taken for Wonders': Community, Identity, and a History of Sumptuary Law." Rev. of *Governance of the Consuming Passions: A History of Sumptuary Law*, by Alan Hunt. *Law & Social Inquiry*. 23 (Summer 1998): 707–728.

Gordon, Andrew. "Performing London: the Map and the City in Ceremony." *Literature, Mapping, and the Politics of Space in Early Modern Britain*. eds. Andrew Gordon and Bernhard Klein. Cambridge: Cambridge University Press, 2001. 69–88.

Gossett, Suzanne. "'Man-maid, begone!': Women in Masques." *English Literary Renaissance*. 18.1 (Winter 1988): 96–113.

Gosson, Stephen. *The Schoole of Abuse*. in *Early Treatises on the Stage*. London: The Shakespeare Society, 1853.

Greenblatt, Stephen J. "Learning to Curse: Aspects of Linguistic Colonialism in the Sixteenth Century." *First Images of America: The Impact of the New World on the Old*. eds. Fredi Allen Chiappelli, J.B. Michael, Robert C. Benson, Robert S. Lopez. Berkeley: University of California Press, 1976. 561–580.

Greene, Juana Irene. *Desired Properties: Materializing and Managing Social Relations in Early Modern City Comedy*. Diss. Columbia University, 1999. Ann Arbor: UMI, 2002.

Greene, Thomas. "Ben Jonson and the Centered Self." *SEL: Studies in English Literature*. 10.2 (Spring 1970): 325–348.

Haec Vir (1620). Ann Arbor, MI:University Microfilms.

Hakluyt, Richard. *Voyages and Discoveries: The Principal Navigations, Voyages, Traffiques and Discoveries of the English Nation*. ed. Jack Beeching. London: Penguin Books, 1972.

Hallahan, Huston D. "Silence, Eloquence, and Chatter in Jonson's *Epicoene*." *Huntington Library Quarterly: A Journal for the History and Interpretation of English and American Civilization*. 40 (1977):117–127.

Harman, Thomas. *A Caveat for Common Cursitors Vulgarly Called Vagabonds* (1567). Ann Arbor: University Microfilms.

Hawkes, Terence. *Shakespeare's Talking Animals: Language and Drama in Society*. London: Edward Arnold, 1973.

Hayes, Carol Lise. *Mapping City Comedy: Topographies of London and the Anomalous Woman*. Diss. University of California—Irvine, 2000. Ann Arbor: UMI, 2002.

Hazard, Mary E. *Elizabethan Silent Language*. Lincoln, NE: University of Nebraska Press, 2000.

Heinemann, Margot. *Puritanism and Theatre: Thomas Middleton and Opposition Drama Under the Early Stuarts*. Cambridge: Cambridge University Press, 1980.

Helgerson, Richard. *Forms of Nationhood: The Elizabethan Writing of England*. Chicago: University of Chicago Press, 1992.

Heller, Herbert Jack. *Penitent Brothellers: Grace, Sexuality, and Genre in Thomas Middleton's City Comedies*. Diss. Louisiana State University, 1997. Ann Arbor: UMI, 2002.

Helms, Lorraine. "Roaring Girls and Silent Women: The Politics of Androgyny on the Jacobean Stage." *Women in Theatre: Themes in Drama, vol.11*. Cambridge: Cambridge University Press, 1989. 59–73.

Henderson, Katherine Usher and Barbara F. McManus. *Half-Humankind: Contexts and Texts of the Controversy about Women in England, 1540–1640*. Urbana, IL: University of Illinois Press, 1985.

Hic Mulier (1620). Ann Arbor, MI: University Microfilms.

Hirsch, James, ed. *New Perspectives on Ben Jonson*. Madison, NJ: Fairleigh Dickinson University Press, 1997.

Holdsworth, R.V. "Antedatings and Additions for *OED* from *Epicoene*." *Notes and Queries*. 28:226.3 (1981): 242–245.

Holzknecht, Karl J. *Outlines of Tudor and Stuart Plays, 1497–1642*. New York: Barnes & Noble, Inc., 1959.

Howard, Jean. "Crossdressing, The Theatre, and Gender Struggle in Early Modern England." *Shakespeare Quarterly*. 39.4 (Winter 1988): 418–440.

———. "Scripts and/versus Playhouses: Ideological Production and the Renaissance Public Stage." *Renaissance Drama XX*. Evanston, IL: Northwestern University Press, 1989. 31–49.

———. "Sex and Social Conflict: The Erotics of *The Roaring Girl*." *Erotic Politics: Desire on the Renaissance Stage*. ed. Susan Zimmerman. New York: Routledge, 1992. 170–190.

———. "Shakespeare and the London of City Comedy." *Shakespeare Studies*. 39 (2001):1–21.

———. *The Stage and Social Struggle in Early Modern England*. London: Routledge, 1994.

———. "Women, Foreigners, and the Regulation of Space in *Westward Ho*." *Material London, ca. 1600*. ed. Lena Cowen Orlin. Philadelphia, PA: University of Pennsylvania Press, 2000. 150–167.

Huebert, Ronald. "A Shrew Yet Honest: Manliness in Jonson." *Renaissance Drama XV*. Evanston, IL: Northwestern University Press, 1984. 31–68.

Jackson, Gabriele Bernhard. *Vision and Judgment in Ben Jonson's Drama*. New Haven: Yale University Press, 1968.

Jackson, J.A. "'On forfeit of your selves, think nothing true': Self-Deception in Ben Jonson's *Epicoene*." *Early Modern Literary Studies*. 10.1 (May 2004) 28 par. http://www.shu.ac.uk/emls/10–1/jacksons.ht 29 June 2006.

Jones, Ann Rosalind. "'Rugges of London and the Divell's Band': Irish Mantles and Yellow Starch as Hybrid London Fashion." *Material London, ca. 1600*. ed. Lena Cowen Orlin. Philadelphia, PA: University of Pennsylvania Press, 2000. 128–149.

Jones, Ann Rosalind and Peter Stallybrass. *Renaissance Clothing and the Materials of Memory*. Cambridge: Cambridge University Press, 2000.

Jones, Richard Foster. *The Triumph of the English Language: A Survey of Opinions Concerning the Vernacular from the Introduction of Printing to the Restoration*. Palo Alto, CA: Stanford University Press, 1953.

Jonson, Ben. *Ben Jonson*. eds. C.H. Herford and Percy and Evelyn Simpson. 11 vol. Oxford: Clarendon Press, 1966.

———. *Ben Jonson*. The Oxford Authors. ed. Ian Donaldson, Oxford: Oxford University Press, 1985.

———. *Ben Jonson's Plays and Masques*. ed. Robert M. Adams. New York and London: W.W. Norton, 1979.

———. *The Complete Masques*. ed. Stephen Orgel. New Haven: Yale University Press, 1969.

———. *Epicoene*. ed. R.V. Holdsworth. New York: The New Mermaids—W.W. Norton & Co., Inc., 1979.

———. *The Staple of News*. ed. Anthony Neil Parr. Manchester: Revels Plays—Manchester University Press, 1988.

Joseph, James Earl. *Eloquence and Power: The Rise of Language Standards and Standard Languages*. London: Frances Pinter, 1987.

Kay, W. David. "Jonson's Urbane Gallants: Humanistic Contexts for *Epicoene*." *Huntington Library Quarterly: A Journal for the History and Interpretation of English and American Civilization*. 39 (1976):251–266.

Keene, Derek. "Material London in Time and Space." in *Material London, ca. 1600*. ed. Lena Cowen Orlin. Philadephia, PA: University of Pennsylvania Press, 2000. 55–74.

Kifer, Devra Rowland. "*The Staple of News*: Jonson's Festive Comedy." *SEL* 12 (1972): 329–344.

Knights, L.C. *Drama and Society in the Age of Jonson*. London: Chatto & Windus, 1937.

Lakoff, Robin Tolmach. *Language and Woman's Place*. New York: Harper & Row, 1975.

Lambert [Lambarde], William. *A Perambulation of Kent* (1570). Ann Arbor, MI: University Microfilms.

Lanier, Douglas. "Brainchildren: Self-Representation and Patriarchy in Ben Jonson's Early Works." *Renaissance Papers* 1986. eds. Dale B.J. Randall and Joseph A. Porter. Durham, NC: The Southeastern Renaissance Conference, 1986. 53–68.

———. "Masculine Silence: *Epicoene* and Jonsonian Stylistics." *College Literature*. 21.2 (June 1994):1–18.

Larsen, Virginia Lee Larsen. *Thomas Middleton as Social Critic: A Study of Three Plays.* Diss. University of California—Santa Cruz, 1995. Ann Arbor: UMI, 2002.

Leinwand, Theodore B. *The City Staged: Jacobean City Comedy, 1603–1613.* Madison, WI: University of Wisconsin Press, 1986.

Lever, Ralph. *The Arte of Reason, Rightly Termed, Witcraft.* London, 1573. *Early English Books Online.* University of Washington Libraries. 11 March 2004. <http://eebo.chadwyck.com/eebo/image/15541/>

Levin, Harry. "Notes Toward a Definition of City Comedy." *Renaissance Genres: Essays on Theory, History, and Interpretation.* ed. Barbara K. Lewalski. Cambridge, MA: Harvard English Studies 14—Harvard University Press, 1986. 126–146.

Levin, Richard. "*The Staple of News,* The Society of Jeerers, and Canter's College" *Philological Quarterly* XLIV. (Oct. 1965): 445–453.

———. "The Structure of *Bartholomew Fair.*" *PMLA* 80.3 (June 1965): 172–179.

Lippi-Green, Rosina. *English with an Accent.* New York and London: Routledge, 1997.

Loxley, James. *The Complete Critical Guide to Ben Jonson.* London and New York: Routledge, 2002.

Luckyj, Christina. '*A Moving Rhetoricke': Gender and Silence in Early Modern England.* Manchester and New York: Manchester University Press, 2002.

Mandy, Judith Kovacs. *City Women: Daughters, Wives, Widows and Whores in Jacobean and Restoration City Comedy.* Diss. Lehigh University, 1996. Ann Arbor: UMI, 2002.

Manley, Lawrence. "From Matron to Monster: Tudor-Stuart London and the Languages of Urban Description." *The Historical Renaissance: New Essays on Tudor and Stuart Literature and Culture.* eds. Heather Dubrow and Richard Strier. Chicago and London: University of Chicago Press, 1988. 347–374.

———. *Literature and Culture in Early Modern London.* Cambridge: Cambridge University Press, 1995.

Marcus, Leah. "Of Mire and Authorship." *The Theatrical City: Culture, Theatre and Politics in London, 1576–1649.* eds. David L. Smith, Richard Strier, and David Bevington. Cambridge: Cambridge University Press, 1995. 170–182.

Mardock, James. "Hermaphroditical Authority in Jonson's City Comedies." *Ben Jonson Journal.* 9 (2002):69–85.

Martin, Matthew R. *Between Theater and Philosophy: Skepticism in the Major City Comedies of Ben Jonson and Thomas Middleton.* Newark, DE: University of Delaware Press, 2001.

Mazzio, Carla. "Sins of the Tongue." *The Body in Parts: Fantasies of Corporeality in Early Modern Europe.* eds. Carla Mazzio and David Hillman. New York: Routledge, 1997. 53–79.

McDonald, Russ. *The Bedford Companion to Shakespeare: An Introduction with Documents.* New York: Bedford Books of St. Martin's Press, 1996.

McLuskie, Kathleen. *Renaissance Dramatists.* Atlantic Highlands, NJ: Humanities Press International, Inc., 1989.

McMullan, John L. *The Canting Crew: London's Criminal Underworld 1550–1700.* New Brunswick, NJ: Rutgers University Press, 1984.

Mehl, Dieter, Angela Stock, and Anne-Julia Zwierlein, eds. *Plotting Early Modern London: New Essays on Jacobean City Comedy.* Hampshire and Burlington: Ashgate, 2004.

Merritt, J.F. ed. *Imagining Early Modern London: Perceptions and Portrayals of the City from Stow to Strype, 1598–1720.* Cambridge: Cambridge University Press, 2001.

Middleton, Thomas. *The Works of Thomas Middleton.* ed. A.H. Bullen. 8 vol. Boston: Houghton-Mifflin, 1885–1886.

Middleton, Thomas and Thomas Dekker. *The Roaring Girl* (1611). ed. Paul A. Mulholland. Manchester: The Revels Plays—Manchester University Press, 1987.

Mikalachki, Jodi. "Gender, Cant, and Cross-talking in *The Roaring Girl.*" *Renaissance Drama XXV.* Evanston, IL: Northwestern University Press,1994. 119–143.

Miller, Shannon. "Consuming Mothers/Consuming Merchants: The Carnivalesque Economy of Jacobean City Comedy." *Modern Language Studies.* 23.2–3 (Spring-Summer 1996): 73–97.

Milroy, James and Lesley Milroy. *Authority in Language: Investigating Language Prescription and Standardization.* London, Boston: Routledge & K.Paul, 1985.

Mirabelli, Philip. "Silence, Wit, and Wisdom in *The Silent Woman.*" *SEL: Studies in English Literature, 1500–1900.* 29.2 (Spring 1989):309–336. .

Montrose, Louis. *The Purpose of Playing: Shakespeare and the Cultural Politics of the Elizabethan Theatre.* Chicago: University of Chicago Press, 1996.

Mugglestone, Lynda. *'Talking Proper': The Rise of Accent as Social Symbol,* 2nd edition. Oxford and New York: Oxford University Press, 2003.

Mulcaster, Richard. *The Elementarie* (1582). Ann Arbor: University Microfilms.

Mullaney, Steven. *The Place of the Stage: License, Play and Power in Renaissance England,* 2nd edition. Ann Arbor, MI: University of Michigan Press, 1995.

Newman, Karen. "City Talk: Women and Commodification in Jonson's *Epicoene.*" *English Literary Renaissance.* 53 (1989): 503–518.

———. "Engendering the News." *The Elizabethan Theatre.* 14 (1996): 49–69.

———. *Fashioning Femininity and English Renaissance Drama.* Chicago and London: University of Chicago Press, 1991.

Norden, John. *Speculum Britanniae pars: The Description of Hertfordshire* (1598). Ann Arbor, MI: University Microfilms.

Ong, Walter J. "Latin Language Study as a Renaissance Puberty Rite." *Studies in Philology.* 56.2 (1959):103–124.

———. *Orality and Literacy: The Technologizing of the Word,* 2nd edition. London and New York: Routledge, 1991.

Orgel, Stephen. "The Subtexts of *The Roaring Girl.*" *Erotic Politics: Desire on the Renaissance Stage.* ed. Susan Zimmerman. New York: Routledge, 1992.

———. "Why Did the English Stage Take Boys for Women?" *Teaching Shakespeare Through Performance.* ed. Milla Cozart Riggio. New York: Modern Language Association, 1999. 102–113.

The Oxford English Dictionary, 2nd edition. Oxford and New York: Oxford University Press, 1989.

The Oxford English Dictionary Online, 2nd edition. 2004. http://dictionary.oed.com.

Parker, Patricia. *Literary Fat Ladies: Rhetoric, Gender, Power*. London and New York: Methuen, 1987.

Partridge, Edward B. *The Broken Compass: A Study of the Major Comedies of Ben Jonson*. London: Chatto & Windus, 1958.

Paster, Gail Kern. *The Idea of the City in the Age of Shakespeare*. Athens, GA: University of Georgia Press, 1985.

———. "Leaky Vessels: The Incontinent Women of City Comedy." *Renaissance Drama* XVIII. Evanston, IL: Northwestern University Press, 1987. 43–65.

Pigman, G.W. "Versions of Imitation." *Renaissance Quarterly.* 33 (1980):1–32.

Preussner, Arnold. "Language and Society in Jonson's *Epicoene*." *Thoth: Syracuse University Graduate Students in English.* 15.2 (1975):9–20.

Richter, David H. ed. *The Critical Tradition: Classic Texts and Contemporary Trends*, 2nd edition. Boston: Bedford Books, 1998.

Roland-Leone, Erin. "Jonson's Vessels Runneth Over: A Look at the Ladies of *Bartholomew Fair.*" *English Language Notes.* 33.1 (Sept. 1995): 12–15.

Romaine, Suzanne. *Communicating Gender.* NJ: Lawrence Erlbaum, 1999.

Rose, Mary Beth. "Women in Men's Clothing: Apparel and Social Stability in *The Roaring Girl.*" *English Literary Renaissance.* 14.3 (Autumn 1984): 367–391.

Salgado, Gamini. *The Elizabethan Underworld.* Totowa, NJ: Rowman and Littlefield, 1977.

Salingar, Leo. "Crowd and Public in *Bartholomew Fair.*" *Renaissance Drama X*. Evanston, IL: Northwestern University Press, 1979.141–159.

———. "Farce and Fashion in *The Silent Woman.*" *Essays and Studies.* 20 (1967):29–46.

Sanders, Eve Rachele and Margaret Ferguson. "Literacies in Early Modern England." *Critical Survey* 14.1 (2002): 1–8.

Sanders, Julie. *Ben Jonson's Theatrical Republics.* New York: St. Martin's Press; London: Macmillan Press, 1998.

———. "'Wardrobe Stuffe': Clothes, Costume and the Politics of Dress in Ben Jonson's *The New Inn.*" *Renaissance Forum.* 6.1 (Winter 2002): 1–15. 12 September 2003 http://www.hull.ac.uk/renforum/v6no1/sanders.ht.

Sanders, Julie, Kate Chedgzoy, Susan Wiseman. *Refashioning Ben Jonson: Gender, Politics, and the Jonsonian Canon.* New York: St. Martin's, 1998.

Sarup, Madan. *An Introductory Guide to Post-Structuralism and Postmodernism*, 2nd edition. Athens, GA: University of Georgia Press, 1993.

Schneider, Jane. "Fantastical Colors in Foggy London: The New Fashion Potential of the Late Sixteenth Century." in *Material London, ca. 1600.* ed. Lena Cowen Orlin. Philadelphia, PA: University of Pennsylvania Press, 2000. 109–127.

Scott-Warren, Jason. *Early Modern English Literature.* London: Polity Press, 2005.

Shakespeare, William. *The Complete Works of Shakespeare*, 5th Edition. ed. David Bevington. New York: Pearson/Longman, 2004.

Shargel, Raphael. "A Stewed Comedy: Chaos and Authority in *The Staple of News*." *The Ben Jonson Journal*. 12 (2005): 45–72.

Sharpe, Kevin. *Reading Revolutions: Politics of Reading in Early Modern England*. New Haven, CT: Yale University Press, 2000.

Shepherd, Simon. *Amazons and Warrior Women: Varieties of Feminism in 17th Century Drama*. New York: St. Martin's, 1981.

Sherman, Stuart. "Eyes and Ears, News and Plays: The Argument of Ben Jonson's *Staple*." *The Politics of Information in Early Modern Europe*. ed. Brendan Dooley and Sabrina A. Baron. *Routledge Studies in Cultural History 1*. London: Routledge, 2001. 23–40.

Sinfield, Alan. "*Poetaster*, the Author, and the Perils of Cultural Production." *Material London, ca. 1600*. ed. Lena Cowen Orlin. Philadephia, PA: University of Pennsylvania Press, 2000. 75–89.

Sisson, C.J. "King James the First of England as Poet and Political Writer." *Seventeenth Century Studies Presented to Herbert Grierson*. Oxford: Clarendon Press, 1938. 50–61.

Slights, William. "*Epicoene* and the Prose Paradox." *Philological Quarterly*. 49 (1970):178–187.

Smith, David L., Richard Strier, and David Bevington. *The Theatrical City: Culture, Theatre, and Politics in London, 1576–1649*. Cambridge: Cambridge University Press, 1995.

Speaght, George. *Punch and Judy, A History*. London: Studio Vista Ltd., 1970.

Spender, Dale. *Man Made Language*. London: Routledge & Kegan Paul, 1980.

Spenser, Edmund. *The Works of Edmund Spenser: A Variorum Edition*. eds. Edwin Greenlaw. 11 vol. Baltimore: Johns Hopkins University Press, 1932–57.

Stallybrass, Peter and Allon White. *The Politics and Poetics of Transgression*. Ithaca, NY: Cornell University Press, 1986.

Stow, John. *The Survey of London*. ed. Henry B. Wheatley. London: JM Dent & Sons, Ltd., 1945.

Stubbes, Philip. *The Anatomie of Abuses*. ed. Margaret Jane Kidnie. Tempe, AZ: Renaissance English Text Society, 2002.

Sullivan, Jim. "'Language Such as Men Do Use': The Ethnic English of Ben Jonson's *The Irish Masque at Court*." *Michigan Academician*. 31 (1999):1–22.

Swann, Marjorie. "Refashioning Society in Ben Jonson's *Epicoene*." *SEL: Studies in English Literature, 1500–1900*. 38.2 (Spring 1998): 297–315.

Tompkins, Jane. "A Short Course in Post-Structuralism." *Conversations: Contemporary Critical Theory and the Teaching of Literature*. eds. Charles Moran and Elizabeth F. Penfield. Urbana, IL: NCTE Press, 1990. 19–37.

Tydeman, William. "The Image of the City in English Renaissance Drama" *Essays and Studies* 38 (1985): 29–44.

Underdown, D.E. "The Taming of the Scold: The Enforcement of Patriarchal Authority in Early Modern England." In *Order and Disorder in Early Modern England.* eds. Anthony Fletcher and John Stevenson. Cambridge: Cambridge University Press, 1985. 116–136.

van den Berg, Sara. "The Passing of the Elizabethan Court." *Ben Jonson Journal.* 1:31–61.

———. "Reading Dora Reading: Freud's 'Fragment of an Analysis of a Case of Hysteria." *Literature and Psychology.* 32.3 (1986): 27–35.

Ward, Joseph P. *Metropolitan Communities: Trade Guilds, Identity, and Change in Early Modern London.* Palo Alto, CA: Stanford University Press, 1997.

Watt, Tessa. *Cheap Print and Popular Piety, 1550–1640.* Cambridge: Cambridge University Press, 1991.

Wells, Susan."Typicality and Indeterminacy in Jacobean City Comedy." In *The Dialectics of Representation.* Baltimore and London: Johns Hopkins University Press, 1985. 103–132.

West, William N. "Talking the Talk: Cant on the Jacobean Stage." *English Literary Renaissance.* (Spring 2003):228–251.

Womack, Peter. *Ben Jonson.* New York: B. Blackwell, 1987.

Woodbridge, Linda. "Patchwork: Piecing the Early Modern Mind in England's First Century of Print Culture." *English Literary Renaissance.* 23 (1993): 5–45.

———. *Women and the English Renaissance: Literature and the Nature of Womankind, 1540–1620.* Urbana, IL: University of Illinois Press, 1984.

Wrightson, Keith. *English Society 1580–1680.* London: Hutchinson and Co., 1982.

Yachnin, Paul. *Stage-Wrights: Shakespeare, Jonson, Middleton, and the Making of Theatrical Value.* Philadelphia, PA: University of Pennsylvania Press, 1997.

Zucker, Adam. "The Social Logic of Ben Jonson's *Epicoene.*" *Renaissance Drama.* 33 (2004): 37–62.

Zwager, Nicolaas. *Glimpses of Ben Jonson's London.* Folcroft, PA: Folcroft Library Editions, 1976.

Index